The
LOST KING
of FRANCE

ALSO BY DEBORAH CADBURY

Terrible Lizard

Altering Eden

The
LOST KING
of FRANCE

A TRUE STORY OF REVOLUTION,
REVENGE, AND DNA

Deborah Cadbury

ST. MARTIN'S PRESS
NEW YORK

www.stmartins.com

ISBN 0-312-28312-1

First Edition: October 2002

10   9   8   7   6   5   4   3   2   1

For my mother and Martin,
the first readers,
with love

Contents

ACKNOWLEDGMENTS

In writing this book, I am grateful to many specialists for making a wealth of information available to me. I would particularly like to thank the historians Dr. John Hardman and Ian Dunlop for finding the time to read and comment on the manuscript and offering expert guidance. Professor Jean-Jacques Cassiman and his colleagues at the University of Leuven in Belgium patiently dealt with all my questions and provided key information on the forensic and genetic testing. I am also indebted to Professor Sir Alec Jeffreys at the University of Leicester for advice on the genetics history and to Adrian Radulescu for commenting on the final chapter.

In Paris, thanks are due to historian Philippe Delorme for a most inspiring discussion on the mystery of Louis XVII and for sharing his expertise on the historical issues. At the Museum of Saint-Denis, Rodolphe Huguet and Dominique Blangis supplied details of the strange odyssey of the stolen heart and kindly traced Philippe-Jean Pellatan's remarkable narration for me. I owe a great deal to the studies of many historians and forensic specialists whose works are cited in the bibliography, especially Michel Fleury at the Commission du Vieux Paris, who provided information on the most recent exhumations at Sainte-Marguerite. The staff at Versailles, the *Con-*

ciergerie and the Musée Carnavalet gave invaluable assistance with inquiries, as did the staff at the Bodleian Library in Oxford and the British Library in London. They traced many historical texts without which I could not have completed my research.

I am particularly grateful to Christopher Potter at Fourth Estate in London and Charles Spicer at St. Martin's Press, New York, for giving me the opportunity to write this book and for their continued encouragement. Leo Hollis at Fourth Estate has been a wonderful support in seeing the manuscript through to its final version and providing skilled editorial judgment on each chapter. Many thanks to Jane Bradish-Ellames at Curtis Brown for her friendship and valued advice over the years as literary agent and to Giles Gordon for taking on this book and seeing it through to the final stages.

Finally, heartfelt thanks to friends and family without whom I could not have completed this book. I would particularly like to thank Martin Surr and Julia Lilley for their excellent judgment as the first readers in commenting on the drafts and for our many inspiring discussions on the history, the characters and the emerging narrative.

❧ *Introduction* ❧

THE HEART OF
STONE

On April 19, 2000, the *New York Times* reported that:

GENETICS OFFERS DENOUEMENT TO
MYSTERY OF PRINCE'S DEATH

The question has intrigued historians for 200 years. Was the disease-riddled little boy who died in 1795 after years alone in a prison cell really the son of Louis XVI and Marie Antoinette? Or had royalists managed at the height of the French Revolution to spirit the young heir from harm after his parents were sent to the guillotine. . . . Through the years, more than 500 books had been written about the young Dauphin, and many theories emerged about his possible escape and presumed exile. . . .

Today, two scientists, after examining all that remains [of the supposed prince]—a dried heart—said they had been able to extract three samples of mitochondrial DNA from the heart and compare them with samples from locks of hair taken from Marie

Antoinette, two of her sisters and two living maternal relatives. . . .

The scientists, Jean-Jacques Cassiman of the University of Leuven in Belgium and Bernard Brinkmann of the University of Munster in Germany, are both specialists in human genetics. . . . Professor Cassiman was at first unsure that any DNA testing could be accomplished because the heart was in such bad shape. The story of how it survived is a crazy saga that can hardly be a scientist's dream . . .

Behind the headline in the *New York Times* is the true account of a young boy who inherited the hostility and hatred of a nation during the French Revolution. From his portrait, Louis-Charles, Duc de Normandie, looks out confidently on the world with large blue eyes in a sensitive face framed by fair hair; the perfect storybook prince happily unaware that destiny had marked him out for a rather different story. His life had begun in 1785, four years before the revolution and his early years had been spent safely cocooned in the gilded palace of Versailles near Paris. At the age of four, on the death of his older brother, he had become the royal heir, the dauphin, in whose small frame was centered all the hopes of the continuing Bourbon dynasty that had sat on the French throne since the sixteenth century. With his good looks and sunny nature he was a much-loved child, Marie-Antoinette's treasured little *"chou d'amour."*

However, this charmed childhood, played out in the beguiling walkways of Versailles, led only to a life of mounting terror, as he was, all too soon, encompassed by the fierce extremes of the revolution. When his father, Louis XVI, and his mother, Marie-Antoinette, were taken from him and executed at the guillotine in 1793, the "wolf cub" or "son of a tyrant" as he was now known, was isolated in solitary confinement, taught to forget his royal past and punished for the errors and extravagances of his ancestors. Forbidden to see his sister, Marie-Thérèse, the only other surviving member of his immediate family, the boy king became the victim of brutal physical and emotional abuse in his filthy, rat-infested cell. He was thought to have died in the Temple prison in Paris at the age of ten, unrecognizable as the royal prince, his body covered with scabies and ulcers.

In 1795, when leaders of the French Revolution announced that Louis-Charles, the boy king, had mysteriously died in the Temple prison, rumors immediately began to circulate that he was still alive. Many were convinced that he had been spirited out of the prison by royalist supporters and escaped to safety abroad, ready to reclaim the throne. After all, there was no tomb to mark his official burial site; his death certificate drawn up by revolutionary officials was widely believed to be a forgery; one official's wife even admitted that she had helped to smuggle him from the prison in a laundry basket, leaving a dying substitute child in his place.

As in a fairytale, after the revolution, the young prince sprang to life. He was sighted in Brittany, Normandy, Alsace and the Auvergne. Was he the charming and dignified "Jean-Marie Hervagault" who held court so convincingly and attracted a large and faithful following intent on seeing him attain the throne? Could he have been the rough diamond, "Charles de Navarre," generous-natured, confident, whose love of parties usually ended in drunken bad manners, accounts of which tallied so neatly with the brutalizing treatment meted out to the "son of Capet" in prison? Or was he the suave and smooth talking "Baron de Richemont," who could tell of his childhood in Versailles and the Temple prison in compelling detail and whose epitaph in Gleizé in France acknowledged him as "Louis-Charles of France, son of Louis XVI and of Marie-Antoinette"?

In time, more than a hundred young dauphins stepped forward to claim their inheritance, the constant uncertainty adding to the anguish of Marie-Thérèse, the lost king's sister, who thought her brother was dead. Many an adventurer or vagrant suddenly recalled their blue-blooded descent, and potential princes hopefully presented themselves at the gates of the Palace of the Tuileries in Paris. The missing "little boy the dolphin"—as he was disparagingly called by Mark Twain—appeared in London, America, Russia, even in the Seychelles. In time, dauphins—not necessarily of French origin or even French-speaking—surfaced in all corners of the globe; one was an American Indian half-caste. Some claimants seemed genuine, gaining supporters willing to sponsor their cause, and lived out their days in lavish surroundings, holding court with devoted admirers. Others were thrown in prison or swiftly exposed as frauds.

To the astonishment of Europe, nearly forty years after his official death, a certain Prussian, Karl Wilhelm Naundorff, returned to France and announced that he was the lost king and wished to claim the throne on the restoration of the monarchy. Unlike many other claimants, "Prince" Naundorff could remember his childhood in Versailles with chilling accuracy and vividly describe his escape from the Temple prison. A succession of former courtiers at Versailles, even the dauphin's governess and nursemaid, joyfully confirmed he was telling the truth and begged "his sister" to acknowledge him. Yet Marie-Thérèse refused to meet with him; the French authorities seized his identity documents, rejected his claims and he lived out his years in exile. He founded a parallel dynasty; to this day, Naundorff's descendents resolutely seek to prove that he was the rightful king of France.

There is one remaining clue to the mysterious life of the young prince—a grisly relic inside the great gothic Basilica at Saint-Denis, in a northerly suburb of Paris. By the high altar, almost hidden by the tall pillars, there is a dark passageway leading down to an even darker underground world: "the City of the Dead." Stretching almost the entire length of the Basilica is the vast crypt, with vaulted ceiling and thick shadowy arches, where by tradition the kings and queens of France now rest. At the bottom of the dark passageway, barred from the main crypt by a heavy iron grille bearing the Bourbon coat of arms, there is a side chapel known as *La Chapelle des Princes*. Unlit, except for an ornamental brass ceiling light which casts strange, spiky shapes across the deep shadows of the room, the floor is crammed with wooden coffins.

Beyond these coffins, thin shafts of light direct the eye to a crucifix and stone shelving behind, displaying various brass caskets. These contain the preserved organs, hearts and entrails of various Bourbon kings of France, removed, according to tradition, prior to embalming the bodies. Hard to discern in the dim light, on the bottom shelf behind the crucifix, there is a small, plain crystal urn, marked with the Bourbon *fleur de lys*. It contains a round object that, on first inspection, resembles a stone, shrivelled and dried hard as rock, hanging on a thread. Yet this is no ordinary stone. This is thought to be the actual heart of the ill-fated boy who died in the Temple prison, stolen from his dead body at the height of the revolution.

Now over two hundred years old, this child's heart has had a remarkable journey through time. Cut hurriedly from the supposed dauphin's body during his autopsy in the Temple prison in 1795 and smuggled out in a handkerchief, the heart which once raced and quickened to the Terror of the revolution, even in death became a symbol to be treasured or despised. Preserved merely to be stolen once more, hidden in grand palaces and lost again during the revolution of 1830, only with the passage of time, as the years slowly buried all painful memories, was the child's heart quietly forgotten, eventually coming to rest by the coffins in *La Chapelle des Princes*.

With recent developments in forensic science it has become possible to uncover one of the most enduring secrets of the French Revolution: what actually happened to the dauphin. With improvements in the restoration of ancient DNA and the analysis of special genes inherited from the maternal line, known as mitochondrial DNA, the mummified heart of the child offers a possible end to two hundred years of speculation.

On December 15, 1999, at the Abbey of Saint-Denis, the crystal urn which held the heart was veiled in a purple cloth and brought out from its shadowy tomb in the crypt for scientific testing. A small crowd had gathered in the Basilica, leading scientists such as the geneticist Professor Jean-Jacques Cassiman from Belgium, historians with an interest in the case, notaries to witness the proceedings, the inevitable TV crews and the various pretenders to the French throne: the Naundorff and Bourbon princes. The heart was placed on a small table in front of the high altar. Here, bathed in a fine tracery of stained-glass light, it could be clearly seen: an unprepossessing object, not unlike a garden stone. It was blessed by the priest who led a short ceremony. "I do not know whose heart this is," he said, "but it is certainly symbolic of children anywhere in the world who have suffered. This represents the suffering of all little children caught up in war and revolution."

With great solemnity, the crystal urn was taken in a hearse to the nearby Thierry Coté Medical Analysis Laboratory in Paris. The two-hundred-year-old heart was hard as rock. Anticipating this, Professor Cassiman and his colleague, Dr. Els Jehaes, had brought a sterile handsaw with which they could cut along the bottom tip of the child's heart. It took some time to saw a small strip, barely a centimeter wide; this was then split in two and escorted to two specialist laboratories in Germany and Belgium for genetic testing.

Invisible to the naked eye for over two centuries, the secrets locked within the tissues of this heart could now be revealed to modern science. Did the young son of Louis XVI and Marie-Antoinette die a brutal death during the French Revolution? Or did he escape this fate and survive only to be ridiculed later as an impostor when he returned to claim the throne of France. In the gloved hands of the geneticists, the centuries of time which had slowly buried the terrible story of the owner of the heart could now be rolled back to solve one of the great enigmas in the history of the Revolution.

This is a royal detective story of mystery, fraud and revenge that spans two centuries. From the lavish chambers of Versailles to the grim prisons of Paris at the height of the Terror, it plummets the depths of human nature and reveals the worst that man can bestow on his enemies. Extraordinary feats of heroism, stoic endurance and almost foolhardy courage entwine with hatred, vengeance and cruelty masquerading under the flag of justice. At the center of it all is a family utterly destroyed; a weak but compassionate father, and a headstrong and courageous mother whose terrifying end, at the people's will, ensured that fate would mark her young son for a special retribution. For the first time, the true story of Louis XVI and Marie-Antoinette's son and heir can be told and his memory can finally be laid to rest.

PART I

Chapter One

"THE FINEST KINGDOM IN EUROPE"

Man is born free, and everywhere he is in chains.
— JEAN-JACQUES ROUSSEAU,
SOCIAL CONTRACT, 1762

On Saturday, April 21, 1770, the Austrian archduchess, Maria-Antonia, left her home, the imperial palace of Hofburg in Vienna, forever and embarked on the long journey to France. On departure, in the courtyard in front of the palace, the royal entourage assembled. Two grand *berlines* lavishly upholstered in blue and crimson velvet and decorated with fine embroidery had been provided by the French ambassador to take Maria-Antonia to Paris. These were to be conveyed in a cavalcade of almost fifty carriages, each to be drawn by six horses, and an array of guards and outriders. The whole of the Austrian court, in all its silken and bejewelled finery, attended this auspicious event. Maria-Antonia, the youngest daughter of the distinguished Empress Maria-Theresa and Emperor Franz I, was to marry the future king of France and, it was hoped, consolidate Austria's troubled relationship with France.

Maria-Antonia was slightly built with all the attractiveness of youth. "She has a most graceful figure; holds herself well; and if, as may be hoped, she grows a little taller, she will possess every good quality one could wish for in a great princess," wrote her tutor, the Abbé Jacques de Vermond, adding, "her heart and character are both excellent." Maria-Antonia had large blue eyes, reddish blond hair and a good complexion; many even considered her a beauty. The aging French king, Louis XV, eagerly inquiring about the prospective Austrian bride for his grandson was told by officials that she had "a charming face and beautiful eyes." She had, however, inherited the Habsburg projecting lower lip and prominent brow, which prompted her mother, in preparations for the event, to bring a *coiffeur* from France to arrange her hair to soften the line of her forehead.

Maria-Antonia, the subject of all this detailed scrutiny, had had her future determined when she was thirteen. "Others make war but thou, O happy Austria, makest marriages" was a family motto. Her mother, the Empress Maria-Theresa, who was widely considered to be the best queen in Europe since Elizabeth I of England, ruled the Habsburg Empire. Her territories encompassed most of central Europe, reaching to parts of Romania in the east, regions of Germany in the north, south to Lombardy and Tuscany in Italy and west to the Austrian Netherlands, now Belgium. Some of this success was due to a series of strategic marriages, which were an important part of royal diplomacy. Maria-Antonia was the youngest of sixteen children, and several of her older sisters had already taken part in Austrian foreign policy. One sister was married to the governor general of the Austrian Netherlands, another became the Duchess of Parma, and a third, Maria-Antonia's favorite sister, Maria-Carolina, had become the queen of Naples—a role that at first she deplored. "The suffering is true martyrdom," Maria-Carolina wrote home, "made worse by being expected to look happy . . . I pity Antonia who has yet to suffer it."

For the Empress Maria-Theresa, eclipsing all these marriages was the prospect of an alliance with the French. France was seen as the richest and most powerful state in Europe, and, with twenty-five million people, also the largest. Yet France had been Austria's enemy for over two hundred years. For many, a permanent alliance between the two former long-standing enemies seemed out of the question, even potentially dangerous. However, the empress was determined to secure a match between her youngest daughter and the dauphin of France. Such an important marriage would seal a political alliance and enable the two countries to work as allies against the growing Prussian influence.

Despite the exciting prospects that lay ahead, Maria-Antonia's departure from her home, and her mother in particular, was still an ordeal, according to one witness, Joseph Weber, the son of her former nurse. "The young Maria-Antonia burst into tears and the spectators, touched by the sight, shared the cruel sufferings of mother and daughter. Maria-Theresa . . . took her into her arms and hugged her. . . . 'Adieu, my dear daughter; a great distance is going to separate us, but be just, be humane and imbued with a sense of the duties of your rank and I will always be proud of the regrets which I shall always feel. . . . Do so much good to the people of France that they will be able to say that I have sent them an angel.'" As her carriage departed, Maria-Antonia, "her face bathed with tears, covered her eyes now with a handkerchief, now with her hands, and put her head out of the window again and again, to see once more the palace of her fathers to which she would never return." All she had to represent her future was a miniature portrait of her future husband, Louis-Auguste, the dauphin.

Her magnificent cortège travelled for a week through Austria and Bavaria until finally they reached the frontier with France, on the banks of the Rhine River near Kehl. On an island in the middle of the river, Maria-Antonia had to undergo a ceremony in which she was symbolically stripped of her Austrian roots and was then reborn, robed in French attire. A magnificent wooden pavilion, over a hundred feet long, had been constructed, divided into two main sections. On one side were the courtiers from Vienna and on the other, from France. Once the formal ceremonies were completed the door to the French side was opened, and Maria-Antonia had to make her entrance into the French court, no longer as Maria-Antonia, but Marie-Antoinette. As she realized that the door to the Austrian side had closed behind her on all those familiar faces, she was overwhelmed, and "rushed" into the French side, "with tears in her eyes."

As she continued her journey into France she received a rapturous welcome. Every kind of extravagant preparation had been taken to honor the

[5]

young princess. There were displays of all kinds; fireworks, dances, theater, great triumphal arches built, petals strewn before her feet, floating gardens on the river beneath her window, fountains flowing with wine, endless enthusiastic crowds, cheer upon cheer. If she had left the Austrian court in tears, her slow progress through France to such approbation could only fill her with every possible hope.

By May 14 she arrived at Compiègne, some forty miles northeast of Paris, where she was to meet her future husband, the dauphin, Louis-Auguste. Marie-Antoinette, by now well briefed on etiquette by her new advisor, the eminent Comtesse de Noailles, stepped from her carriage and sank into a deep curtsy before the king. Louis XV was still a handsome man whose regal presence eclipsed that of the shy and somewhat overweight sixteen-year-old standing next to him. If she was disappointed by her first impressions of her future husband, there is no record of it. Others, however, have left a less-than-favorable account. "Nature seems to have denied everything to Monsieur le dauphin," Maria-Theresa's ambassador in France had reported, somewhat harshly. "In his bearing and words, the prince displays a very limited amount of sense, great plainness and no sensitivity." Indeed, the tall, ungainly youth was more than a little awkward with his prospective bride. When Marie-Antoinette politely kissed him he seemed unsure of himself and promptly moved away.

It took twenty-three days from leaving the Hofburg in Vienna before they reached Versailles on May 16, 1770. As the cavalcade of carriages turned into the drive that sunny morning the vast scale of the magnificent chateau came into view. Once the dream of the Sun King, Louis XIV, who had transformed it from a hunting lodge to a sumptuous estate and symbol of royal power, Versailles gave off an immediate impression of classical grandeur, ionic columns, arched windows and balustrades receding into the distance as far as the eye could see. The ornamental façade of the main block alone, in brick and honey-colored stone, stretched over one-third of a mile. This was the administrative center of Europe's most powerful state, nothing less than a town for up to ten thousand people: the royal family and their entourage, several thousand courtiers and their servants, the king's household troops, Swiss guards, musketeers, gendarmes and countless other staff and visitors.

Marie-Antoinette was taken to the ground-floor apartments where her ladies-in-waiting were to prepare her for her wedding. But nothing was to prepare the princess for the lavishness of the palace; the Hofburg in Austria was modest by comparison. The reception rooms were of an unbelievable richness and elegance, and the draped and canopied beds of the royal apartments had more in common with Cleopatra's silken barge than the planks and straw of the common lot. Then there were the endless mirrored panels of the vast *Galerie des Glaces* where courtiers were assembling to greet her. This famous Hall of Mirrors was the talk of Europe, with its four hundred thousand reflected candles, and beyond, the tall western windows; the perfect view with its enchanted blue distance held forever in mirrors, gold and more gold, the sparkle of diamonds and the finest crystal. It could not fail to seduce the senses and beguile the emperor's daughter as to her assured prospects at Versailles.

The marriage ceremony took place later that day in the gilt and white chapel at Versailles. In this regal setting, Bourbon kings were traditionally christened and married, secure in the knowledge of their "divine right" as monarch. Standing before the carved marble altar, the dauphin, dressed in cloth of gold studded with diamonds, found the whole procedure something of an ordeal. "He trembled excessively during the service," wrote one eyewitness. "He appeared to have more timidity than his little wife and blushed up to his eyes when he gave [her] the ring." Marie-Antoinette, her slender figure seeming lost in her voluminous white brocade gown, was sufficiently nervous that when she signed the register, she spilled some ink.

The ceremony was followed by a grand reception in the *Galerie des Glaces* for over six thousand guests, and a sumptuous wedding feast in the Opera House, which was inaugurated in their honor. Afterward, following customary French etiquette, the bride and groom were prepared for bed in a very public ritual where the king himself gave the nightshirt to his grandson.

Yet for all the weeks of imposing preparations in anticipation of this happy moment, when the sheets were checked in the morning, there was no evidence that the marriage had been consummated.

The aging king "was enchanted with the young dauphine," observed her First Lady of the Bedchamber, Henriette Campan; "all his conversation was about her graces, her vivacity, and the aptness of her repartees." But her new husband was not so appreciative. Rumors soon began to circulate that the dauphin was impotent or had difficulty making love. He showed only "the most mortifying indifference, and a coldness which frequently degenerated into rudeness," continued Madame Campan, whose memoirs as the queen's maid convey many intimate details of Marie-Antoinette's early years in France. "Not even all her charms could gain upon his senses; he threw himself, as a matter of duty, upon the bed of the dauphine, and often fell asleep without saying a single word to her!" When Marie-Antoinette expressed her concerns in a letter to her mother, the empress advised her not to be too impatient with her husband, since increasing his uneasiness would only make matters worse. Nonetheless, Marie-Antoinette was worried and "deeply hurt" by his lack of physical interest in her.

The dauphin was in fact a serious, well-intentioned young man who suffered from a chronic lack of confidence and self-assertiveness. As a child, Louis had felt himself to be in the shadow of his brothers; first his brilliant older brother who had died at the age of ten, and then his younger brothers, the clever and calculating Comte de Provence—who wanted the throne for himself—and the handsome Comte d'Artois. To add to his sense of insecurity, when Louis was eleven, his father had died of tuberculosis, to be followed soon afterward by his mother—a loss which he felt deeply. Increasingly anxious about whether he was equal to his future role, he withdrew, absorbing himself in his studies, especially history, or pursuing his passion for the hunt. Somewhat incongruously for a future king, he also loved lock-making and had a smithy and forge installed next to his library. Marie-Antoinette did not share his interest in history or reading and thought his smithying quite ridiculous. "You must agree that I wouldn't look very beautiful standing in a forge," she told a friend. Her mother, the empress, was increasingly concerned about their apparent incompatibility.

For the public, however, the fortunate young couple symbolized all the promise of a new age. When Louis and Marie-Antoinette made their first ceremonial entrance into Paris on June 8, 1773, there was jubilant cheering. Their cortège clattered across the streets of the capital, which had been strewn with flowers. "There was such a great crowd," wrote Marie-Antoinette, "that we remained for three-quarters of an hour without being able to go forwards or backwards." When they finally appeared on the balcony of the Palace of the Tuileries, the crowds were ecstatic and their cheers increased as the dauphine smiled. Hats were thrown in the air with abandon, handkerchiefs were waving and everyone was enthusiastic. "Madame, they are two hundred thousand of your lovers," murmured the governor of Paris, the Duc de Brissac, as he saw the sea of admiring faces.

The following year, their protected lives were to change dramatically. On April 27, 1774, Louis XV was dining with his mistress when he became feverish with a severe headache. The next day, at Versailles, he broke out in a rash. The diagnosis was serious: smallpox. Within a few days, as his body became covered with foul-smelling sores, it was apparent that the king was suffering from a most virulent form of the disease. Louis and Marie-Antoinette had no chance to pay their last respects; they were forbidden to visit him. In less than two weeks, the once handsome body in his exquisite gilded bed festooned in gold brocade appeared to be covered in one huge, unending black scab.

For those who could not come near the sickroom, a candle had been placed near the window, which was to be extinguished the instant the king died. Louis and Marie-Antoinette were waiting together, watching the flickering light at the window with growing apprehension. When the flame went out, "suddenly a dreadful noise, absolutely like thunder," wrote Madame Campan, was heard in the outer apartment. "This extraordinary tumult . . . was the crowd of courtiers who were deserting the dead sovereign's antechamber to come and bow to the new power of Louis XVI." The courtiers threw themselves on their knees with cries of *"Le roi est mort: vive le roi."* The whole scene was overwhelming for the nineteen-year-old king and his eighteen-year-old queen. "Pouring forth a flood of tears, [they] exclaimed: 'God guide and protect us! We are too young to govern.'"

The coronation ceremony was held on a very hot day in June 1775. Louis-Auguste walked up the aisle of Rheims Cathedral dressed in stately splendor. He was anointed with oil and bore the sword of Charlemagne as the crown of France was solemnly lowered onto his head. Such was the magnificence of the occasion and the jubilation of the crowds that Marie-Antoinette was overwhelmed and had to leave the gallery to wipe away her tears. When she returned, the spectators in the packed cathedral cheered once again and the king's eyes were full of appreciation for his young wife. "Even if I were to live for two hundred years," Marie-Antoinette wrote ecstatically to her mother, she would never forget the wonderful day. "I can only be amazed by the will of Providence that I, the youngest of your children, should have become queen of the finest kingdom in Europe."

However, "the finest kingdom in Europe" that they had inherited was not all that it appeared. The visible outward signs of great wealth that greeted Marie-Antoinette every day in the sheer size and opulence of Versailles disguised a huge national debt. Their predecessors, Louis XIV and Louis XV, had pursued policies that had driven France to the verge of bankruptcy. A succession of expensive wars had aggravated the problem. In the War of Austrian Succession spanning 1740 to 1748, France had fought as an ally of Prussia against Austria, the Netherlands and Britain. Eight years later, between 1756 and 1763, Louis XV reversed France's historic hostility to Austria by allying with them against Britain and Prussia in the Seven Years' War. These two wars alone cost France 2.8 billion livres, much of which could only be paid by borrowing.

These problems were compounded by an ancient system of taxation that exacted more from the poor than the rich. The fast-growing population of France was divided into three "Estates." The First Estate consisted of around 100,000 clergy. Almost half a million nobility comprised the Second Estate.

The Third Estate were the commoners, the vast majority of the population, consisting of the peasants, wage earners and bourgeoisie. Under this increasingly despised system, the first two Estates, the clergy and nobility, were largely exempt from taxes, even though they were the wealthiest. They also enjoyed traditional privileges over the Third Estate, whose members could rarely achieve high rank, such as officer in the army.

As a result of tax exemptions for the nobility and clergy, the tax base was small and fell disproportionately on those least able to pay. Louis XV had repeatedly failed to tackle the problem of taxation reform; time and time again, he faced opposition from nobles and clergy who were not going to give up their tax concessions. Since he could not raise money by increasing taxation, he was obliged to borrow still more. Far from inheriting a wealthy nation, by the 1770s, the king faced a government deficit that was huge and growing, as annual expenditure continued to exceed revenue.

The unjust system of taxation underlined huge disparities in wealth. Peasants felt increasingly insecure as many found that their incomes were dwindling and their debts were rising. Their problems were compounded by the fact that France was still almost entirely an agricultural nation. Only around half a million people produced manufactured goods, so there were few exports to cover the cost of imports of wheat when the harvest failed. One traveller, François de La Rochefoucauld, commenting on the incredible hardships of the peasants he observed in Brittany, declared, "They really are slaves. . . . Their poverty is excessive. They eat a sort of porridge made of buckwheat; it is more like glue than food." Indeed, the extreme wealth of the nobles in their magnificent chateaux in contrast to the wretched poverty of many of the people could not have been more plain for all to see.

In eighteenth-century France, there was no institutional framework that would readily allow Louis XVI to tackle these fundamental problems. Administratively it was a fragmented nation, each region with completely separate customs, taxes, even different measurements and weights. Each region jealously protected its own interests and independence, which had grown up around local *parlements*, thirteen *parlements* in all. These *parlements* were not like the English parliament of elected representatives. They were law courts of magistrates and lawyers who had paid for their seats and who used them, not to represent the people, but principally to further their own interests. Although the king could formally overrule a *parlement* or dissolve it, conflicts with *parlement* had been a feature of Louis XV's reign and had stifled modernizing reforms.

As absolute monarch, the king had authority over the military and the national system of justice, and he could determine levels of taxation and influence the clergy. The difficulty was in exercising this power when the country was politically divided. Louis XVI faced a situation where no section of society was satisfied. The nobles wanted to restore ancient rights and to resist any tax changes, the bourgeoisie resented the privileges of the nobles, and the commoners criticized the tax system. The British ambassador, Lord David Murray Stormont, captured the difficulties: "Every instrument of faction, every court engine is constantly at work, and the whole is such a scene of jealousy, cabal and intrigue that no enemy need wish it more." As a young, rather idealistic man, Louis XVI earnestly wished to enhance the reputation of the monarchy and build a more prosperous France, yet he knew this would require major unpopular reforms.

One of the king's first priorities was to cut back the nation's debt. To do this he had to reduce state expenditure, starting with Versailles. Versailles just soaked up money; the palace was in need of repair and some servants had not been paid for years. Even before he was king, Louis spent nearly a quarter of his allowance in back payment to staff. He continued to be strict about the royal family's spending and repaying debts. Provence, Artois and their wives were ordered to eat with him and the queen at Versailles to minimize demands on their own expensive households, and he discouraged the many extravagant noblemen at court from living beyond their means.

He appointed as finance minister Anne-Robert Jacques Turgot, who tried to increase state revenue by stimulating the economy. He removed restrictions on the grain trade between the thirteen different regions and promoted light industry by suppressing the powerful guilds that would not allow nonmembers to practice a trade. This was achieved with some success. Louis was also able to introduce other reforms. He passed measures to improve the appalling state of prisons in France and abolished the barbaric practice of torturing accused prisoners which, up until then, had been regarded as a legitimate means to get at the truth of a man's innocence or guilt. However, for all his humanitarian instincts, he failed to get to grips with tax reform, and the nation's debt continued to rise.

While Louis XVI was trying to come to terms with his role as king, Marie-Antoinette was creating her new life as queen. She quickly understood that she was barred from politics but soon found there were other ways of exercising her power at Versailles. As dauphine she had made no secret of the fact that she disliked the time-consuming exacting etiquette and formality of the French court where, she felt, her life was lived "in front of the whole world." Depending on their rank, courtiers could attend the rising or *lever* of the monarch and his family, and in the evening the ceremony for undressing, or *coucher*. For the all-too-frequent public meals, or *grand couvert*, the royal family could be watched dining by any member of the public who was suitably attired.

The queen's disregard for ceremony shocked the more traditional courtiers in Versailles, who observed her on occasion to yawn or giggle during an event, perhaps disguising her expression with her fan. Needless to say, the young queen was continually reproved by her advisor on social etiquette, Madame de Noailles. Yet "Madame Etiquette," as Marie-Antoinette called her, failed to inspire her protégée with the significance of these rituals. "Madame de Noailles held herself bolt upright with a most severe face," observed Madame Campan, and "merely succeeded in boring the young princess." It wasn't long before Madame Etiquette lost her post altogether and this was followed by many relaxations in court ceremony. Madame Campan, who had lived at Versailles since her youth when she was employed as reader to the princesses of Louis XV, was concerned at the harm this might do her mistress: "An inclination to substitute by degrees the simple customs of Vienna for those of Versailles proved more injurious to her than she could have possibly have imagined." Her insensitivity to the French way of doing things was adding to the slowly creeping distrust of a foreign queen.

As Marie-Antoinette gained confidence, she began to place her own stamp on court life. She soon found she could patronize friends of her own choosing, such as the Princesse de Lamballe, of the royal House of Savoy. They had become friends at a winter sleigh party, where according to Madame Campan, the princess, "with all the brilliancy and freshness of youth, looked like Spring peeping from under sable and ermine." Lamballe had been widowed at nineteen, when her husband died of syphilis. Marie-Antoinette found in her a sensitive confidante and soon appointed her Superintendent of the Queen's Household, a move that caused uproar since there were others whose rank made them much more suited for the post. Unlike the Princesse de Lamballe, another intimate friend, Gabrielle de Polignac, was drawn from the impoverished nobility. Gabrielle was a generous-spirited, levelheaded girl with a taste for simplicity. The queen found her husband an official position at Versailles so that Gabrielle, too, could live at the court. It wasn't long before the queen was bestowing favors to numerous other members of the Polignac family.

With her newfound friends, Marie-Antoinette's life became more fun and increasingly indulgent: a whirlwind of masked balls, plays and operas in Paris, as well as race meetings and hunting parties. Even Madame Campan, who invariably wrote appreciatively of her mistress, was critical. "Pleasure was the sole pursuit of everyone of this young family, with the exception of the king," she wrote. "Their love of it was perpetually encouraged by a crowd of those officious people, who by anticipating their desires . . . hoped to gain or secure favor for themselves." Who would have dared, she asks, to check the amusements of this young, lively and handsome queen? "A mother or husband alone had the right to do it!" Although the king rarely joined her for these social events, he threw no impediment in her way. "His long indifference had been followed by feelings of admirations and love. He was a slave to all the wishes of the queen." However, her mother, hearing of these indulgences, was quick to warn her daughter in frequent letters from Austria: "I foresee nothing but grief and misery for you."

Gambling soon became another irresistible occupation for the young queen, who managed to accumulate heavy debts, which her husband settled from his private income. Constantly frugal himself, Louis failed to impose this self-discipline on his young wife.

Worse criticism was to come when she began to ring up bills for diamonds, followed by more diamonds, in ever increasing size and quantity until her mother in some distraction wrote, "A queen can only degrade herself by such impossible behavior and degrades herself even more by this sort of heedless extravagance, especially in difficult times. . . . I hope I shall not live to see the disaster which is all too likely to occur." Marie-Antoinette replied, "I would not have thought anyone could have bothered you about such bagatelles."

Inevitably, all this played into the hands of the rumormongers. Malicious gossip soon spread about how much money she was spending. Apart from jewels and clothes—around 170 creations a year, not to mention her famous hairdresser, Leonard Hautier, who came out from Paris each day to create a powdered, coiffured fantasy up to three feet high—she also lavished money on the Petit Trianon. This was an elegant neoclassical pavilion about a mile from Versailles given to her by the king, which she refurbished to her own taste, including the creation of an English-style garden. This little private heaven was a place where Marie-Antoinette could escape the suffocating etiquette of court and enjoy being informal with her friends; but of course, the money poured into the Petit Trianon, together with enormous sums spent on generously favoring her friends, created jealousy and hostility among those who were not so favored. Courtiers frustrated not to be part of her inner circle maliciously called the Petit Trianon "Little Vienna."

Her Austrian blood still rankled with many in France. All too many nobles had had relatives killed by Austrians in recent wars or at least had fought against Austrian troops. The queen's apparent contempt for French customs soon made her enemies among the nobility. "Apart from a few favorites . . . everyone was excluded from the royal presence," complained one nobleman, the Duc de Lévis-Mirepoix. "Rank, service, reputation, and birth were no longer enough to gain admittance." Some nobles, he said, stayed away from Versailles, rather than endure snubs from such a young, apparently light-headed and frivolous foreigner.

Yet she was not without admirers; she particularly cultivated the good-looking and fashionable men, such as the king's youngest brother, Artois. With his cosmopolitan air and ease with women, he was only too happy to oblige the king and escort the queen to countless social events. On one occasion, in January 1774, at a masquerade at the Opera in Paris, through her grey velvet mask, Marie-Antoinette found herself talking to a tall, attractive man with a somewhat serious expression. He was finishing a European grand tour and, as he talked, she realised he had a delightful Swedish accent. Always drawn to foreigners, she became interested in this aristocratic stranger who was so at ease in Parisian high society. The glamorous Count Axel Fersen made an instant impression.

Not surprisingly, her relationship with her husband was under strain. Anxious about his new role as king, he seemed intimidated by this sophisticated and beautiful wife whom he could not satisfy. "The king fears her, rather than loves her," observed one courtier, who noticed the king seemed much happier and more relaxed when she was absent. Marie-Antoinette, in turn, chose the company of young men full of energy and wit who would flatter and amuse her; she found it difficult to be patient with such a dull and unexciting husband. Yet they both wanted the marriage to succeed and, in particular, they both wanted an heir.

However, as the years passed, no heir was produced, which incited much malicious gossip. In the autumn of 1775, five years into the marriage, Parisian women were heard shouting revolting obscenities at Marie-Antoinette at a race meeting, mocking her for not giving birth to a dauphin. In the same year she wrote to her mother to tell her about the birth of Artois's first son, the Duc d'Angoulême, now third in line to the throne. "There's no need to tell you, dear Mama, how much it hurts me to see an heir to the throne who isn't mine." Despite this pressure, Louis remained, to say the least, rather uninterested in sex. The best doctors were consulted and various diagnoses were made, although no serious impediment to the match was found. Marie-Antoinette told her mother that she tried to entice her husband to spend more time with her, and reported enthusiastically early in 1776 that "his body seemed to be becoming firmer."

The empress, however, required much more than this to seal the all-important political alliance. The following year, in April 1777, Marie-Antoinette's brother, now the Emperor Joseph, came to visit Versailles, charged, amongst other things, with trying to ascertain why no heir was forthcoming. Joseph was enchanted with his sister, whom he described as "delightful . . . a little young and inclined to be rash, but with a core of honesty and virtue that deserves respect." It would appear from Joseph's private letters afterwards to his brother Leopold of Tuscany that during his six-week stay he did not shrink from probing the intimate details of their marriage: "In the conjugal bed, here is the secret. He [Louis] has excellent erections, inserts his organ, remains there without stirring for perhaps two minutes, and then withdraws without ever discharging and, still erect, he bids his wife goodnight. It is incomprehensible." Joseph continued, "He ought to be whipped, to make him ejaculate, as one whips donkeys!" As for Marie-Antoinette, he wrote that she is not "amorously inclined," and to-gether they are "a couple of awkward duffers"!

Joseph reproved his sister for not showing her husband more affection. "Aren't you cold and disinterested when he caresses you or tries to speak to you?" he challenged her. "Don't you look bored, even disgusted? If it's true, then how can you possibly expect such a cold-blooded man to make love to you?" Marie-Antoinette evidently took his advice to heart. That summer, she was elated to tell her mother that at last she had experienced "the happiness so essential for my entire life." The king and queen's sexual awak-ening brought them closer together and, early the following year, she re-ported that "the king spends three or four nights a week in my bed and behaves in a way that fills me with hope." Some weeks later, Marie-Antoinette proudly announced to her husband that she was at last expecting a baby. Louis was overjoyed.

On December 19, 1778, Marie-Antoinette went into labor. At Versailles, a royal birth, like eating or dressing, was a public ritual, open to spectators who wished to satisfy themselves that the new baby was born to the queen. As the bells rang out, "torrents of inquisitive persons poured into the cham-ber," wrote Madame Campan. The rush was "so great and tumultous" that it was impossible to move; some courtiers were even standing on the furniture. "So motley a gathering," protested the First Lady of the Bedchamber, "one would have thought oneself in a place of public amusement!" Finally, when the baby was born, there was no sound, and Marie-Antoinette began to panic, thinking it was stillborn. At the first cry, the queen was so elated and exhausted by the effort that she was quite overcome. "Help me, I'm dying," she cried as she turned very pale and lost consciousness.

The Princesse de Lamballe, horrified by the agony of her friend, also collapsed and was taken out "insensible." The windows, which had been sealed to keep out drafts, were hurriedly broken to get more air, courtiers were thrown out, the queen was bled, hot water fetched. It took some time for the queen to regain consciousness. At this point "we were all embracing each other and shedding tears of joy," writes Madame Campan, caught up in "transports of delight" that the queen "was restored to life." A twenty-one-gun salute rang out to announce the birth of a daughter: Princesse Marie-Thérèse-Charlotte, or Madame Royale. "Poor little girl," the queen is reported to have said as she cradled her daughter. "You are not what was desired, but you are no less dear to me on that account. A son would have been the property of the state. You shall be mine."

Despite this success, there was still great pressure on Marie-Antoinette to conceive a male heir. To her delight, early in 1781, she found she was pregnant again. After the traumas of Marie-Thérèse's very public delivery, spectators were banned from the next birth. In fact, there was such deep silence in the room as the newborn emerged that the queen imagined she had again only produced a daughter. Then the king, overwhelmed with pride and delight, "tears streaming from his eyes," came up to the queen and said, "Madame, you have fulfilled my wishes and those of France. You are the mother of a dauphin."

A hundred and one cannon heralded the long awaited birth of a son, Louis-Joseph. The news was greeted by wild celebrations: fireworks, festivities and fountains of wine in Paris. There was such "universal joy," said Madame Campan, that complete strangers "stopped one another in the street and spoke without being acquainted." A delegation of Parisian artisans and craftsmen came to Versailles with generous gifts for the young child. The king, at last showing confidence, was all smiles, remaining on the balcony a long time to savor the sight and constantly taking the opportunity to say with great pleasure, "my son, the dauphin." The royal line had an heir and the continuity of the monarchy seemed assured.

Nevertheless, for all triumphant public displays, the monarchy was being imperceptibly undermined, sinking slowing beneath an ocean of debt. Furthermore, like his forebears, Louis XVI had found himself drawn into policies that added to the debt. He had agreed to provide secret funds to help General Washington's army in America against Britain and soon sent troops and supplies as well. Support for the American Revolution against the British was popular in France. Many wanted to retaliate for the defeats suffered in Seven Years' War, such as the Marquis de La Fayette, whose father had been killed by the British. La Fayette set sail for America in 1777 and was soon appointed major general, serving George Washington. His daring exploits were widely reported in France as he led his men in several victorious campaigns.

Louis XVI had found himself increasingly involved in the American war. In 1778, he recognized the American Declaration of Independence and signed a military alliance with the Americans. The eight thousand French soldiers who went to America made a significant difference in the war against England. Much to her disappointment, the queen's favorite, Count Fersen, was one of many who volunteered to join the French expeditionary corps. However, as the fighting dragged on, the French government was forced to spend heavily to finance the military campaign against England.

A succession of finance ministers came and went, seemingly unable to get to grips with the deficit. Instead of reforming the tax system, Louis tried to solve the problem without alienating the aristocracy. Each year he was forced to borrow more to balance the budget, sinking further and further into debt. When his reforming finance minister, Turgot, tried to change this, he became so unpopular at court, especially with Marie-Antoinette, that he was dismissed.

His successor, Jacques Necker, a Swiss banker appointed in June 1777, attempted to reorganize the tax system but soon became embroiled in further borrowing at increasingly exorbitant interest rates. In 1781, in an attempt to win the confidence of creditors, he published the *Compte Rendu*, a highly favorable report of the state's finances. His ambitious plan failed. His figures were challenged and in the ensuing furor, finding he did not have the full support of Louis XVI, he resigned.

He was succeeded in 1783 by his rival, Charles Alexandre de Calonne. Calonne tried to tackle the problem by boosting the economy with increased state spending, especially on manufacturing. This only served to deepen the crisis, and he was forced to contemplate further taxes. To add to the difficulties, a long agricultural depression gripped the country and inflation was rising. All this was exacerbated by the effects of the American war.

Although the French secured a victory against England in the American War of Independence, aid to the Americans between 1776 and 1783 had added around 1.3 billion livres to the spiralling national debt. And there was another hidden cost of supporting America: the returning men, inspired by what they had seen overseas, brought back revolutionary ideas.

During the Enlightenment of eighteenth-century France, writers like Voltaire and Jean-Jacques Rousseau had set out radical new ideas in political philosophy. Voltaire's *Philosophical Letters* of 1733 indicted the French system of government and were suppressed. He continued to challenge all manifestations of tyranny by the privileged few in church or state. Rousseau's *Social Contract*, published in 1762, tackled the great themes of liberty and virtue and the role of the state, creating a new sense of possibilities and opportunities. Intellectuals began to reject established systems of government; "reason," they argued, had greater value than the king's claim to a "divine right," and they no longer saw the monarch's rights and privileges as unchallengeable. Political issues became much more widely debated in the salons and academies of Paris. Why support a system that had the great mass of the populace in chains to their abject poverty? Surely the people, rather than the king, should determine levels of taxation? Is a republic morally superior to a monarchy? Educated Frenchmen began to see in America's Declaration of Independence a better model to follow. With the establishment of the American constitution there was a practical alternative to the monarchy of France.

The growing discontent with the government found a tangible focus in the popular press through the increasingly vitriolic portrayal of the queen. Although with the responsibilities of motherhood she had begun to moderate her earlier excesses and spent much time with her children, she had many enemies at court and the slanders continued unabated. In the streets of Paris, pornography, cartoons, prints and *libelles* poured out an endless barrage of spiteful criticism which, before long, became common truths throughout France. The production of these pamphlets was a commercial enterprise, and writers fought to outdo each other in their ever-more-outrageous copy. The queen was portrayed as wildly frivolous and extravagant with no care for the welfare of her people. Much was made of her seven years of childlessness and she was accused of lesbian relationships, especially with her favorites, Gabrielle de Polignac, and the superintendent of the household, the Princesse de Lamballe: "In order to have children, Cupid must widen Aphrodite's door. This Antoinette knows, and she tires out more than one work lady widening that door. What talents are employed! The superintendent works away. Laughter, games, little fingers, all her exploits proved in vain."

Even when she fulfilled her role as mother, she was portrayed as unfaithful, turning the king of France into a "perfect cuckold."

> *Our lascivious queen*
> *With Artois the debauched*
> *Together with no trouble*
> *Commit the sweet sin*
> *But what of it*
> *How could one find harm in that?*

These calumnies demonizing the queen became increasingly explicit and obscene. *The Love Life of Charlie and Toinette*, published in 1779, outlines in graphic detail the "impotence of L------- whose matchstick . . . is always limp and curled up," and how "Toinette feels how sweet it is to be well and truly fucked" by Artois. In the pamphlets and *libelles*, the queen's voracious sexual appetite required more than one lover; Fersen, Artois and others were implicated. There was even a fake autobiography, *A Historical Essay on the Life of Marie-Antoinette*, which first appeared in the early 1780s and proved so popular it was continually updated, purporting to be her own confession as a "barbaric queen, adulterous wife, woman without morals, soiled with crime and debauchery, these are the titles that are my decorations." Yet for many her worst crime was undeniable: she was Austrian. To the gutter press of Paris, in addition to all her other failings, she was invariably *"l'Autrichienne,"* stressing the second half of the word, *chienne,* or bitch.

In March 1785, Marie-Antoinette had a second son, Louis-Charles, Duc de Normandie. Could Count Axel Fersen have fathered this child, as some historians have suggested? He was the only man out of the many named in the *libelles* with whom the queen might have had an affair. There is no doubt of their mutual attraction, yet historians cannot agree over the nature of their relationship. Was this a courtly romance, where Fersen discreetly adored the queen from a distance? Or was this a romantic passion with many secret rendezvous in the privacy of her gardens at Trianon? The many deletions in Marie-Antoinette's correspondence with Fersen, made years later by the Fersen family, make the matter impossible to resolve. The most likely conclusion is that, although it is likely that they had an affair, there is no evidence that Louis XVI was not Louis-Charles's father. Quite the reverse. Courtiers noted that the date of conception did indeed neatly coincide with the dates of the king's visits to his wife's bedroom.

However, so successfully had lampoonists demolished the queen's reputation that when she made her traditional ceremonial entry into Paris after the birth of her second son, there was not a single cheer from the crowd. As she walked though the dark interior of Notre Dame toward the great sunlit western door and square beyond, the awesome silence of the crowd was the menacing backdrop as the clatter of horses' hooves rang out in the spring air. It was in stark contrast to the tumultuous celebrations that had greeted her on her arrival in Paris as a young girl. The queen, distraught by this hostility, returned to Versailles crying out, "What have I done to them?"

She could no longer turn to her mother in Austria for advice. The Empress Maria-Theresa never had the satisfaction of knowing that her daughter had finally provided two male heirs. After a short illness, she had died of inflammation of the lungs. Marie-Antoinette was inconsolable, reported Madame Campan. "She kept herself shut up in her closet for several days . . . saw none but the royal family, and received none but the Princesse de Lamballe and the Duchesse de Polignac." Even at a distance, her mother had been a powerful influence in her life, constantly providing shrewd and critical guidance. She felt her isolation now, in a foreign court, with all the responsibilities of queen, wife and mother.

Marie-Antoinette did have one treasured memento of her mother, a lock of her hair, which she wore close to her skin. And in Austria, concealed in the empress's rosary, there was a small token of her distant daughter. The delicate chain of black rosary beads was entwined with sixteen gold medallions, each one encasing locks of hair from her children. After her death, the rosary passed to her oldest daughter, the invalid, Maria-Anna, who lived in the Elizabethinen convent in Klagenfurt. These small symbols of the empress's children were all but forgotten. In time, they would assume great significance.

❦ Chapter Two ❦

"GRÂCE POUR MAMAN"

*"This is a revolt?" asked the King, hearing of the fall of the Bastille.
"No, sire, it is a Revolution" came the reply.*

At Versailles, Louis-Charles, Duc de Normandie, lived a charmed life, well protected from the "trifling disturbances"—as they were sometimes known at court—beyond the palace gates. In the royal nursery, under the sensitive administration of the Governess of the Children of France, the Duchesse de Polignac, his little empire was well endowed with servants. Apart from Cécile, his wet nurse, there was a cradle rocker, Madame Rambaud, and his personal rocker, Madame Rousseau, otherwise known as Rocker to the Children of France, whose sister, Madame Campan, worked in the queen's household. Valets were appointed, such as Hanet Cléry, a particularly loyal and discreet servant who had been in service to the royal family since 1782. In addition, the Duc de Normandie had two room boys, four ushers, a porter, a silver cleaner, a laundress, a hairdresser, two First Chamber Women, eight Ordinary Women and a periphery of minor staff all vying for importance.

The nursery on the ground floor of Versailles opened out onto the large terraces and acres of ornamental gardens beyond; rows of orange trees and neatly trimmed box bushes receded into the distance, geometrically arranged around circular pools with tall fountains cascading onto statues, gilded each year. Any infant tumble from the prince as he took his first steps would bring a kaleidoscope of riches to view; wherever he looked, his soft and silken world was perfect. His mother watched his excellent progress with delight. Louis-Charles was glowing with vitality, "a real peasant boy, big, rosy and plump," she wrote. This contrasted sharply with his brother, Monsieur le Dauphin who, although more than three years older, was constantly prone to infections.

Monsieur le Dauphin was eventually moved out of the nursery and established in his own official suite on the ground floor of Versailles, ousting his uncle Provence. His older sister, Madame Royale, also had her own apartment near Marie-Antoinette, under the Hall of Mirrors. Apart from occasional state duties, such as the *grand couvert*, where they would dine in public—Madame Royale with her hair powdered and wearing a stiff panniered gown, the Duc de Normandie usually sitting on his mother's lap—their lives were shielded from the public. The Duc de Normandie was taken on carriage trips around the park, visits to the farm at the Trianon or he could play in his little garden on the terrace. Occasionally there would be trips to nearby palaces at Marly, Saint-Cloud or Fontainebleau.

Nonetheless, the "gilded youth" of Versailles, in the words of one nobleman, the Comte de Ségur, walked "upon a carpet of flowers which covered an abyss." France's deepening financial crisis was beginning to dominate public life. In 1787 interest on the national debt alone had risen to almost *half* of all state expenditure. Louis and his finance minister, Charles Alexandre de Calonne, were fast approaching a point where it was no longer possible to borrow more money except at excessive interest rates. They faced no alternative but to raise taxes.

Calonne, like his predecessors, urged the king to reform the tax system and abolish the partial exemption from direct taxation enjoyed by the nobility and clergy. The king, always anxious to create a consensus for change rather than appear to act as autocratic leader, wanted to introduce Calonne's reforms without confrontation. Consequently, rather than present his proposals to the *parlements*—which he knew would be hostile—he decided to take a chance and call a special Assembly of Notables, composed of leading figures in society, hand-picked for the occasion.

However, when the Assembly of Notables gathered in Versailles in February 1787, far from accepting and popularizing the tax reforms as the king had hoped, they were suspicious. The clergy and nobles, who owned most of the land, were largely exempt from the principal land tax, the *taille*, yet under the new measures they would pay up to five percent of their own income. As news spread of the proposed tax reforms and soaring deficit, Calonne became the focus of the passionate criticism. In Paris his effigy was burned in the streets. By April 1787, the king was forced to dismiss his unpopular minister, and the following month he dissolved the Assembly of Notables.

His new finance minister, Loménie de Brienne, prepared a revised package of tax reforms and boldly decided he would try to win approval directly from the *parlement* of Paris. However, *parlement*, like the Assembly of Notables, rejected the equalization of taxation. Ironically, this revolutionary measure, which would have benefited the vast majority of people, was perceived to be an act of despotism by the monarchy. Since the king had to raise money somehow, to pay staff and honor debts, he was becoming increasingly desperate. In August 1787, he exiled the entire *parlement* of Paris to the country at Troyes. This caused uproar; There were demonstrations in Paris and crowds gathered outside *parlement* crying for "liberty." Although Louis had reduced court spending, the increase in taxes for the nobles and clergy was inextricably linked in the public's mind with the demands made by the royal family on the public purse to fund their extravagant lifestyle. The public's growing hostility began to focus on Louis and, inevitably, his Austrian wife, Marie-Antoinette.

A large diamond necklace would prove the queen's undoing: 647 brilliants, two thousand eight hundred carats, arranged in glittering layer upon layer, a piece of jewellery to dazzle the eye and empty the purse. It was the dream creation of the court jewellers, Böhmer and Bassenge, and they hoped to sell this diamond fantasy to Marie-Antoinette. To their disappointment, by the late 1780s, the "Queen of the Rococo" was now much more restrained; she repeatedly refused to buy the necklace.

Böhmer would not give up. He offered his 1.6-million-livre "superb necklace" to the king, hoping he would buy it for Marie-Antoinette. The king, it seems, was not in a necklace-buying mood. Faced with constant if polite refusals, the worried Böhmer, increasingly looking bankruptcy in the eye, decided on a rather theatrical appeal to the queen as he waylaid her at court. "Madame, I am ruined and disgraced if you do not purchase my necklace," he cried as he threw himself on his knees. "I shall throw myself into the river." The queen spoke with him severely. "Rise, Böhmer. I do not like these rhapsodies." She urged him to break up the necklace and sell the stones separately.

It was the queen's misfortune that the Grand Almoner of France, one Cardinal de Rohan, had long dreamed of enhancing his standing with the royal family. The cardinal fell prey to a con artist posing as a friend of the queen, a certain charming Comtesse Jeanne de La Motte-Valois. Knowing that the cardinal wished to ingratiate himself and be part of the queen's elite circle, Jeanne de La Motte hired a woman to dress like Marie-Antoinette and meet him secretly one night in the palace grounds. This false queen pressed a rose into the cardinal's hand and hurried away, leaving him under the delightful impression that he had indeed met with the queen's favor.

Encouraged by this, when Jeanne de La Motte told the cardinal that the queen wished him to purchase Böhmer's famous necklace on her behalf, he obligingly did so. He duly passed the fabulous necklace to Jeanne de La Motte, who went to London posthaste to make her fortune as the gems emerged in brooches, earrings, snuff boxes, and other trifles.

There was just the outstanding sum of 1.6 million livres. When the court jewellers demanded payment, the shocking scandal began to unravel. The king arrested the cardinal and he was sent to the Bastille, only to be tried and acquitted of theft later before a sympathetic *parlement*. There were cries of *"Vive le Cardinal"* in the streets as people thought he was the foolish victim of a tyrant king. Eventually brought to justice, Jeanne de La Motte was sent to the prison of *La Salpetrière* and condemned to a public flogging. She was to be branded with a V for *voleuse*, or thief, on her shoulder. In front of a huge crowd, the iron rod slipped as she struggled and she was burned on the breast. She, too, successfully portrayed herself as victim in the "Diamond Necklace Affair" in her memoirs, in which she claimed only to have confessed to the theft to protect the queen, with whom she had had an affair.

Although Marie-Antoinette was entirely innocent, as the unbelievable saga unfolded before the amazed public in the late 1780s, it was *her* reputation that became the most sullied. Her love of beautiful jewels had been widely reported. It was easy to believe that she had accepted the necklace, refused to pay for it and then spitefully passed the blame onto others. Under the relentless onslaught of outrageous *libelles* that poured onto the streets of Paris, her image became irrevocably tarnished. It was claimed that she and her favored friends continued to spend recklessly and that she had handed over millions of livres to her Austrian family.

She was portrayed as the real power behind the throne who pushed Austrian interests on a weak king. The degree to which she was seen as out of touch with the realities of the poor came when she was attributed as saying, "Let them eat cake," when bread was in short supply. There is no evidence that she said this; the remark is more likely to have been made a century before, by Louis XIV's queen. Yet the queen began to receive pointed demonstrations of disapproval when she ventured out in public. Trips into Paris could turn quickly into frightening undertakings.

With France teetering on the edge of bankruptcy and the king demanding yet more taxes, the queen began to emerge as the prime culprit. The "Austrian whore" or "Austrian bitch" was transformed into the root cause of the country's financial plight. At a watershed in the destruction of her image she was dubbed the wildly extravagant "Madame *Déficit*." Due to her unpopularity, her latest portrait was not hung in the Royal Academy of Paris. In the blank frame remaining, someone had written, "Behold the deficit!"

The once pleasure-loving queen retreated from public gaze. Occasional rides into the country around the Trianon with Count Axel Fersen were one of the few consolations at a time when she was increasingly preoccupied with motherhood. In the summer of 1787, her fourth child, Sophie, born the year before, died suddenly from tuberculosis. As she struggled with this loss, it was becoming increasingly evident that the dauphin, too, was showing signs of tuberculosis. He began to lose weight and suffered attacks of fever.

As the autumn and winter months wore on, the king was losing control of the political situation. Under continued financial pressure, Louis recalled the *parlement*. However, the king's insistence that he wanted a fairer system of taxation fell on deaf ears. He seemed unable to get his message across, and was even opposed by his own relative, his distant cousin, the scheming Philippe d'Orléans, head of the Orléanist line of the Bourbon family. It was becoming clear to Louis that the tax issue was being used as a pretext for a wider challenge to his authority as the king. A system of rule that had existed in France for generations was now at risk. At stake was not just balancing the budget and pushing through a fairer system of taxation, but more fundamentally who had the right to make these decisions and govern France.

Determined to reestablish his authority, on May 8, 1788, Louis gambled yet again. He suspended not only the *parlement* of Paris but also the other twelve provincial *parlements* as well. This prompted a wave of rioting across France. There was an outpouring of support for the *parlements* and all sections of society seemed ranged against a king who was increasingly portrayed as a tyrant. Louis began to doubt his own ability and, according to his youngest sister, Madame Élisabeth, was wracked with indecision. "My brother has such good intentions," she wrote, "but fears always to make a mistake. His first impulse over, he is tormented by the dread of doing an injustice." Both he and his finance minister became ill with the stress as the government's financial position continued to deteriorate. Many people refused to pay any taxes at all until the king backed down. Loménie de Brienne, now unable to raise money either by credit or taxes, was obliged to print money to pay government staff. It was, in effect, an admission of bankruptcy. He was losing command of the situation and by August he was fired.

In the hope of bringing order to the disintegrating condition of the state, Louis came under increasing pressure to summon an ancient institution known as the Estates-General. This comprised elected representatives of three great medieval orders or estates: the clergy, the nobles and the commoners. The Estates-General was only summoned in times of crisis; Louis was only too aware that such a meeting might undermine his authority still further. The last time the Estates-General had sat, in 1614, they had only become a forum for disagreement and conflict. Yet the whole nation seemed to be demanding its recall. In late August, responding to popular demand, he reappointed his former finance minister, Jacques Necker. Lurching from one policy to another, increasingly unable to stave off bankruptcy, Louis became trapped. Finally, he agreed to summon the Estates-General to Versailles the following year. It was a desperate gamble.

When the Estates-General had last met 174 years previously, it had had an equal number of representatives from each Estate, in which the First Estate (the clergy) and the Second Estate (the nobility) could always combine together to outvote the Third Estate (the commoners). When the restored *parlement* demanded the same arrangement this time, there was outrage and further riots. Louis decided to right this imbalance by giving the commoners as many representatives as the nobility and clergy together, but he neglected to say whether the voting would be by "order" or by head. What had initially begun as a protest by the clergy and nobles against the powers of the king to raise their taxes had now set in motion a chain of events in which all sections in France sought to exert greater political power. Even the elements seemed ranged against Louis. A very bad harvest was followed in 1788 by a viciously cruel winter in which many of the poor died of cold or starved. Unrest was growing; robber bands pillaged the countryside. To many ordinary people the whole system in France seemed rotten; feelings against the king and queen hardened as deeply felt grievances were aired.

As the debates raged about the Estates-General, Marie-Antoinette watched anxiously over the declining health of her eldest son. "The young prince fell, in a few months, from rude health into a condition which curved his spine, distorted and lengthened his face, and rendered his legs so weak that he was unable to walk without being supported like some broken old man," wrote Madame Campan. Still only six years old, his little body slowly became pitifully deformed as his tuberculosis spread. "He has one leg shorter than the other, and his spine is twisted and sticks out unnaturally," the queen confided to her brother, Emperor Joseph II, in February 1788. The next month, the dauphin was sent to the Château de Meudon with his governor, in the hopes that his health would recover with the fresh country air. The king visited his son no less than forty times over the summer months, eagerly looking for any sign of improvement. There was none.

The queen took comfort from her other two children. Marie-Thérèse, the eldest, she nicknamed *Mousseline la Sérieuse* on account of her serious, thoughtful manner. The Petite Madame took after her father in temperament, although she could be dignified sometimes to the point of seeming haughty. The queen reserved her strongest endearments for her youngest, Louis-Charles, *mon chou d'amour*. His blue eyes and blond hair resembled his mother's, and with his affectionate and playful personality he proved a most rewarding child. In the nursery with his friends he enjoyed games of "wedding" and playing with sand or horses—his great aunts had given him eight small black ponies, which had been specially trained so he could ride them. Madame Campan observed, "His ruddy health and loveliness did, in truth, form a striking contrast to the languid look and melancholy disposition of his elder brother." Increasingly, the king and queen's hopes for the future of their line were now concentrated on this charming little ruler of the nursery who, at four and a half, was already wearing coat and trousers.

May 4, 1789. The streets of Versailles were hung with tapestries for the magnificent opening procession to mark the historic gathering of the Estates-General. With great ceremony to mark this rebirth of France—as some believed—the parade of two thousand people filed though the crowded streets for a service at the Church of St. Louis. The king walked behind the archbishop of Paris, followed by the royal family, then representatives of the three Estates, each with lighted candles.

[31]

Marie-Antoinette, sumptuously bejewelled in a silver dress, looked sad as she passed. Unable to take part, but watching the proceedings from a balcony, was her seven-year-old son; his twisted little body stretched on a daybed. She now knew he was dying and could scarcely hold back her tears as he smiled valiantly at her. At that moment, some "low women," according to Madame Campan, "yelled out '*Vive le Duc d'Orléans!*' in such a rebellious manner that the queen nearly fainted." Many of the representatives, she wrote, arrived in Versailles with the "strongest prejudices" against the queen, certain she "was draining the treasury of the State in order to satisfy the most unreasonable luxury." Some demanded to see the Trianon, convinced that there was at least one room, "totally decorated with diamonds, and columns studded with sapphires and rubies." Disbelieving representatives searched the pavilion in vain for the diamond chamber.

The first session of the Estates-General met the next day in the opulent surroundings of the *Salle des Menus Plaisirs* in the palace. The clergy, in imposing scarlet and black ecclesiastical robes, were seated on benches on the right. The nobles, richly dressed in white-feathered hats and gold trimmed suits, took the benches on the left. The commoners sat furthest from the king at the far end, dressed simply in black. One of those among them taking in the scene—the large ornate chamber, the symbolic ranking of the representatives with the Third Estate in plain clothes at the back— was a young lawyer called Maximilien Robespierre.

At the age of eleven, Robespierre had won a scholarship to one of the most prestigious schools in France, Louis-le-Grand, in Paris. He had graduated in law in 1780 and returned to practice in his hometown, Arras, in the northern province of Artois. When the Estates-General were summoned, he seized his chance to further his career and successfully secured a position as one of eight Third Estate deputies for Artois. Like many commoners, he arrived in Versailles determined to challenge the structures of privilege at the heart of French society and create social equality.

As the speeches and debates began, the great expectations that had preceded the opening of the Estates-General soon disintegrated. Far from even attempting to resolve the all-important financial crisis, which Necker outlined at great length, there were increasingly bitter arguments about voting procedures, with each Estate continually plotting for positions of power over the others. As the weeks of May passed, rather than resolving the issue of tax reform, the meeting served as a catalyst, crystallizing grievances at the very heart of the constitution of France.

At this time, the queen was almost completely preoccupied with the young dauphin. The young prince suffered as his illness slowly destroyed every trace of childish vitality. When the Princesse de Lamballe visited him at Meudon with her lady-in-waiting, they could hardly bear to look at his "beautiful eyes, the eyes of a dying child." The queen watched helplessly as his emaciated body became covered in sores. "The things that the poor little one says are incredible; they pierce his mother's heart; his tenderness toward her knows no bounds," observed a friend. On the second of June, services were held for him across France and prayers were said. It was to no avail. Two days later he died in his mother's arms.

The significance of these events was lost on the four-year-old Louis-Charles playing in the nursery at Versailles. He wept to hear of the death of his older brother, now lying in state at Meudon in a silver and white room, his coffin covered with a silver cloth, his crown and sword. All around him, the chambers of Versailles resounded to the acrimonious debates of the deputies. Louis-Charles had now become the symbol of the royal future of France, "Monsieur le Dauphin," next in line to a throne increasingly devoid of authority as well as funds.

The king, somewhere during these events, private and public, missed his opportunity to rally the deputies and inspire their support. Overwhelmed with grief, he and the queen left Versailles to mourn their oldest son. In his absence, the deputies of the Third Estate seized the initiative. At a pivotal meeting, on June 17, 1789, they passed a motion that since they represented 95 percent of the people, the Third Estate should be renamed as a new body, called the National Assembly, which had the right to control taxation. With flagrant disregard for the king, they planned to proceed, with or without royal approval.

While the king vacillated, hopelessly torn between the advice of ministers such as Necker who counselled compromise, and that of his wife and brothers who argued for a tougher line, the Third Estate went even further. When the deputies of the new National Assembly found themselves locked out of their usual meeting room, they adjourned to an indoor tennis court. Here each member solemnly swore not to separate until France had a new constitution. This became known as the "Tennis Court Oath."

The king's power was collapsing. His specially appointed Assembly of Notables had defied him, the *parlement* had defied him, now the Third Estate was defying him. With each successive swipe at the monarchy, the king was racked with indecision. "All goes worse than ever," Madame Élisabeth reported frankly to her friend, the Marquise de Bombelles, as she confided her despair at her brother's lack of the "necessary sternness." Foreseeing disaster, she wrote, "The deputies, victims of their passions . . . are rushing to ruin, and that of the throne and the whole kingdom. As for me," she told the marquise ominously, "I have sworn not to leave my brother and I shall keep my oath."

As support grew rapidly for the new National Assembly, the king was obliged to recognize it. He ordered the other two Estates to join the Third. As a result, the commoners, who had had their representation doubled, now held a majority. Many took the Third's victory and the king's acquiescence as a sign that his authority had completely broken down. There was rioting on the streets; civil war seemed imminent. The king summoned extra regiments to Paris. He told the deputies of the National Assembly that the troops were stationed as a precaution, to protect the people. The Assembly, however, saw the presence of twenty-five thousand troops in and around the capital differently and feared that they themselves were under direct threat from the king. One of its members spoke out: "These preparations for war are obvious to everyone and fill every heart with indignation."

On July 12, following the dismissal of the popular finance minister, Necker, crowds gathered to hear rousing revolutionary speeches against the tyranny of the monarchy, whom it was feared was seeking to destroy the new National Assembly that represented the people. "Citizens, they will stop at nothing," urged one speaker, the journalist Camille Desmoulins, a school friend of Robespierre. "They are plotting a massacre of patriots." People rushed to arm themselves. As a wave of panic swept the Paris streets, armorers and gunsmiths were raided—one later reported that he was looted no less than thirty times. The monastery of Saint-Lazare, a depot for grain and flour, was sacked. The next day, at the Hôtel de Ville, the Marquis de La Fayette, a hero of the American war, set out to enroll a new National Guard with himself as colonel, creating a new citizens' army. Early the next morning, on July 14, around eighty thousand people gathered at the Invalides, the army's barracks, where they overwhelmed the troops and managed to obtain thirty thousand muskets and some cannon. Faced with rumors that royal troops were on the move, the citizens' army needed gunpowder, and this was in the Bastille. The crowd swept forward, to rousing cries of "To the Bastille!"

The grey stone walls and menacing towers of this fourteenth-century fortress rose as a great, dark edifice on the Rue Saint-Antoine on the eastern side of Paris. For years, any enemies of the crown could be detained in this prison without a judicial process, merely by a royal warrant, the notorious *lettres de cachet*. Consequently, the almost-windowless walls, five feet thick, rising sheer from the moat, had come to represent a mighty symbol of royal tyranny and oppression. The cry went up to seize the Bastille, take the gunpowder and release the prisoners. Revolt was fast turning into revolution.

As nine hundred men gathered around the Bastille, the atmosphere inside was tense. The governor, Marquis Bernard-René de Launay, gave orders for his guards to defend the prison at all cost. After midday, the mob broke through the first drawbridge and behind a smoke screen formed by burning two carts of manure, they aimed their guns at the gate and the second drawbridge. With the fortress under siege, the garrison fought back, killing almost one hundred of the assailants and injuring many more. Yet the mob continued to attack. The guards eventually surrendered, defying de Launay's orders, and lowered the second drawbridge. The crowds, now out of control, surged forward into the fortress, breaking windows and furniture, and killing any guards who had not put down their weapons. The prisoners were released; for all the furor, there were only seven—including one madman.

With the people eager for revenge, the governor, de Launay, was seized and dragged toward the Hôtel de Ville, the excited crowd wanting his death and kicking him down until the governor, unable to endure another moment, screamed, "Let me die!" As he lashed out, the crowd finished off their victim with hunting knives, swords and bayonets. Finally a cook named Désnot cut off his head with a pocket knife. The still-dripping head was twisted onto a pike and paraded around the streets to the cheering crowd. He was described on a placard as "Governor of the Bastille, disloyal and treacherous enemy of the people." For patriots, the fall of the Bastille created a wave of euphoria, and it would not be long before it was demolished entirely.

Faced with this new crisis, the king went to the National Assembly and effectively surrendered, promising to withdraw his troops from Paris. As the sense of desperation grew, many senior members of the Versailles court now fled. On the night of July 16, the king's young brother, Artois, and the queen's close friend, Gabrielle de Polignac, left the palace with their families. "Nothing could be more affecting than the parting of the queen and her friend," wrote Madame Campan. The queen "wished to go and embrace her once more" after they had parted, but knowing that her movements were watched, was too frightened that she might give her friend away. The duchess "was disguised as a *femme de chambre,*" and instead of travelling in the waiting *berline,* stepped up in front with the coachman, like a servant.

After long discussions with his ministers, the king decided that the royal family would stay at Versailles. Madame Campan saw the queen tear up the papers ordering preparations for departure "with tears in her eyes." She was in no doubt about the danger they faced. In the event of an attack on the palace, they might not even be able to count on the loyalty of the guard at Versailles to protect them. In a bold attempt to defuse the situation, Louis agreed to a request by the National Assembly to visit Paris. Marie-Antoinette begged him not to go. Locked in her rooms with her family, she sent for members of the court, only to find they had already fled. "Terror had driven them away," said Madame Campan; no one expected the king to return alive. "A deadly silence reigned throughout the palace."

It was dark before the king returned. He had faced the crowd and was now wearing the red, white and blue cockade—soon to be the badge of the revolutionary—as he made his way back to his palace escorted by a citizens' army. "Happily no blood has been shed," he told his family, "and I swear that never shall a drop of French blood be shed by my order."

Only five days later, Joseph Foulon, one of his ministers brought in to replace Necker, was recognized by the crowd and dragged to the Hôtel de Ville. "After tormenting him in a manner the particulars of which make humanity shudder," reported Campan, he was hanged. "His body was dragged about the streets and his heart was carried—by women—in the midst of a bunch of white carnations!" It had been rumored that Foulon had said, "If the rogues haven't any bread, they can have hay." Now hay was stuffed in his mouth as his head was thrust on a pike and borne through the streets of Paris.

The terror in Paris ricocheted around the country in a wave of panic known as *la Grande Peur*. Angry mobs invaded the Bastilles at Bordeaux and Caen; fighting broke out in the streets of Lyon, Rennes, Rouen and Saint-Malo. With the harvest not yet in, the price of bread soared. Many feared that there was a plot to starve the people into submission. As the poor left their homes to scavenge for food it was widely believed that these vagrants were paid by the nobility to cause disruption and steal bread. Rumors were rife that the food shortages were exacerbated by the stockpiling of grain by the wealthy, including the royal family. As panic spread, peasants invaded the chateaux to exact bloody revenge on their masters.

At Versailles, the queen was increasingly concerned about the safety of her children. Following the departure of Gabrielle de Polignac, she chose as their governess the Marquise de Tourzel, a woman who combined "an illustrious ancestry with the most exemplary virtue," according to the king. However, the marquise hesitated; she had children of her own and was under no illusion of the "perils and responsibilities" of the post. It was only the "spectacle of desertion" by so many of their friends that persuaded her to accept.

On July 24, the queen wrote to the marquise with practical details of her new charges. "My son is two days short of being four years and four months old. . . . His health has always been good, though even in his cradle we noticed that he was very nervous and upset by the slightest sudden noise. . . . Because of delicate nerves he is always frightened by any noise to which he isn't accustomed and, for example, is afraid of dogs after hearing one bark near him." Despite these sensitivities, she portrays Louis-Charles as a good-natured child "with no sense of conceit," although he could, on occasion, be a little thoughtless. His greatest defect, wrote the queen, was his indiscretion. "He easily repeats what he has heard; and often without intending to lie, adds things according to his imagination. This is his greatest fault and must be corrected."

"My son has no idea of rank in his head and I would like that to continue: our children always find out soon enough who they are. He is very fond of his sister and has a good heart. Every time something makes him happy, a trip somewhere or a gift, his first impulse is to request the same for his sister. He was born cheerful; for his health he needs to be outside a great deal, and I think it is best for him to play and work on the terraces rather than have him go any further. The exercise taken by little children playing and running about in the open air is far healthier than making them go for long walks which often tire their backs." The queen instructed her new governess never to let him out of her sight. Finding the virtuous marquise stricter than her predecessor, it wasn't long before the dauphin dubbed her "Madame Sévère."

In August 1789, the National Assembly moved quickly to destroy many of the pillars of the *ancien régime*, the previous or old order of France. On the night of the fourth, in a highly charged and emotional sitting, the nobles and clergy capitulated and agreed to relinquish all feudal privileges. All exemptions from taxation and a multitude of dues that peasants owed their landlords were abolished. It was the overthrow of feudalism. Over the next two weeks, the National Assembly went further to try to establish equality throughout France in a *Declaration of the Rights of Man and of the Citizen*. In this declaration, it was said "all men are born free and equal" and every citizen had the right to decide what taxes should be imposed. It also set out a definition for fundamental human rights: freedom of speech, freedom from unlawful imprisonment, freedom of the press and religious liberty. The declaration was then given to the king at Versailles for his formal assent. He played for time and delayed approving the documents.

Feeling increasingly vulnerable at Versailles, in mid-September, Louis summoned a thousand troops that he knew to be loyal from the northern frontier: the Flanders regiment. According to tradition, the king's body-guards held a celebratory dinner to welcome officers of the new regiment to Versailles. On the first of October a lavish banquet was prepared by the royal chef, and set up beneath the gold and blue canopies of the Opera House. "There were numerous orchestras in the room," says Madame Campan. "The rousing air, *'O Richard! O mon Roi'* was played and shouts of *'Vive le Roi!'* shook the roof for several minutes."

The king and queen, who had not planned to attend, made an unexpected entrance with the dauphin. Immediately the orchestra struck up. "People were intoxicated with joy," wrote Madame Campan. "On all sides were heard praises of Their Majesties, exclamations of affection, expressions of regret for what they had suffered, clapping of hands and shouts of *'Vive le Roi!' 'Vive La Reine!' 'Vive le Dauphin!'* " A highly charged atmosphere was created with many tears and officers dramatically saluting the king with their swords. At one point, the young dauphin was lifted onto the horseshoe table at the center of the stage. Rising to the occasion, he walked the length of the table, smiling at everyone as he carefully picked his way through the fine china and glassware. When the king and queen finally left, the theater resounded with defiant shouts of "Down with the Assembly! Down with the Assembly!" Yet there were spies everywhere and reports of the grand banquet spread like fire around Paris.

It was an incendiary piece of news: while people were almost starving in

Paris, banquets were apparently being organized for counterrevolutionaries in Versailles! Reports became wildly exaggerated. The feast was no less than an orgy at which red, white and blue cockades were crushed underfoot, to gleeful shouts of "Down with the Nation!" Did not the queen personally distribute white rosettes to each person at the banquet? That week in Paris, bread was becoming increasingly scarce with many bakeries completely out of supplies. By Sunday, October 4, bread riots even led to one baker being hanged, accused of hoarding flour in the expectation of higher prices. Increasingly bitter charges were made against the queen. It was widely rumored that she was planning the counterrevolution and had given instructions for the stockpiling of flour at Versailles, hoping to crush the people with famine. The queen became a lightning conductor for much of the fury and frustration in Paris.

Monday, October 5. Church bells rang out around the Place de Grève by the Seine in Paris, traditionally the place used for executions and hangings. Women began to gather; the *poissardes*—or fishwives—and market women, servants and washerwomen converged on the square united by their desperate poverty and equally desperate need for bread, their anger and resolve strengthened by the sight of their own hungry children. Despite the rain, by early afternoon, more than six thousand women had assembled, armed with anything they could find: pitchforks, scythes, kitchen knives, even skewers and sticks. Nothing could deter them; they had nothing to lose as they began to march the twelve miles to Versailles, with the now-driving rain soaking their ill-clad bodies. Soon after they left, the National Guard of Paris, eager to support the women's march, also began to assemble. By the late afternoon, fifteen thousand guardsmen set out for Versailles, reluctantly led by La Fayette.

Marie-Thérèse, the queen's daughter, still only ten years old, later wrote vividly of "that too-memorable day," which for her marked the beginning of the "outrages and cruelties" that her family was to endure. That morning, everything was tranquil at the palace; she was having her lessons, her aunt Elisabeth had ridden out to her property at Montreuil, her father was hunting, her mother was in her gardens at Trianon. Madame Élisabeth was the first to hear that Paris was on the march and rushed to Versailles, in great agitation, to warn the queen. Her father raced back at three in the afternoon. The wrought-iron gates of the chateau were swung tightly shut against the people.

Soon after this, the army of women, soaked and splashed with mud, arrived at the gates, demanding bread and shouting violent abuse at *l'Autrichienne*. Marie-Thérèse was in no doubt of their intentions. "Their [principal] purpose was to murder my mother," she wrote, "also to massacre the bodyguards, the only ones who remained faithful to their king." Terror reigned at Versailles.

The captain of the guard asked the king for authority to disperse the crowd. Louis could not bring himself to fire against women and agreed to meet a delegation. Their spokesperson, a demure seventeen-year-old called Pierrette Chabry, in spite of fainting at the critical moment, managed to get across the need for bread. The king reassured her that he had given orders already for any grain held up on the roads around Paris to be delivered at once. Gratefully, she asked to kiss the king's hand.

Outside the palace, the crowd were not so easily appeased and shots rang out. Marie-Antoinette begged Louis to flee Versailles with his family. The king delayed, tormented with indecision. "A fugitive king, a fugitive king," he said over and over again, unable to come to terms with such a momentous defeat. How could he be driven from his palace merely by a crowd of hungry women? He missed his moment. When he finally decided on flight, the crowd was prepared and would not allow him to depart. They mounted the carriages, cut the harnesses and led the horses away.

As dusk fell, the crowd camped around the palace; bonfires were lit, a horse was roasted. The arrival of the National Guard of Paris was ambiguous. Would they protect the king or further the interests of the crowd? At midnight, La Fayette was presented before the king and reassured him that the National Guard would stop the mob from attacking the palace. Comforted by this, finally, at two in the morning the royal family attempted to get some rest. "My mother knew that their chief object was to kill her," wrote her daughter. "Nevertheless in spite of that, she made no sign, but retired to her room with all possible coolness and courage . . . directing Madame de Tourzel to take her son instantly to the king if she had heard any noise in the night."

However, at five in the morning, some women discovered that the gate to the *Cour des Princes* was not properly locked. There was a call to action. The crowd surged into the palace, and entered the inner courtyard, the *Cour de Marbre*, by the royal quarters. Many rushed straight up the stairs leading to the queen's apartments, yelling obscenities. A guard later reported that he heard, "We'll cut off her head . . . tear her heart out . . . fry [*fricasser*] her liver . . . make her guts into ribbons and even then it would not be all over." One of the bodyguards tried to defend the stairway. He was stabbed with pikes and knives and dragged half alive into the courtyard where his head was chopped off with an axe. Inside the palace, according to Marie-Thérèse, another guard, "though grievously wounded, dragged [himself] to my mother's door, crying out for her to fly and bolt the doors behind her." Just at this point, the queen's *femme de chambre* opened the door of the queen's antechamber and was horrified to see this bodyguard holding a musket valiantly across the door as he was struck down by the mob. "His face was covered with blood," wrote Madame Campan. "He turned round and exclaimed, 'Save the queen, Madame! They are come to assassinate her.' She hastily shut the door on the unfortunate victim of duty and fastened it with a great bolt." Seconds later, "the wretches flung themselves on him and left him bathed in blood."

Hearing firing and shrieks outside her door, "my mother sprang from her bed and, half dressed, ran to my father's apartment, but the door of it was locked within," wrote Marie-Thérèse. Within moments, the rioters had burst into the queen's empty bedroom and cut her bedclothes to shreds with their sabers and knives, to cries of "kill the bitch," or "kill the whore!" Those protecting the king did not realize it was the queen herself—not rioters—at the door. For several terrifying minutes she was trapped, hammering on the door, unable to enter the king's apartments. "Just at the moment that the wretches forced the door of my mother's room, so that one instant later, she would have been taken without means of escape . . . the man on duty . . . recognized my mother's voice and opened the door to her."

In the frenzy of the night, the king was trying to reach the queen's apartment to bring her to safety; Madame de Tourzel was trying to protect the dauphin; the queen went in frantic search of Marie-Thérèse. Gradually, they all reunited in the *Salon de l'Oeuil de Boeuf,* where they could hear axes and bars thumping against the door as the guards tried to drive the rioters away with their bayonets. It was only after they had driven the rioters outside to the courtyard that La Fayette finally emerged with his men and managed to save the bodyguards.

Outside in the marble courtyard, the crowd demanded to see the king. He emerged onto the balcony, but this did not appease the crowd who began to shout for the queen. Inside, Marie-Antoinette turned white. "All her fears were visible on her face." Dazed and numbed by the attempt on her life, she hesitated. Everyone in the room urged her not to face the crowd. Outside, the yells echoed ever more insistently around the courtyard and rose in a great cry, "The queen to the balcony!" Summoning extraordinary courage, she stepped out, her hair dishevelled, in a yellow striped dressing gown, her children by her side. For Marie-Thérèse and Louis-Charles, looking through the familiar gilded balustrade on the sea of hostile faces staring at them, it was a terrifying glimpse of the full force of the hatred of the French people. "The courtyard of the chateau presented a horrible sight," recalled Marie-Thérèse. "A crowd of women, almost naked, and men armed with pikes, threatened our windows with dreadful cries."

There were cries of "No children! No children!" The queen ushered her children inside to safety. For a few minutes, she faced out the murderous, armed crowds alone with incredible nerve. "She expected to perish," reported her daughter, but happily "her great courage awed the whole crowd of people, who confined themselves to loading her with insults, without daring to attack her person." No one fired. After a while, she simply curtsied and went back into the palace, gathered her son into her arms and wept.

However, their ordeal was not over. The menacing cry went up, "The king to Paris." The king felt he had no alternative but to agree, in order to avoid further bloodshed. He decided he must take his family with him as it was too dangerous to leave them behind. "I confide all that I hold most dear to the love of my good and faithful subjects," he told the vengeful mob in the courtyard.

By one o'clock in the afternoon, everything was ready for the departure of the royal family. "They wished to prevent my father from crossing the great guard rooms that were inundated with blood," reported Marie-Thérèse. "We therefore went down by a small staircase . . . and got into a carriage for six persons; on the back seat were my father, mother and brother; on the front seat . . . my Aunt Elisabeth and I, in the middle my uncle Monsieur and Madame de Tourzel. . . . The crowd was so great it was long before we could advance."

It was the most extraordinary and grotesque procession. News had spread that the royal family was forced out of Versailles and thirty thousand, at least, had gathered to escort the king to Paris. The scene was terrifying; a great swirling mass of humanity, most intent on harm, some so drunk with hatred that any form of violent disturbance could erupt within seconds. Leading the "horrible masquerade"—in the words of one courtier—was the National Guard, with La Fayette always in view near the royal coach. The *poissardes*, market women and other rioters followed like so many furies, brandishing sticks and spikes, some with the heads of the king's murdered guardsmen on their pikes. These gruesome trophies were paraded with dev-ilish excitement as they danced around the royal coach, all too conscious that power was indeed an intoxicating mixture as they endlessly threatened obscene and imminent death to the queen. Many had loaves of bread from the kitchens of Versailles stuck on their bayonets and were chanting, "We won't go short of bread anymore. We are bringing back the Baker, the Baker's wife and the Baker's boy." Behind were the household troops and Flanders regiment, unarmed; many obliged to wear the revolutionary cock-ade. They were followed by innumerable carriages bearing the remnants of the royal court and deputies from the new National Assembly. Count Axel Fersen, who was in one of the carriages following the king, wrote of their six-

and-a-half-hour journey to Paris: "May God preserve me from ever seeing again so heartbreaking a spectacle as that of the last few days."

For the royal family, forced to take part in this terrifying and, until then, almost unimaginable procession, it was a definitive end of an era. In the distance behind them, glimpsed only through a forest of pikes and a sea of hostile faces, the Palace of Versailles, which for more than a century had epitomized the Bourbon's absolute power, slowly retreated from view, quietness descending, the only sound the hammers of workmen fastening the shutters. Now the king, impassive and silent, was a consenting victim to the barbarity of the mob, as he allowed his family to be led in humiliation to Paris. Inside the coach, he held a handkerchief to his face to hide his shame and tears. Next to him was the queen, clutching her four-year-old son tightly, her expression bearing "the marks of violent grief." She tried to ignore the *poissardes* who climbed onto the carriage, yelling still more insults and abuse at her. "Along the whole way, the brigands never ceased firing their muskets . . . and shouted *Vive la Nation*!" wrote Marie-Thérèse. Occasionally the young dauphin—terrified as this horrific grown-up world suddenly burst in on his orderly life with such force—bravely leaned out of the window and pleaded with the crowds not to harm his mother. *"Grâce pour Maman! Grâce pour Maman,"* he cried. "Spare my mother, spare my mother."

Chapter Three

THE TUILERIES

The Tuileries Palace, a large jail filled with the
condemned, stood amid the celebration of destruction.
Those sentenced also amused themselves as they waited
for the cart, the clipping, and the red shirt they had
put out to dry. And through the windows, the queen's
circle could be seen, stunningly illuminated.

—CHATEAUBRIAND, *MÉMORIES D'OUTRE-TOMBE*

The royal family was taken to the Tuileries, a sixteenth-century palace in the heart of Paris by the Seine. For over sixty years it had been abandoned as a royal residence, and servants and artisans had settled into the rabbit warren of dark chambers and seemingly endless, dimly lit galleries and stairways. The place was crowded and in disrepair. Rooms were hurriedly prepared for the royal family, but it was soon found that the doors to the dauphin's room would not close and had to be barricaded with furniture. "Isn't it ugly here, Mama," said Louis-Charles. Marie-Antoinette replied, "Louis XIV was happy here. You should not ask for more." Yet he was clearly anxious. The young child who had lived surrounded by richness and elegance, with never a cross word, found, in the space of a few days, his world had become an unrecognizable, frightening chaos. The queen asked the Marquise de Tourzel to watch over him all night.

Woken by the clamor of the crowd outside their windows in the gardens of the Tuileries, Louis-Charles was still terrified. "Good God, Mama! Is it still yesterday?" he cried as he threw himself in her arms. Struggling to understand their change in fortunes, later he went up to his father and asked why his people, who once loved him so well, were "all at once so angry with him and what he had done to irritate them so much?" The king took his young son on his lap. "I wanted money to pay the expenses occasioned by wars," he replied. He carefully tried to explain how he had tried, unsuccessfully, to raise money through the *parlements* and then through the Estates-General. "When they were assembled they required concessions of me which I could not make, either with due respect for myself or with justice to you, who will be my successor. Wicked men, inducing the people to rise, have occasioned the excesses of the last few days; the people must not be blamed for them."

The king and queen were forced to face the fact that they were now detained in Paris indefinitely—at the people's pleasure. They no longer had their own bodyguards; the Tuileries was surrounded by the National Guard who answered to the Assembly. With six armed guards constantly tailing them and their movements closely monitored, the queen quickly made the young prince understand the importance of treating everyone about him politely and "with affability"—even those whom they distrusted. The dauphin "took great pains" to please any visitors. When he had an opportunity to speak to any important dignitaries, he often looked for reassurance from his mother, whispering in her ear, "Was that all right?" With his customary charm, he soon made friends with the sons of National Guards and established his own pretend "Royal Dauphin Regiment" with himself as colonel. People flocked to see him when he was allowed outside where he kept his own pet rabbits and tended a small garden.

Marie-Antoinette struggled to keep up a semblance of normalcy and various possessions claimed from Versailles helped as she set about making it as comfortable as possible. She drew strength from devoting herself to her children. "They are nearly always with me and are my consolation," she wrote to Gabrielle de Polignac, who was now safely out of the country. "*Mon chou d'amour* [the dauphin] is charming and I love him madly. He loves me very much too, in his way, without embarrassment. He is well, growing stronger and has no more temper tantrums. He goes for a walk everyday which is extremely good for him." The queen still had a few of her friends around her, such as the loyal Princesse de Lamballe, who invariably accompanied her when she had to receive deputations of *poissardes* and others, who had come for a hundred reasons, but mostly to air their grievances. Count Axel Fersen also remained discreetly in Paris, in case he could be of any use to the queen.

The king desperately allowed himself to hope that all these arrangements would be temporary, and that he would eventually be restored to Versailles with full power. But power lay in the Assembly, renamed the Constituent Assembly, and gallingly, now installed in the building opposite the Tuileries and flying the new flag which bore the words FREEDOM. NATION. LAW. KING. Although Louis was still king, his authority to pass laws had been effectively taken over by the Assembly. In principle, he retained a delaying veto, yet in the intimidating atmosphere of his confinement in the Tuileries, he was fearful of using even this remaining influence.

For several months the king could not face the meetings of the Assembly, and took refuge in family life, spending more time with his children. While the deputies debated the future of France, he had a smithy installed in the Tuileries, and worked at making locks in his smithy, alone. For Louis, in his virtual prison, terrible despair and fragile hope had become the bread and butter of his daily life as he sank into helpless depression. "The late Grand Monarch makes a figure as ridiculous as pitiable," commented the English writer Edmund Burke. Burke was struck by "the portentous state of France—where elements which compose Human Society seem all to be dissolved, and a world of Monsters to be produced in the place of it." Stripped of the glory of Versailles and the powers of an absolute monarch, the king seemed a spent political force.

Royal authority was also undermined by the continuous outpouring of vicious slander, especially against the queen. Absurdly, even while under the close scrutiny of the National Guard at the Tuileries, she was accused of every conceivable sexual obsession and debauchery: with the guards themselves, courtiers, actors, there was no limit to her superhuman appetite. In an updated version of Madame de La Motte's *Mémoires* published in 1789, her passion for women was also set out in explicit detail. "Her lips, her kisses followed her greedy glances over my quivering body," claimed La Motte. "What a welcome substitute I made, she laughed, for the lumpish, repulsive body of the 'Prime Minister'—her mocking name for the king." The image of her as an insatiable, tyrannical queen was invariably linked to her bloodthirsty lust for revenge on the French people for the uprising. "Her callous eyes, treacherous and inflamed, radiate sheer fire and carnage to gratify her craving for unjust revenge. . . . Her stinking mouth harbors a cruel tongue, eternally thirsty for French blood." Letters were "found," allegedly written by her and intercepted by spies. "Everything goes well, we shall end by starving them," she was quoted as having written to Artois, one of her accomplices. The extremists in the Assembly knew that this skillfully orchestrated propaganda against the queen greatly advanced their political aims to slay royal power. She became the focal point, the hate object of all who were opposed to the monarchy.

As the moderates were forced out of the Assembly and radicals gained the upper hand, royal power continued to decline. Some extremists wished to abolish the monarchy altogether; others to limit its powers still further. It wasn't long before the king found his religious beliefs were to come under attack and, for Louis, this was the final straw. The Assembly increasingly saw the clergy as a pillar of a now-discredited *ancien régime*, loyal to the king. Fearing it was a threat to the survival of the revolution, they searched for a way to reduce its powers. They still had to deal with the problem of the national debt and staving off bankruptcy and realized this problem could be tackled at a stroke. In November 1789, they simply nationalized all the church land, valued at a colossal three billion livres. The Assembly then moved swiftly to introduce the "civil constitution" of the clergy in which the state took responsibility for the administration of the clergy. By November 1790, it was decreed that every priest in the land had to swear an oath of loyalty to the state.

As a devout Roman Catholic, Louis's instincts were to oppose this latest dictate from the Assembly. Yet fearful of where this might lead, finally that

Christmas he felt coerced into signing the decree. This prompted the pope, Pius VI, to intervene, opposing the revolution. Any priest who took the oath was suspended, decreed the pope, unless he retracted the oath within forty days. Once more the Paris mobs took to the streets; an effigy of the pope was burned and the king was denounced for treason for having received communion from a priest who had not sworn the oath. Louis came close to nervous collapse in the spring of 1791, and his doctors advised him to take a rest away from Paris. With the approval of the Assembly, the King resolved to take his family to Saint-Cloud.

On April 18, 1791, at one o'clock, the king, queen, Marie-Thérèse, Louis-Charles and their entourage were in their *berline* in the courtyard of the Tuileries, ready to depart. However, a large, menacing crowd had gathered at the gates and blocked their path. Far from protecting the royal family, the National Guard refused to disperse the rioters. "They mutinied, shut the gates, and declared they would not let the King pass," recorded Madame Campan. Hearing of the emergency, La Fayette hurried to the Tuileries and ordered the guards to allow the king's carriage to depart. It was impossible. The rioters became angry and abusive. The Marquise de Tourzel, who was in the carriage, wrote of the "horrible scene" as she observed the king himself, trying to appeal to the people. "It is astonishing that, having given liberty to the nation, I should not be free myself," he pleaded. It was no use. The crisis lasted two hours. Some of the king's attendants were dragged away; one was violently assaulted. At this point, the dauphin became frightened. He rushed to the window and cried out, "Save him! Save him!" The royal family was obliged to admit defeat and go back inside the Tuileries, the king deeply depressed. There was no escaping the fact that had been evident for months: they were prisoners.

The king felt his position was becoming untenable. Politically, he had been systematically stripped of his powers, sidelined and humiliated. The events of that "cruel day" had provided unnerving evidence that the National Guard could not be trusted to enforce the law and defend the royal family against a hostile mob. Up until this point, despite pressure from his wife and others, the king had been unwilling to reconcile himself to the idea of fleeing from his own people. Now, at last, the urgent need for escape began to take shape in his mind.

Six hundred National Guardsmen, increasingly more loyal to the nation rather than the king, were now patrolling the Tuileries, and spies were everywhere. However, the king and queen could count on one very loyal and capable ally: Count Axel Fersen. Determined to rescue the queen from her impossible position, he told his father, "I should be vile and ungrateful if I deserted them now that they can do nothing for me and I have hope of being useful to them."

Axel Fersen advised the king and queen to escape separately, in light, fast carriages, but they insisted on travelling together with the children, in a more capacious, but much slower, *berline*. They aimed to reach Montmédy, a border town almost two hundred miles to the east by the Austrian Netherlands. Here, protected by a garrison led by his faithful general, Marquis Louis de Bouillé, the king hoped to unite his supporters and challenge the right of the Assembly to usurp his authority.

Fersen coordinated arrangements for their escape. Fresh horses were needed at staging posts every fifteen miles from Paris. For the last eighty miles, once they had passed Châlons in the Champagne region, troops would be waiting at various points from the Pont de Somme-Vesle to escort them to the border. Throughout the spring meticulous arrangements were in progress. At the palace, secret doors were constructed to assist the escape. Disguises and passports were obtained for the royal family. The Marquise de Tourzel would pose as a wealthy Russian woman, "Baronne de Korff," travelling with her two "daughters," Marie-Thérèse as Amélie and Louis-Charles as Aglae. The king would be dressed simply as her valet and the queen, in black coat and hat, was to be the children's governess.

On the planned day of departure, June 20, 1791, the king and queen tried to keep a semblance of normalcy but their anxiety did not pass unnoticed. Marie-Thérèse was only too aware that her mother and father "seemed greatly agitated during the whole day," although she had no idea why. Her anxiety only increased when in the afternoon her mother found an opportunity to take her aside and whisper that "I was not to be uneasy at anything that I might see," and that "we might be separated, but not for long. . . . I was dumbfounded."

"I was hardly in bed before my mother came in; she told me we were to leave at once," wrote Marie-Thérèse. Marie-Antoinette had already woken the dauphin. Although more asleep than awake, Louis-Charles was annoyed to find himself being dressed as a girl. His daytime games were all of soldier heroes and now he thought he was about to command a regiment, shouting for his boots and sword. At half past ten Marie-Antoinette escorted them downstairs and out through an empty apartment to a courtyard where Fersen was waiting, dressed as a coachman and even smoking tobacco.

The dauphin, in his plain linen dress and bonnet, hid at the bottom of the carriage under Madame de Tourzel's gown. To attract less attention, the carriage made several turns around the nearby streets before waiting near the Tuileries for the king and queen. "We saw Monsieur de La Fayette pass close by us, going to the king's *coucher*," recalled Marie-Thérèse. "We waited there a full hour in the greatest impatience and uneasiness at my parents' long delay." Eventually, to her alarm, "I saw a woman approach and walk around our carriage. It made me fear we were discovered." However, it was her aunt Élisabeth, disguised as a nurse to Baronne de Korff. "On entering the carriage she trod upon my brother, who was hidden at the bottom of it; he had the courage not to utter a cry."

At last the king was able to make his escape through a secret passage to Marie-Antoinette's room and then down the staircase, straight past the guards, and out of the main palace entrance. For over two weeks before this, a friend, the Chevalier de Coigny, had visited the Tuileries each evening in similar clothes to those planned for the king's escape. The guards, seeing the same corpulent figure in a brown and green suit, grey wig and hat, assumed this was the Chevalier de Coigny once more, and let him pass. With uncharacteristic cool, Louis even stopped in full view of the guards to tie up one of his shoe buckles. He had left a declaration behind in his rooms at the Tuileries, revealing why he had felt compelled to leave Paris. He argued that the country had deteriorated while he had not been in control; the deficit was ten times bigger, religion was no longer free, and lawlessness was commonplace. He called upon all Frenchmen to support him and a constitution that guaranteed "respect for our holy religion."

Everyone in the escape carriage was waiting for Marie-Antoinette. Just as she ventured out of the palace, another carriage passed right in front of her. It was La Fayette and some guards on their nightly security round. She stepped back quickly, pressing herself against a wall. They had not seen her, but she was so shaken that she mistook her route through the palace and was soon lost in a warren of narrow dark passages. For almost half an hour she frantically tried to get her bearings while at the same time avoiding the armed guards patrolling the corridors.

Meanwhile, La Fayette approached the carriage again, as he left the palace. To their relief, he did not stop to check the passengers; it was not uncommon to see carriages waiting in the Petit Carrousel. When the queen finally made her escape, the king was so delighted, wrote Madame de Tourzel, that he "took her in his arms and kissed her." Fersen urged the horses on cautiously and the carriage moved forward, slipping out of the Tuileries unnoticed.

At last, they made their way through Paris and once through the customs post discarded their escape coach for the specially built *berline*. Unfortunately, at the next change of horses, Fersen had to leave the party. The king feared that if their escape were discovered, it would make their position untenable if a foreigner had escorted the royal party to the border. With the cool and capable Fersen now gone, they were much more vulnerable. The three bodyguards riding on top were junior officers, more used to receiving orders than giving them, and leading the expedition was the king, a man not noted for his decisive action. The *berline*, smartly painted in green, black and lemon and drawn by six horses, with its lavishly appointed interior, "a little house on wheels," was the sort of vehicle that would draw attention to itself as it trundled through the countryside.

Everything went as planned. Six fast horses were waiting at every staging post and by early morning, with Paris now several hours behind him, Louis smiled to think of his valet at the Tuileries, entering his bedroom and raising the alarm. "Once we have passed Châlons there will be nothing to fear," he told Marie-Antoinette with great confidence in his waiting troops. However, the *berline* was three hours behind schedule. Apart from the delay in leaving the palace, some of the relays had taken a little longer than they had planned. Worse still, while crossing a narrow bridge at Chaintrix, the horses fell and the straps enabling the carriage to be drawn were broken. They improvised a repair but more precious minutes were lost. Nonetheless, they passed Châlons successfully at around five in the afternoon. Their armed escort was to be waiting for them at the next stop: Pont de Somme-Vesle.

As they approached the town, their eyes discreetly scanning the horizon from behind the green taffeta blinds, there were no soldiers to be seen. The village was silent. The king did not dare knock on the doors to find out if the troops had been waiting there. He sensed something had gone terribly wrong. Had the escape plan been discovered? Were their lives now at risk? "I felt as though the whole earth had fallen from under me," he wrote later.

The soldiers had, in fact, arrived in Pont de Somme-Vesle early in the afternoon under the leadership of the Duc de Choiseul. As they waited in the village for the king, the local people became alarmed at the sight of so many armed men. Since the peasants assumed that the soldiers were there to enforce the collection of overdue rent, a huge crowd gathered, armed with pitchforks and muskets, preparing to fight if necessary.

When the king had still not arrived by late afternoon, Choiseul had panicked. He feared that the king's escape had been foiled somewhere on the road and that the armed peasants would attack his men. Rashly, not only did he give orders that his own men must disperse but also passed these instructions to the other staging posts down the line. "There is no sign that the treasure will pass today," he wrote. "You will receive new instructions tomorrow." Barely half an hour after Choiseul's departure, the king's *berline* drove into the village.

Without their armed escort, the carriage wound its way for a further two hours along the country road to the next town, Sainte-Menehould, the anxious passengers inside still daring to hope that all was not lost. When they arrived, once again, there was still no evidence of any dragoons. At last,

Captain d'Andouins, who had been in command of the soldiers in this village, approached the *berline*. The captain told the king briefly that the plan had gone awry but he would reassemble his troops and catch up with the king. Unfortunately, as he moved away, he saluted the king.

The vigilant postmaster of the village, one Jean-Baptiste Drouet, noticed that the captain saluted the person in the carriage. Even more surprising, as the carriage departed, he thought he recognized the king leaning back inside. Drouet sounded the alarm. A roll call of drums summoned the town's own National Guard, who stopped the king's soldiers leaving the village.

By this time, on the streets of Paris there was commotion as news of the daring escape spread. "The enemies of the revolution have seized the person of the king," La Fayette announced and gave orders that the king must be found and returned at once to the capital. A dozen riders were found to spread this message quickly throughout France. Meanwhile, the postmaster at Sainte-Menehould, Jean-Baptiste Drouet, had obtained permission from the local authorities to set off at speed and detain the *berline*.

In the lumbering *berline*, the royal family continued on their way "in great agitation and anxiety." By eleven o'clock that night they were approaching Varennes, just thirty miles from the border and safety. Unknown to the royal party, their driver had been overheard giving instructions to take the minor road to Varennes and this had been duly passed on to Drouet. With the pursuit closing in on them, they stopped, as arranged, in the upper part of Varennes for their fresh horses. These were nowhere to be seen and the postilions—responsible for the horses—refused to take the tired horses any further. A dispute began between the postilions and the drivers of the coach. In desperation, the king, queen and Madame Élisabeth stepped out, frantically searching in the pitch black for the new horses themselves. These were, in fact, in the lower part of the town beyond the river Aire, being held by officers who had no idea the king was so near. Just at this point, Drouet came racing past the carriage, and went straight to find the mayor of Varennes to alert him to the royal fugitives in his village.

The king finally persuaded the drivers that the horses must be in the lower part of the village, and the *berline* set off down the steep slope. Suddenly there was a jolt. "We were shocked by the dreadful cries around the carriage, 'Stop! Stop!' Then the horses' heads were seized and in a moment the carriage was surrounded by a number of armed men with torches," recalled Marie-Thérèse. "They put the torches close to my father's face and told us to get out." When the royal party refused, "they repeated loudly that we must get out or they would kill us all, and we saw their guns pointed at the carriage. We were therefore forced to get out."

As alarm bells resounded round the village, the royal party was led to the mayor's house, up a narrow, spiral stairway to a small bedroom where they were detained. "My father kept himself in the farthest corner of the room, but unfortunately his portrait was there, and the people gazed at him and the picture alternately," wrote Marie-Thérèse. They evidently did not believe Madame de Tourzel, who "complained loudly of the injustice of our stoppage, saying that she was travelling quietly with her family under a government passport, and that the king was not with us." As the accusations became increasingly confident and acrimonious, the king was obliged to admit the truth. During the night, as the news spread through the region, hundreds of armed National Guardsmen began to arrive, some with cannon, making escape increasingly impossible. Eventually, at around five in the morning, two agents of Monsieur de La Fayette arrived. They presented the king with a decree from the Assembly ordering his return to Paris.

"There is no longer a king in France!" Louis declared as he heard the decree, in effect demanding his arrest.

Marie-Antoinette was less accepting. "Insolence!" she declared. "What audacity, what cruelty," and she threw the document on the floor. She was overcome by rage and despair, by the bungling and lack of decisiveness, as events had slowly shaped themselves into disaster. When the agents of La Fayette put pressure on the king, saying Paris was in uproar over his departure and women and children might be killed, Marie-Antoinette replied, "Am I not a mother also?" Her anxiety for her two children was her paramount concern.

The royal family tried to play for time. Surely General de Bouillé would send a detachment to rescue them? As the king's young daughter points out, they could so easily have been carried off to the frontier "if anyone had been there who had any head." However, by daybreak all they could hear was the sound of some six thousand people gathering outside, jeering and demanding that the king turn back. At last, at seven in the morning, "seeing there was no remedy or help to be looked for," wrote Marie-Thérèse, "we were absolutely forced to take the road back to Paris."

It took almost four terrifying days in the stifling heat to make the dismal and humiliating return journey under heavy guard. The crowds lining the roads back to Paris were aggressive and threatening; their mood was unpredictable. The people wanted to see the king, so the windows were open, the blinds drawn back; they were "baked by the sun and suffocated by the dust." "One cannot imagine the suffering of the royal family on this luckless journey," wrote Madame de Tourzel. "Nothing was spared them!" On top of their carriage were three of their bodyguards handcuffed in fetters and in danger of being dragged down and killed.

For the king it was a terrible defeat. Yet again, he had failed. He had failed as a king, and brought his country to revolution. He had failed as a husband to protect his wife: she was now subject to even worse unknown terrors. He had failed as a father to bring his precious children to safety. Travelling with his loyal wife, his devoted sister and his young children, he knew that any words of assurance to them were empty promises; events had moved beyond his control. And somehow the failures had piled up despite his best efforts. He had always tried to avoid bloodshed; he couldn't bear anyone to be hurt on his behalf. Yet his very gentleness and compassion had led inexorably to this utterly terrifying point in their lives. "I am aware that to succeed was in my hands," he wrote later to General de Bouillé. "But it is needful to have a ruthless spirit if one is to shed the blood of subjects. . . . The very thought of such contingencies tore my heart and robbed me of all determination."

During the midafternoon, a local nobleman, the loyal Comte de Dampierre, rode up to salute the king, "in despair at the king's being stopped." The crowd was enraged at Dampierre's proroyalist gesture and tried to pull him off his horse. According to Marie-Thérèse, "Hardly had he spurred his horse, before the people who surrounded the carriage fired at him. He was flung to the ground. . . . A man on horseback rode over him and struck him several blows with his saber; others did the same and soon killed him." The scene was horrible, wrote Marie-Thérèse, "but more dreadful still was the fury of these wretches who, not content with having killed him, wanted to drag his body to our carriage and show it to my father." Despite his entreaties, "these cannibals came on triumphantly round the carriage holding up the hat, coat and clothing of the unfortunate Dampierre . . . and they carried these horrible trophies beside us along the road."

Worse was to come at Épernay the following day. At one point the royal family was obliged to abandon their carriage to enter a hotel, struggling through a crowd of angry people armed with pikes "who said openly that they wished to kill us," wrote Marie-Thérèse, shocked by their bloodcurdling threats. "Of all the awful moments I have known, this was one of those that struck me most and the horrible impression of it will never leave me. . . . My brother was ill all night and almost had delirium so shocked was he by the dreadful things he had seen."

Ahead, a hostile reception was waiting for them in Paris. Following orders from La Fayette, the people lining the streets kept their heads covered and remained absolutely silent, to show their contempt for this monarch who had tried to flee. La Fayette's orders were so strictly observed that "several scullery boys without hats covered their heads with their dirty, filthy handkerchiefs," recorded Madame de Tourzel. As they made their way down the Champs-Élysées and across the Place Louis XV, it was like an unspoken, public decoronation, as the citizens of Paris refused to acknowledge the royal status of their king and queen.

The crowds were so great it was evening before they finally reached the Tuileries. As they stepped down from the carriage someone tried to attack the queen. The dauphin was snatched from her and whisked to safety by officials as others helped the queen into the palace. Louis-Charles was becoming increasingly terrified at the violence targeted directly at the royal family. "As soon as we arrived in Varennes we were sent back. Do you know why?" he asked his valet, François Hüe, as he struggled to make sense of it all. He was not easily comforted and that night, once again, he was woken with violent nightmares of being eaten alive by wolves.

As the dauphin fell into a fitful sleep, "guards were placed over the whole family, with orders not to let them out of sight and to stay night and day in their chambers." The next day the Assembly provisionally suspended Louis from his royal functions. The once-untouchable king and queen were now finally reduced to the powerless symbols of a vanishing world.

The king's support collapsed after his abortive flight to Varennes. Those who had remained loyal to the monarchy now questioned the motives of a king who had tried to flee, exposing his people to the risk of civil war. Those who had opposed the monarchy had a tangible weapon: here was evidence that the king would betray his people. Imprisoned in the Tuileries, with little support in the Assembly or outside it, in September 1791, the king reluctantly signed the new constitution. The once-supreme Bourbon ruler was now, by law, no more than a figurehead, stripped of his powers.

Louis still clung to the hope that this would mark an end to the revolution and that France would settle down as a constitutional monarchy. Yet when he inaugurated the new Legislative Assembly in October, demands for still further change gathered momentum. Conflicts grew between the moderates and the extremists in the Assembly. The key battlegrounds were over the growing number of émigrés and the clergy. What measures should be taken to protect France from the émigrés who might be plotting counter-revolution? How could the clergy who had refused to swear the oath of allegiance to the constitution be brought into line?

The king found himself facing a crisis in November, when the Assembly introduced a punitive decree: any priest who had not signed the oath would lose his pension and could be driven from his parish. This was presented to the king for his approval under the new constitution. As crowds gathered menacingly outside the Tuileries demanding that he sign, Louis wrestled with his conscience. His only remaining power was a delaying veto. If he used this he would infuriate the Assembly and the Parisian people, but how could he approve such a measure when the constitution promised "freedom to every man . . . to practice the religion of his choice?" The king vetoed the decree.

The news outraged deputies at the Assembly. The extremists, largely drawn from a political club known as the Jacobins, sought to limit the king's power still further. Maximilien Robespierre was not a member of the Legislative Assembly, but was highly influential in the Jacobin Club and could exploit its powerful network throughout the country to influence opinion. Although he was not a good speaker, he was a skilled strategist, whose passionate appeals for *"patrie"* and "virtue" stirred political activists. "I will defend first and foremost the poor," he declared, as he campaigned against the privileges of the nobility and the monarchy. He found support in other prominent republicans such as the barrister Georges Danton, leader of the extremist Cordeliers' Club.

Those opposed to the monarchy could turn to militant journalists such as Camille Desmoulins and Jacques-René Hébert to whip up public opinion in their favor. Hébert was a zealot for the cause and, with killing cruelty, week after week in his journal, *Le Père Duchesne*, he stirred up loathing of the royal tyrants. They were dehumanized and turned into hate objects. The king, for so long the "royal cuckold" or "fat pig," was now "the Royal Veto," an animal "about five feet, five inches long . . . as timid as a mouse and as stupid as an ostrich . . . who eats, or rather, sloppily devours, anything one throws at him." The "Female Royal Veto" was "a monster found in Vienna . . . lanky, hideous, frightful . . . who eats France's money in the hope of one day devouring the French, one by one." Marie-Thérèse was "designed like the spiders of the French Cape, to suck the blood of slaves." As for "the delphinus . . . whose son is he?" The endless stream of vituperation soaked into the consciousness of Parisians. It became easy to see the royal family as the terrible Machiavellian enemy gorged from preying on innocent French people.

The queen, drawing on all the strength of her character, was indeed now playing a formidable, duplicitous role. Determined to save the throne, that autumn she charmed the moderates in the Assembly with her apparent support for the constitution, while she was, in fact, in secret correspondence with foreign courts and her devoted Fersen. Count Fersen had escaped to Brussels where he joined the king's brother, Provence, and was devastated to hear of the royal family's recapture at Varennes. "Put your mind at rest; we are alive. . . . I exist," the queen reassured him as she adapted to life closely surrounded by spies and enemies; just to see her own son, an army of guards would follow her. "My only hope," she said, "is that my son at least can be happy. . . . When I am very sad, I take my little boy in my arms, I kiss him with all my heart and this consoles me for a time."

While Marie-Antoinette was writing in code to her brother, the Emperor Leopold, asking him to support the French monarchy, Fersen went on a desperate diplomatic tour of European capitals. In February 1792, he risked his life in a daring mission to return to France in disguise to see the queen in the Tuileries. Despite their efforts, in March the Austrian Emperor Leopold II died suddenly, to be replaced by Marie-Antoinette's nephew, Francis II. Marie-Antoinette could not be sure that Emperor Francis would intervene on her behalf and feared betrayal.

By spring 1792, the new powers in France were growing increasingly militaristic, convinced that neighboring countries would be forced to act against their own population's possible political awakening. Rumors were rife of an immediate attack against France by an alliance of Austrians and Prussians, supported by émigré forces. Soon there were calls upon all patriots to defend their country as the warmongering verged on hysteria. In April, France declared war on Austria. Marie-Antoinette's position became intolerable. Many people were convinced that *l'Autrichienne* who wished to "bathe in the blood of French people" was an enemy agent, betraying the nation. When a French campaign in the Netherlands went badly, fears were mounting that the Austrians and Prussians would march on Paris and restore the "royal tyrants."

Despite the pressures of war the Assembly continued to persecute the clergy. Any priest still loyal to Rome denounced by more than twenty citizens was to be deported to the French colony of Guiana, a fate that was certain death, since leprosy and malaria were endemic in the colony. This decree was sent to the king for his approval. After much heart searching and anguish, he again used his veto and refused to sign this decree.

The very next day, June 20, 1792, thousands of citizens, angered by the king's use of his veto, gathered around the palace. "This armed procession began to file before our windows, and no idea can be formed of the insults they said to us," wrote Marie-Thérèse. On their banners was written, TREMBLE TYRANT; THE PEOPLE HAVE RISEN, and we could also hear cries of "Down with the veto! And other horrors!" Thirteen-year-old Marie-Thérèse witnessed what happened next. "Suddenly we saw the populace forcing the gates of the courtyard and rushing to the staircase of the chateau. It was a horrible sight to see and impossible to describe—that of these people with fury in their faces, armed with pikes and sabers, and pell-mell with them women half unclothed, resembling furies." In all the turmoil, Marie-Antoinette tried to follow the king but was prevented. "Save my son!" she cried out. Immediately someone carried Louis-Charles away and she was unable to follow. "Her courage almost deserted her, when at last, entering my brother's room she could not find him," wrote Marie-Thérèse.

Meanwhile, the crowd surged upstairs armed with muskets, sabers and pikes. Madame de Tourzel describes the ordeal. "The king, seeing that the doors were going to be forced open, wanted to go out to meet the factionists and try to control them with his presence." There was no time. The doors to the king's rooms were axed down in seconds and the crowd burst in shouting, "The Austrian, where is she? Her head! Her head!" Élisabeth stood valiantly by her brother, and Madame de Tourzel describes her great bravery as she was mistaken for the queen. "She said to those around her, these sublime words: 'Don't disabuse them. If they take me for the queen, there may be time to save her.' "

The revolutionaries turned on the king and demanded that he sign the decrees of the Assembly. For over two hours, Louis tried to reason with them. He pointed out that he had acted in accordance with the constitution and in all conscience, he believed his actions were right. At the insistence of the crowd, to prove his loyalty to the revolution, he wore a *bonnet rouge*, the symbol of liberty, and toasted the health of the nation. After some hours, it became clear that the king would not yield.

Meanwhile, Marie-Antoinette, finally reunited with both her son and daughter, was forced to flee from the dauphin's rooms as they could hear doors to the antechambers being hacked down. Accompanied by a few loyal allies, the Princesse de Lamballe and Madame de Tourzel, they tried to escape to the king's bedroom, without success. Clinging to her children, she took refuge in the Council Chamber. Trapped behind a table before the hostile crowds, they were protected by just a few guards. For two hours they endured taunts and jeers as the angry hordes paraded past, some bearing "symbols of the most unspeakable barbarity," wrote Madame Campan. There was a model gallows, "to which a dirty doll was suspended bearing the words *'Marie-Antoinette à la lanterne,'* " to represent her hanging. There were model guillotines and a "board to which a bullock's heart was fastened," labelled "Heart of Louis XVI." The seven-year-old dauphin, who was "shrouded in an enormous red cap," was crying.

After several hours, the mayor of Paris, Jérôme Pétion, arrived and dispersed the mob, pretending "to be much astonished at the danger the king had faced," observed Marie-Thérèse. Traumatized, the royal family was finally reunited. Louis-Charles was so shocked by the day's events that his usual sunny personality was stunned into complete silence as he clung to his parents in great relief. As for Marie-Thérèse, the endless succession of traumatic ordeals was rapidly undermining her. Already by nature Madame Sérieuse, she was losing "all the joy of childhood," observed Madame de Tourzel's daughter, Pauline, and she would lapse into deep and gloomy silences like her father.

For the next few days, the king's bravery caused a popular swing in his favor. Nevertheless, behind the scenes the political landscape was changing fast. Robespierre, voted vice-president of the Jacobin Club in July, with well-argued cold cunning, persuaded his followers that the royal family was the main obstacle to establish his democracy—along with the constitution and Legislative Assembly that recognized the role of the king. Together with radicals drawn from the Cordeliers' Club such as George Danton, Camille Desmoulins, Jean-Paul Marat, and Jacques-René Hébert, they played on people's terror of a foreign invasion. The king and queen in the Tuileries were portrayed as being at the scheming center of interests that wanted to destroy France. When the Prussians entered the war, promising vengeance if the king and queen were harmed, collusion seemed only too likely. While moderates like La Fayette left the capital, National Guardsmen from the provinces poured into Paris. The highlight came on July 30, when five hundred National Guardsmen from Marseilles, recruited for their radicalism by their local Jacobin club, arrived in Paris singing the rousing *Marseillaise*. The revolutionaries became known as *sans-culottes*—meaning literally "without breeches"—since they were dressed in working men's clothes: baggy trousers, *carmagnole* jackets and hats. Whipped up into a frenzy of hatred by the militant journalism of Hébert, Desmoulins, and others, the *sans-culottes* shared a common interest in inciting an insurrection against the "despicable tyrant" and the "colossus of despotism" in the Tuileries.

Inside the palace, clinging onto the last semblance of royalty, the queen was only too aware of the dangers. "On all sides," wrote Madame Campan, "were heard the most jubilant outcries of people in a state of delirium almost as frightful as the explosion of their rage." The queen wrote to Fersen in early August, "Our chief concern is to escape the assassin's knives and to fight off the plotters who surround the throne on the verge of collapse. The factions no longer bother to hide their plans about murdering the royal family. . . . They merely disagree about the method."

Events came to a head during the night of August 10, when an Insurrectionary Commune was established at Hôtel de Ville, and began to give orders to the National Guard, in effect challenging the Legislative Assembly and creating a revolutionary government. Soon after midnight, bells rang out across Paris—the insistent sound a call to arms and a death toll for the French monarchy. The insurgents began to gather and soon the streets around the Tuileries Palace were bristling with at least twenty thousand armed citizens.

Inside the palace, they could hear the tocsin ring out and the ominous sounds of the impending attack. The king had summoned nine hundred

[64]

Swiss guards in addition to the nine hundred gendarmes and 2,500 National Guards on duty at the palace, but only the Swiss guards could be relied upon to remain loyal. No one slept, except the little dauphin whose "calm and peaceful slumber formed the most striking contrast with the agitation which reigned in every heart," wrote the Marquise de Tourzel. The queen, true emperor's daughter, wanted to stand her ground and fight to the last. The king, in helpless despair, could see no solution to the impasse. The Attorney General of the department of Paris, Pierre Roederer, arrived and informed them they had no choice but to flee before they were murdered. "Imagine the situation of my unhappy parents during that horrible night," wrote Marie-Thérèse, "expecting only carnage and death." Early in the morning the king tried to rally his troops. The queen heard in despair as the king, dishevelled and downtrodden, was greeted with hoots of derision and shouts of *"Vive la Nation!"* by some of the palace National Guards, many of whom were now fraternizing with the protesters. "Some artillery men," reported Marie-Thérèse, "dared turn their cannon against their king . . . a thing not believable if I did not declare that I saw it with my own eyes!"

At seven in the morning, Roederer insisted that they escape and take refuge in the Legislative Assembly, urging that "all of Paris was on the march." The queen, bitterly frustrated at the prospect of fleeing to the lion's den, held out against the idea. But the king would not risk bloodshed. *"Marchons!"* he said, raising his hand. "There's nothing to be done here."

There was no time for preparations, no time to gather together treasured possessions or mementos, even a change of clothes; the royal family fled with nothing from the palace. Marie-Antoinette followed Louis, holding her son and daughter by the hand, Louis-Charles disconsolately kicking out at leaves that had fallen early. The Princesse de Lamballe, Princess Élisabeth and the Marquise de Tourzel—in some agitation because she had been obliged to leave Pauline behind—followed, discreetly protected by a few Swiss guards. "The terrace . . . was full of wretches who assailed us with insults. One of them cried out, 'No women or we will kill them all!' " recalled Marie-Thérèse. "At last we entered the passage to the Assembly. Before being

[65]

admitted we had to wait more than half an hour, a number of deputies opposing our entrance. We were kept in a narrow corridor, so dark that we could see nothing and hear nothing but the shouts of the furious mob. . . . I was held by a man whom I did not know. I have never thought myself so near death, not doubting that the decision was made to murder us all. In the darkness, I could not see my parents, and I feared everything for them. We were left to this mortal agony more than half an hour."

Finally they were permitted to enter the hall of the Assembly. "I have come here," the king declared, "to prevent the French nation from committing a great crime." The royal family were hurriedly ushered into a journalist's box, a small room, ten feet long, with a window with iron bars looking out onto the public gallery. Absolutely terrified, prisoners in this tiny hiding place, looking out through bars on their enemies debating their future, it was the end of hope. There was no chance of preserving even a semblance of royal dignity. Through the tiny window they could only watch helplessly, hour after hour, impassive witnesses to the end of the monarchy. "We had hardly entered this species of cage," wrote Marie-Thérèse, "when we heard the cannon, musket-shots and the cries of those who were murdering in the Tuileries."

Louis had assumed that by leaving the Tuileries he would stop an attack and help to prevent any bloodshed. However, the revolutionaries, armed with sabers and pikes, stormed the palace and attacked the red-uniformed Swiss guards. The Swiss fired back and the *sans-culottes* took casualties. Hearing of the slaughter, the king sent his last order, instructing his faithful Swiss guards to lay down their arms. They obeyed, only to be massacred as the "populace rushed from all quarters into the interior of the palace." The Tuileries became a bloodbath, with guards and nobles chased up onto the parapets fighting to the last as they were stabbed, shot or sabered. The dead or dying were flung from windows, some grossly mutilated, others impaled on pikes as trophies. Madame Campan, trapped inside the palace, reported, "I felt a horrid hand thrust down my back to seize me by the clothes." She had sunk to her knees and was aware of "the steel suspended over my head" by a "terrible Marseillais," when she heard another voice yelling, "We don't kill women!" She escaped.

As people fled from the palace, anyone who had defended the king—or was even dressed like a noble—was mercilessly hunted down. One woman reported glimpsing through the blinds of a house "three *sans-culottes* holding a tall handsome man by the collar." When they had "finished him off with the butt of a rifle," at least "fifteen women, one after the other, climbed up on this victim's cadaver, whose entrails were emerging from all sides, saying they took pleasure in trampling the aristocracy under their feet." During the day, over nine hundred guards and three hundred citizens became victims of the hysterical slaughter. Sixty Swiss guards were taken prisoner, only to be led away to the Hôtel de Ville and brutally killed. A young Corsican by the name of Napoleon Bonaparte, who witnessed the events of that day, was filled with a sense of horror at the power of the mob. For Maximilien Robespierre, it was a "glorious event . . . the most beautiful revolution that has ever honored humanity." By nightfall, the entire gruesome spectacle was illuminated by the orange glow of the Tuileries in flames.

Cowering at the Assembly, with murder and mayhem all around them, the royal family feared for their lives. Throughout the day their possessions, including the queen's jewels, spoils from the Tuileries and the heads of the king's supporters were paraded before them as patriots called for a republic and the death of the king and queen. Louis-Charles clung to his mother, whose dress was damp with perspiration. There was nothing to eat or drink, no way of leaving this confined space and no way of consoling his mother. "We witnessed horrors of all kinds that took place," continued Marie-Thérèse. "Sometimes they assailed my father and all his family with the most atrocious insults, triumphing over him with cruel joy, sometimes they brought in gentlemen dying of their wounds; sometimes they brought in my father's own servants, who with the utmost impudence, gave false testimony against him. . . . It was in the midst of these abominations that our entire day, from eight in the morning until midnight, passed, through all gradations of whatever was most terrible, most awful."

The Legislative Assembly held the royal family for two days while deliberating over a suitable residence for them. Meanwhile, the newly formed Paris Commune, to which Robespierre had been elected as a member, seized the initiative. Louis should no longer be treated as king, declared the Commune, but held in a jail as a common prisoner. Faced with the prospect of widespread rioting, the Legislative Assembly panicked and backed down. The king and his family was now entrusted, in the words of the Commune, "to the safekeeping and virtues of the citizens of Paris." They were to be taken to a former medieval fortress known as the Temple, in the east of Paris, not far from the Bastille.

This was a temple in name only. A large twelfth-century tower overshadowed the complex of lodgings, which had been owned by the Comte d'Artois. The queen "shuddered when she heard the Temple proposed," said the Marquise de Tourzel. "She said to me under her breath, 'They will put us in the Tower, you will see, and they will make it a real prison for us. I have always had an absolute horror of that tower, which I have asked Monsieur le Comte d'Artois a thousand times to pull down.' "

Marie-Thérèse described the ordeal of crossing central Paris on the evening of the thirteenth of August, 1792. "Our drivers themselves feared the people so much that they would not let the carriage stop for a moment; yet it took two hours before we could reach the Temple through the immense crowds. On the way they had the cruelty to point out to my parents things that would distress them—the statues of the kings of France thrown down, even that of Henry IV. . . . We did not observe on our way any feeling souls touched by our condition, such terror was now inspired in those who still thought rightly." As their carriage turned into the courtyard of the Temple, and the heavy gates slowly swung shut behind them, their remaining freedom—for so long a sham—was now finally and irrevocably taken away from them.

❧ *Chapter Four* ❧

"GOD HIMSELF HAS FORSAKEN ME"

Madame mounts into her Tower
When will she come down again?
Mironton, Mironton, Mirontaine . . .

—SATIRICAL FRENCH SONG,
SUNG BY THE GUARDS

Once behind the Temple walls, as the clamor of the city streets receded, the royal family found themselves in a small city within a city, a complex of lodgings and passageways that had developed around an old medieval fortress. The first courtyard led to a magnificent seventeenth century palace, Comte d'Artois's former Paris residence, where the elegant rooms were lavishly and fashionably appointed. These rooms opened out onto a second imposing courtyard surrounded by arcades on one side, and on the other, to a large garden planted with high trees. In marked contrast to the elegance of the palace and the charm of the garden there rose, behind some trees, a grim, square fortresslike tower that had about it an air of menace and foreboding, known as the Great Tower. Its solid, almost windowless walls, blackened over the centuries, overshadowed the surrounding buildings, rising more than sixty feet high, a daunting edifice of towers and turrets beneath a steeply pointed, dark slate roof. Through the north turret of the Great Tower it was possible to gain access to a second tower, a five-storied building known as the Little Tower.

To the king's great relief, they were shown into his younger brother's former palace, where extravagant preparations to greet the royal party were under way in the hall, *La Salle des Quatre Glaces*. The palace and courtyards were brightly lit with candles and torches as though for an important function, and the king became convinced they were to be held in the comfortable surroundings of his brother's former home. All innocence, he asked to be shown around, allotting various rooms in the palace to members of his family as he went. He didn't appear to notice the discomfort of the mayor, Pétion, who went hurrying back to the Commune to try to persuade deputies to change their minds. Nor were his suspicions aroused when the Marquise de Tourzel, inquiring repeatedly whether she could settle the exhausted Louis-Charles for the night, was told to wait. His room was not quite ready.

It was eleven before the Marquise de Tourzel was permitted to take him to his room. She followed the guards through an interminable series of vaulted corridors and passageways, up steep winding stone steps and then a wooden stairway until the door finally opened out onto a small, sparsely furnished room with a low ceiling. There were two folding beds and she carefully placed Louis-Charles in one, trying not to disturb his sleep.

Two hours later, the rest of the family was escorted through the same series of passageways. As they left the gracious rooms of the palace behind, it was clear that the queen's earlier fearful apprehension about the Tower had been correct. They found themselves in small, dingy rooms where, as Marie-Thérèse observed, "nothing had been prepared for us. . . . The lodging was bare of everything." The queen was to sleep in the room next to the dauphin, where a camp bed had been set up for Marie-Thérèse. The Princesse de Lamballe was in an antechamber and the king and his valets were led to a room on the third floor. In the cramped, overcrowded conditions, space was found for Madame Élisabeth, Pauline de Tourzel and other waiting women in the kitchen, where they were awake all night, hearing the guards in the room next door.

Before retiring, Marie-Antoinette checked on her son, watching him for a few moments while he slept. It was as she had suspected all along: They were indeed to be held as prisoners in the Great Tower. Since this was unfit for habitation, the Commune had found temporary rooms in the Little Tower, while the main tower was converted into a secure prison. It was now painfully evident that she was powerless to provide even the most basic freedoms for her beloved son, sleeping so peacefully, unaware of how precarious his fate might be. The Commune's choice of location was all too clear. In a palace, Louis would still be a king. In the Tower at the bottom of the palace's garden, which had the appearance of some grim feudal jail, the king and queen were most certainly prisoners. The royal family began their first night of imprisonment behind no less than eight locked iron doors.

They had arrived at the Temple virtually destitute, but the Assembly made available a financial allowance and they were able to buy some linen, bedclothes, kitchen equipment and other necessities. Their barren and confined surroundings were in stark contrast to the palatial splendour of Versailles or even the Tuileries, and in the first few days they tried to brighten up their rooms. Additional furniture was found, along with some hangings of a white cretonne patterned with pink roses. New clothes were ordered, and toys for Louis-Charles: a set of ninepins, rackets, kites, draughts and dominoes.

Less than a week after the royal family arrived at the Little Tower, at around midnight on August 19, guards entered the rooms with a decree from the Commune. All friends and attendants of the royal family were to be removed for interrogation. "They ordered Madame de Lamballe to rise," wrote Marie-Thérèse. "My mother tried to oppose it by urging that she was a relative, but in vain. They replied that they had orders to take her away." The Marquise de Tourzel and her daughter Pauline were also ordered to leave. "Obliged to submit, we all rose with death in our hearts to bid these ladies farewell," said Marie-Thérèse. In the king's room, his valet, Monsieur Hüe, and other staff were taken. Since the dauphin was now alone, he was carried into his mother's room. Inevitably he could not get back to sleep and they stayed awake all night, fearing the worst. They soon heard the worrying news that the Princesse de Lamballe, the Marquise de Tourzel and her daughter had been taken to the prison of *La Force*.

Two new members of staff were to be appointed to serve the royal family. By chance, the dauphin's former valet de chambre, the loyal Hanet Cléry, heard of this and was determined to resume his place "at the service of the young prince." Cléry had escaped the massacre at the Tuileries on August 10. In his plain clothes he had been mistaken for a revolutionary; one eager *sans-culottes* had even offered him a weapon. With his customary resourcefulness, Cléry soon obtained permission to serve the royal family and on August 26, he entered the Tower of the Temple. Many of the details of this period of their captivity come from Cléry's account, written ten years later. "As the sole and continual witness of the injurious treatment the king and his family were made to endure," he wrote, "I alone can write it down and affirm the exact truth."

Cléry almost betrayed his concern for the royal family on his very first day. The princesses, who had been a week without staff, asked if he could help with their hair. "I replied that I would do whatever they desired of me," said Cléry, only to find that a guard immediately warned him to be much more circumspect. He was to show no sign of attachment for his former masters. "I felt frightened at such a beginning," wrote Cléry. Four municipal guards appointed by the Commune watched the king obsessively night and day. Full of suspicion, one guard even insisted on peaches being cut in half and their stone opened to check that they concealed no illicit correspondence. Nonetheless, Cléry and the king's loyal chef, Louis François Turgy, developed ways of getting messages and news to the royal family. Secret notes were passed around, sign languages developed and codes worked up. "I kept on my guard to avoid any imprudence," wrote Cléry, "which would most certainly have ruined me."

The royal family's hopes of any rescue were centered on the Prussian and Austrian alliance. Prussian forces invaded France on August 19 and made rapid progress, approaching Verdun, in Lorraine, an important stronghold before Paris, by the end of the month. As the news of the Prussian army's success reached Paris early in September, a wave of terror gripped France. People panicked at the prospect of terrible retribution from foreign armies and were convinced that the royal family was in league with France's enemies. Recriminations and counterrecriminations began with rousing talk of saving *la patrie* and death to all "traitors within," as Paris succumbed to the urgent beat of the *Marseillaise*. The Commune called people to arms and *sans-culottes* roamed around the city, breaking into the overcrowded prisons, seeking out all "enemies of France"—royalists, aristocrats, nonjuring priests—to mete out brutal justice with their pickaxes and knives. Revolutionary leaders such as Georges Danton, the Minister of Justice, and Maximilien Robespierre, leader of the Jacobins, simply ignored the savage massacre that followed. "What do I care about the prisoners!" declared Danton. "Let them fend for themselves." In five dark days, one thousand four hundred helpless inmates, almost half the prison population of Paris, were slaughtered in cold blood.

On September 2, the royal family was in the Temple compound for their daily walk, but they were hurriedly ushered back inside as the threatening sounds of the uprising grew nearer. One of the municipal officers, named Matthieu, turned on the king, "with all that fury could suggest," wrote Marie-Thérèse. The country was in mortal danger, Matthieu said angrily. "We know that we and our wives and children will perish. But the people will have their revenge. You will die before we do!" He spoke with such vengeance that "my brother was so terrified he burst into tears and ran into the next room," continued Marie-Thérèse. "I did my best to console him, but in vain, he imagined he saw my father dead."

That night, it was difficult for the captives to sleep. They could hear drums beating immediately outside the Temple throughout the small hours; the massacre of that day was soon under way. Later they heard the most bloodthirsty cries of an angry rabble at the gates of the Temple, clamoring to be let in. As the noises drew ever nearer, it was apparent that the crowds had overwhelmed the sentries and burst in, crossing the forecourt in a great mass and making their way to the Tower. Cléry was dining downstairs with two servants and saw the full horror of the scene. "We were hardly seated before a head at the end of a pike was presented at the window," he wrote. "It was that of the Princesse de Lamballe." He immediately recognized her beautiful face, her rather soft and gentle features looking so incongruous in that situation. "Though bloody, it was not disfigured; her blond hair, still curling, floated around the pike." One of the servants screamed. Immediately they "heard the frantic laughs of the barbarians," who thought it was the queen screaming.

Cléry ran at once to warn the king, yet "terror had so changed my face that the queen noticed it." Before he had a chance to whisper discreetly to the king, a guard entered the room. Acting with unusual concern for the royal family, he closed the window and drew the curtains, so that they would see nothing; to no avail. The terrifying cries of the crowd with their gruesome trophies were soon immediately below their rooms. Officers of the National Guard suddenly burst in and ordered the king to show himself to the crowd, which prompted Louis to ask whatever was happening outside.

"Well, if you want to know," said a young officer in the "coarsest tone"— according to Cléry—"it is the head of Madame de Lamballe they want to show you, for you to see how the people avenge themselves on tyrants." Marie-Antoinette was "seized with horror; it was the sole moment when her firmness abandoned her," said her daughter. She then fainted. Such was her shock and incomprehension, even as she came round, she "remained motionless, seeing nothing that took place in the room."

The crowd outside started shrieking for Marie-Antoinette's head as well, and summoned her to kiss her dead friend's head. Louis-Charles and Marie-Thérèse were now sobbing hysterically. Cléry heard one of the municipal officers haranguing the crowd. "The head of Marie-Antoinette does not belong to you. . . . France has entrusted its great offenders to the City of Paris; it is your business to help guard them until the justice of the nation avenges its people." For several hours the royal family's lives hung by a thread, apparently at the mercy of madmen bent on vengeance; they waited, never knowing if this was to be the moment when the unstoppable fury of the mob finally turned on them. It was evening before "all was quiet in the neighborhood of the Tower," wrote Cléry, "although across Paris massacres continued for four of five days."

The unfortunate Princesse de Lamballe, as a close friend of the queen trapped in *La Force* at the height of the slaughter, had been spared nothing. Dragged from her cell and hauled before a kangaroo court, when she refused to swear an oath against the queen she had been sentenced to death. There are differing accounts of her horrendous murder. According to some, she was raped before she was hacked to death, and then mutilated, with her genitalia and heart cut out and mounted on pikes. In other versions she was—mercifully—knocked unconscious before her death. Her head was twisted onto a pike and taken to the Tower; her naked body was dragged through the streets. The crowd had wanted to force the door to make the king and queen see the fate of their friend. The officials were only able to prevent them by permitting them to make a tour of the Tower with Madame de Lamballe's head, on the condition that they left her body at the gates.

The Marquise de Tourzel and Pauline had also been held at *La Force*. In an astonishing display of chivalry, a stranger, who may have inspired the stories of the Scarlet Pimpernel, rescued Pauline. "We had scarcely gone to sleep when we heard someone drawing the bolts on our door," Madame de Tourzel wrote in her memoirs. "We saw a man come in, well dressed and mild of aspect, who went up to Pauline's bed and said, 'Mademoiselle de Tourzel, get ready quickly and come with me.' I was in such a state of distress on seeing my daughter taken from me that I remained frozen without the power to move. . . . My poor Pauline came to my bed and took my hand, but the man, seeing that she was dressed, took hold of her arm and dragged her toward the door. I heard the bolts fastened again. I cried after her, 'God help you and protect you, dear Pauline!' "

Although Pauline was safe, Madame de Tourzel was hauled before the same kangaroo court that had condemned the Princesse de Lamballe. However, by now, so many were very much the worse for drink that it had softened their "murderous lust for blood," she wrote. "Those miserable people were so drunk they could no longer stand on their legs and were obliged to go home to sleep, and those who remained softened up considerably." There were roars of *"Vive la Nation!"* and the marquise found herself discreetly ushered to the prison door by the same stranger who had rescued her daughter.

With the September massacres still all too vivid and with increasing fears for the awful unknowable future, the royal family took refuge in filling their

[75]

days with some semblance of order and meaning. "We kept busy in regulating our hours," wrote Marie-Thérèse, "and passed the whole day together." The family usually had breakfast together at nine, after which the king gave the dauphin his lessons. "His father taught him to recite passages from Corneille and Racine, gave him lessons in geography, and taught him to color maps," wrote Cléry, who was impressed by the young dauphin's memory. "The precocious intelligence of the young prince responded perfectly to the attentions of his father." The queen, meanwhile, gave lessons to her daughter and in the late morning they would all go into the Temple compound, where they were permitted to walk along the avenue of horse chestnut trees. "I made the prince play either at quoits or football, or running, or other games of exercise," said Cléry. In the afternoons, after the customary search of their rooms, they would play piquet or backgammon, or join Louis-Charles in ball games or shuttlecock.

After supper, the queen would hear the dauphin's prayers. "He said one especially for the Princesse de Lamballe and another to protect the life of Madame de Tourzel," wrote Cléry. "If the municipals were near, he took the precaution of saying these last two prayers in a very low voice." While Louis-Charles was in the bathroom, Cléry seized his chance to pass on any news to the queen. Cléry's wife had hired a street crier to come near the walls of the Temple every evening to shout out the main stories of the day. The king usually read well into the night, absorbed in the sizable library of books in the Little Tower. On one occasion, he pointed out the works of Voltaire and Rousseau to his valet! "These two men," he said softly, "have been the ruin of France." While the king took comfort in books, and the queen from her son, for Madame Élisabeth, religion had always been the framework of her life, and now more than ever. "How often have I seen Madame Élisabeth on her knees at her bedside, praying fervently," observed Cléry.

The Commune required daily reports of this humdrum routine. Spies were recruited under cover of household servants to report on their conversations. The queen and Princess Élisabeth were attended by a cheerless, neurotic woman called Madame Tison, whose husband also did heavy work around the Tower. Nobody was allowed to enter the Temple site without being provided with a special pass, which was to bear two seals with the words *Officier Municipal*, printed diagonally. To gain access to the prisoners, an additional visa was needed, stamped *Pour le Tour*. The royal family faced a daily battle to obtain brief moments of privacy against the constant and unrelenting scrutiny of the guards. The slightest incident could attract attention. Once, Cléry had drawn up a multiplication table to help the dauphin with his math. A municipal officer objected on the grounds that Louis-Charles was "being shown how to talk in cipher." On another occasion, the queen was deprived of her tapestry work; she was making chair backs for her friends. To the suspicious eyes of their captors, this was surely hieroglyphics.

Many of the guards delighted at the chance to belittle the royal family. "Not only was my father no longer treated as king," observed Marie-Thérèse, "but he was not even treated with simple respect." One of the commissioners, who began to work at the Tower in early October 1792, was a shoemaker called Antoine Simon. According to Cléry, his eager enthusiasm for liberty and equality was matched by his "lowest insolence" whenever he was with the royal family. Invariably wearing his shabby old hat, he would address the king by the name of his distant forebears. "Cléry, ask *Capet* if he wants anything, for I can't take the trouble to come up a second time." The queen was "Madame Capet." The term "Capet" was a deliberate, calculated insult. Simon wished to denote that Louis was no longer king; he was just a common man.

Each took a lead from the behavior of his peers and soon it became open season to hurl insults at them. One guard, named Rocher—*"d'une figure horrible,"* according to Cléry—was particularly dreaded. For Marie-Thérèse, Rocher was nothing less than "a monster, who roamed around us continually with dreadful glances" and never ceased "torturing my father in every way possible." When it was time for the royal family to go out, Rocher revelled in keeping the royal party waiting by the door, as he "rattled his enormous bunch of keys with a frightful noise, pretending to find the right key." Then he would hurry ahead "to take up a position by the last door, a long pipe in his mouth, and puff his tobacco smoke in their faces, especially those of the princesses," wrote Cléry. "Some of the guards who were amused by such insolence shouted with laughter at each puff of smoke and said the coarsest of things." Sometimes they even brought chairs from the guardroom to obstruct the narrow passage still more and "enjoy the spectacle at their ease." When the royal party returned from their walk, they could find violent graffiti on the Temple walls: "strangle the cubs," or even, on one occasion, a drawing of a guillotine with the caption, "Louis spitting into the bucket." Gradually, the little walk in the garden "became a torture," said Cléry, and the king and queen only continued with it because they wanted their children to take the air.

For the dauphin all this was incomprehensible and distressing. By now aged seven and a half years, he had grown into a good-looking, healthy boy, with blue eyes and long strawberry-blond hair, who liked outdoor games. Yet he was becoming increasingly fretful and nervous. The people's anger weighed heavily on his young mind. He just could not understand how his father had so completely lost the affection of his people, and why they were so hated when they had once lived so happily. His nightmares took on such a compelling reality that, on one occasion, he needed to see his mother to believe that she really was still alive. He was visibly distressed by the open hostility targeted at his family and even himself: the "son of a she-ape," according to *Le Père Duchesne*, or "a little wolfling that should be strangled." Although his family tried to shield him from the worst of it, there was no escaping the endless barrage. Guards were only too happy to leave distressing reports lying around; one guard stated pointedly that although the dauphin alone "caused him pity, being the son of a tyrant, he too, must die."

On September 20, 1792, the newly elected Assembly, now known as the National Convention, met to draft a new constitution and determine the fate of the king. Their first step was to abolish the monarchy and proclaim France to be a republic. A week later, among a great flourish of trumpeters and mounted police, deputies arrived at the Tower to announce that the monarchy did not exist and the king had been stripped of his title. Inside, the royal family could hear the proclamation quite distinctly. Jacques-René Hébert, a man who was consumed with a desire to see the royal family ruined, was now a powerful voice in the Commune and, as Deputy-Procurateur, had elected to be on guard that day to savor the king's downfall. According to Cléry, he and the other guards "stared at the king, smiling treacherously." The royal family was equally determined "not to add to their enjoyment." The king, head bowed, did not look up from his book; the queen continued her sewing. Later that same day, when Cléry applied for warmer coverings for the dauphin's bed as winter approached, he began with the usual introduction, "The king requests . . ." He was sharply reproved that the title had been abolished and he was insulting the French people. When new linens did arrive, they were marked with crowned letters and the guards made the princesses pick out the crowns.

The royal family's increasingly fragile hopes that a foreign invasion of France might yet save them were dashed in late September when the Prussian army was defeated at Valmy, in the Argonne. As the foreign armies retreated, in Paris, the family's enemies were closing in on them. Their little circle of safety was daily diminished and by late October, their massively fortified new prison was ready. The whole family was moved across to the Great Tower with the sounds of the echoing bolts behind them shutting out any thoughts of freedom.

The Great Tower, once a fortress occupied by the Knights Templar, was now metamorphosed into some grim and fearsome place, and made an ideal prison. It was an oppressive, square building, with high dark walls, nine feet thick, blotting out the sky, and at each corner of the square a smaller round turret. The royal family was led up to their rooms in one of the corner towers by a winding stone staircase. From the stairs, the king's rooms on the second floor were approached through two doors, one in very thick oak, studded with nails, and the other of iron, both with a strong lock and several padlocked bolts. Originally, this floor had consisted of one large room, about thirty feet square, which had been hurriedly partitioned by cheap wooden boards into smaller rooms to detain the prisoner. The first room was a small antechamber, furnished with some chairs, a card table and a poster of the Declaration of the Rights of Man by way of adornment. From the antechamber, separate doors opened onto to the king's bedroom, which also contained a folding bed for the dauphin, Cléry's bedroom and a dining room. Each of the rooms had a small window, but since the walls were so thick, inevitably the windows were very deeply set; heavy iron bars and shutters on the outside reduced the light still further, and prevented the air from circulating freely. The spiral staircase led on to the third floor where there was a similar arrangement of locked doors and small rooms for the queen, Marie-Thérèse and Princess Élisabeth. Beyond, past a storeroom on the fourth floor, the steps led through a series of wickets to a locked door leading to the battlements of the roof.

There were eight commissioners, selected by the Commune, on duty at any one time and housed in the Council Chamber on the ground floor. During the night, two commissioners were posted on night sentry duty outside the king's and queen's bedrooms. The commissioners were instructed "never to lose sight of the prisoners for a single instant, to speak to them only to answer questions, and never to tell them anything of what is happening." Up to forty soldiers in the guardroom on the first floor provided additional security. Outside, a high wall surrounded the Great Tower with only two gates out to the Temple complex, each with two locks. Beyond, the Temple compound was protected by a garrison of around two hundred soldiers of the National Guard, with cannon, housed in Artois's former palace. Escape, it seemed, was impossible.

Soon after their arrival, a mason came to fix yet another lock to the king's rooms. Louis, trying to make light of their situation for his son's benefit, started to show Louis-Charles how to use a hammer and chisel to make the holes in the wall to insert the bolts. "When you get out of here you can say that you worked yourself, at your own prison," the mason quipped. "Ah," Louis replied, "when and how shall I get out?" The little prince burst into tears, said Cléry. The king let his hammer and chisel fall, and went back into his room, where he "walked up and down with hasty strides."

Marie-Antoinette lived in constant fear that the dauphin would be taken from her and used as a pawn in some wider political game. She also feared that he might be kidnapped and killed by the murderous gangs that roamed Paris; the fate of her friend the Princesse de Lamballe was too terrible and too vivid a memory for her to have any peace of mind. The commissioners noticed her protective interest and the way "she devoted her existence to the care of her son and found some relief to her troubles in his affection and his caresses." They decided to exert their authority. The day after their arrival in the Great Tower, the Commune approved an order that the dauphin should be removed from his mother for most of the day. Under the new regime, Cléry would look after him, under the supervision of the king; the queen could visit her son, but only at certain times and always with a commissioner in attendance. "Her distress was extreme," wrote Cléry. "With what tenderness, she begged me to watch incessantly over his life."

Nonetheless, the dauphin gradually adapted to the new regime and, according to some reports, his winning ways could apparently charm the most hardened and cruel of commissioners. Even Jacques-René Hébert, who publicly demonized the child as a "tyrant's son" or a "wolf cub," is reported to have told a friend, "He is as beautiful as the day and as interesting as can be. He plays with the king marvellously well. . . . The other day he asked me if the people are still unhappy. 'That's a pity,' he replied, when I answered in the affirmative." By his playful nature and his "little rogueries," Louis-Charles often made "his parents forget for a moment their cruel situation," wrote Cléry. "But he felt it himself; though young, he knew he was in a prison and watched by enemies. His behavior and his talk acquired that reserve which instinct, in presence of danger, inspires perhaps at any age. Never did I hear him mention the Tuileries, or Versailles, or any subject that might remind the queen or the king of painful memories."

Cléry was also very touched by the young prince's concern for others. As winter set in, confined in their dingy, airless rooms where the one stove on each floor failed to provide enough heat, the royal party rapidly succumbed to colds and flu. When Cléry also became too ill to leave his bed, the dauphin insisted on nursing him. "During that first day the Dauphin hardly left me," wrote Cléry, "the august child made me drink." Later, his Aunt Élisabeth

[81]

secretly gave Louis-Charles some soothing lozenges to pass on to their loyal valet. At eleven o'clock that night, Cléry was surprised to hear the Dauphin quietly calling him and expressed his concern that he was still awake. "The fact is," replied Louis-Charles, "I did not want to fall asleep until I had given you this little box from my aunt. You were just in time. I've almost dozed off several times."

The royal family waited helplessly for any news of the foreign armies or developments at the National Convention through an increasingly elaborate system of secret signals with their few remaining loyal staff. Louis-Charles and Marie-Thérèse were quick to collude in any secret communication, watching out for guards or playing noisily as information was exchanged; a favorite game was "pony" where Louis-Charles would gallop from one person to another with suitably loud and distracting sound effects. Turgy, the king's waiter, developed a particularly successful code, using his right hand for good news and his left hand for bad news as he waited on the family at dinner. If, for example, he rubbed his right eye, this denoted that the armies of the French Republic were in retreat. During the autumn, they learned that any chance of rescue had all but vanished as the Prussian armies were beaten back across the French frontier and Austrians and émigrés were forced to flee from Brussels as French forces overran Belgium. More worrying still was the news from Paris. When Turgy passed his hand through his hair, this denoted that the National Convention was discussing the future of the royal family. And during November, this issue came to the fore.

Since its first meeting, the National Convention—of which almost half of the 749 deputies were drawn from the legal profession—had been preoccupied with whether the king should be brought to trial. Many of the more moderate members, drawn from the Girondin faction, maintained that according to the constitution, "the person of the king is inviolable and sacred," and therefore, he could not be tried. They were opposed by those, like Maximilien Robespierre and Louis-Antoine Saint-Just, who argued that the king had "violated the constitution" in his "counterrevolution" of August 10 in which good patriots had died, and consequently he had no rights. Robespierre had secured seats for many of his radical allies at the National

Convention; they became known as the *Montagnards*—the Mountain party—because they occupied raised seats. They argued that the only way to consolidate the gains of the Revolution and to "save the *Patrie*" was for the king to die. Since the king was already a guilty man, there was no need even for a trial. Robespierre considered that Louis had already been "judged" on August 10, when those who attacked the palace "stood proxy for the whole of France." These arguments were couched in such forceful terms that any moderates who challenged this view were in danger of being branded as "traitors" of the Republic. The momentum for action gained pace during November when the king's secret correspondence hidden in an iron chest in the Tuileries was discovered. This revealed that Louis XVI had indeed found the constitution "detestable" and he had only agreed to it because he was coerced. It became easy to cast the duplicitous "Louis Capet" as an enemy of the Republic. The mood in France hardened against the former king and by late November the Convention decided to act.

On December 6, 1792, Cléry's wife came to the Tower with a friend for her customary Thursday visit to see her husband. She was only permitted to see him once a week, in the Council Chamber, the commissioners' room on the ground floor. While his wife distracted the jailers by talking in loud voice about domestic matters, her friend whispered to Cléry as distinctly as she dared, "Next Tuesday they take the king to the Convention. His trial will begin. He may get counsel. All this is certain."

Cléry was greatly shocked by this, but it was impossible to find out any more while they were watched by jailors and he could hardly bear to convey this worrying news to the king. That night, as Louis went to bed, he seized a brief chance to pass on what he had heard. The next day, after breakfast, the king had an opportunity to talk to the queen. "I could see by her look of sorrow that he was telling her what I had told him," wrote Cléry.

With news of the impending trial, the mood in the Tower became increasingly desperate. In order not to compromise their loyal valet, the family had agreed to behave as though they knew nothing. On Tuesday, December 11, at five o'clock in the morning, "we were made very anxious by the beating of drums and the arrival of the guards at the Temple," wrote Marie-

Thérèse. Cannons were brought into the garden of the Temple and they could hear the *générale*—call to arms—echoing around Paris. The commissioners told them nothing and the family had breakfast together as usual. "This continual torture for all the family of never being able to show any emotion, any effusion of feeling at a moment when so many fears agitated them was one of the most refined cruelties of their tyrants," observed Cléry, "and the one in which those tyrants took most delight."

That morning, the little dauphin was eager to play *Siam* with his father— a game similar to ninepins. His manner was "so urgent," wrote Cléry, that the king, in spite of growing anxiety, could not refuse him. At eleven, two commissioners entered the room and ordered Louis-Charles to be separated from his father and taken to his mother. Sensing that his father was in danger, Louis-Charles became distressed at leaving him. The former king had to wait a further two hours alone, before the leader of the Commune, Anaxagoras Chaumette, and other officials entered his room with a decree summoning "Louis Capet" before the National Convention for interrogation.

"Capet is not my name," commented Louis. "It is the name of one of my ancestors. I could have wished, Monsieur," he added, "that the commissioners had left my son with me during the two hours I have passed in waiting for you." He was under no illusion that he would see his family again.

The king was taken by carriage to the National Convention and stood at the bar. The president announced, "Louis, the French Nation accuses you of having committed various crimes to reestablish tyranny on the ruins of liberty." A long list of treasonable charges then followed, including attempting to flee the country "in order to return as a conqueror," and firing on his people on three occasions. Much was made of his secret papers in the Tuileries, which were used to allege that Louis was plotting with France's enemies. The most harmful documents were payments to his former bodyguard. Louis had paid them to ease their monetary worries but to his accusers, this was nothing less than payments to a secret army.

At first, Marie-Antoinette was "in a such a state of anxiety," said her daughter, "that it is impossible to express." For the first time, the queen deigned to question the guards, but "these men would tell her nothing." That night, when the king returned to the Temple she begged repeatedly to be permitted to see him. In his rooms, too, the king made urgent requests to see his family. Yet this was denied. "At least," asked the king, "my son can sleep in my room? His bed and personal belongings are here." This, too, was refused. Until the trial was over he was permitted to see his children only if they were separated from their mother. Faced with such a cruel choice, he could not bring himself to take seven-year-old Louis-Charles from his mother and he gave up the chance to see them.

"My brother spent that first night of the king's trial in my mother's room," said Marie-Thérèse. "He had no bed so she gave him hers, and remained up all night in a gloom so great we did not like to leave her." Unable to eat in her state of great anxiety, Marie-Antoinette again begged to see her husband the next day, without success. Meanwhile, Élisabeth took Cléry aside, asking "with a species of terror" if he had heard "anything of what might happen to the queen." Ever resourceful, Cléry was able to help the royal princesses obtain fragments of news; notes were smuggled between rooms hidden in balls of wool or string to conceal them from the watchful eyes of Madame Tison. On December 19, 1792, it was Marie-Thérèse's fourteenth birthday, yet still the family could not meet. Marie-Thérèse, who was close to her father, could hardly endure the "torture" of his trial, and her health began to decline. Some of the more charitable guards tried "to reassure us that my father would not be put to death." However, rumors were rife that he would be condemned, or if he were spared, he and the dauphin would be imprisoned for life.

Alone on Christmas day, unable to see his family and confined in his small, dark room in the Temple, Louis made his will. "I pray to God especially to cast his merciful eyes on my wife, my children and my sister," he wrote, "who have shared for a long time in my sufferings, that He will sustain them with His grace should I be taken from them." He begged his wife, "to forgive me for all the ills she is suffering for me, and the griefs I may have caused her in the course of our union." As for his devoted sister,

Élisabeth, he asked her "to be a mother to my children should they have the misfortune to lose theirs." He urged his children to "remain united with each other . . . and to regard Élisabeth as a second mother." In particular, he asked Louis-Charles "if he has the misfortune to become king," to remember "that he must dedicate himself entirely to the happiness of his fellow-citizens." He urged him "to feel no hate or resentment about the misfortunes his father is suffering," and to care for "those persons undergoing misfortunes on his father's account."

The day after Christmas, the sound of troops and beating drums in the Temple grounds signalled the continuation of the trial. The king was escorted back under guard to the National Convention. His counsel, the brilliant Romain de Sèze, carefully refuted each of the charges held against him, and then Louis himself rose to make a short, dignified speech, "perhaps the last I shall make before you." He explained that he had always loved his people and had not been afraid "to spare any trouble in order to avoid bloodshed." It was indeed a terrible irony, in the words of an American observer, "that the mildest monarch who ever filled the French throne" was defending himself against charges as "one of its most nefarious tyrants." Yet despite the best efforts of his defense, over the next three weeks, "the bloodthirsty party of Robespierre," said the British ambassador, "exert every nerve to excite the Convention and the people to terminate the days of their unfortunate monarch." Injured victims from the insurrection at the Tuileries on August 10 were brought before the deputies to incite anger at the king's "counter-revolution." "I demand that the National Convention declare Louis Capet guilty," roared Robespierre, "and deserving of death."

On January 15 the trial was brought to a conclusion. Louis was found guilty and, in the evening of the following day, voting began to decide on his penalty. Throughout the night, deputies rose in turn to deliver their verdict. Some members wanted to stop short of execution, recommending imprisonment or banishment; others were determined that the king should die. Robespierre, the leader of the Paris delegation, spoke for many when he declared with passion, "You are not passing sentence for or against a man; you are carrying out an act of national providence. . . . I vote for death."

On January 17, when the votes were finally counted, there was a clear majority in favor of death. President Pierre Vergniaud rose to announce the result. "I declare in the name of the Convention that the death penalty is hereby pronounced upon Louis Capet."

That evening, Chrétien de Malesherbes, a most devoted member of the king's counsel, went to see Louis to inform him of the result. He spoke to Cléry first. "All is lost. The king is condemned to death." Cléry, too, was shocked and found "from the moment of Malesherbes's entrance a great trembling seized me." The king was alone in his room, waiting, his elbows on the table, and his head in his hands. Malesherbes threw himself at his feet, choked with sobs and quite unable to speak for some time. However, the king showed no surprise or emotion at the news. "You see now that from the first moment I was not deceived," said Louis, "and that my condemnation had been pronounced before I had been heard." He seemed most affected to hear that his own cousin, the Duc d'Orléans, now known as "Philippe Égalité," had voted for his death. The loyal Malesherbes still harbored hopes that the king could yet be saved at the last moment. "All honest men will now come forward to save your Majesty or perish at your feet." The king would have none of it. "Monsieur de Malesherbes," he said, "that would compromise a lot of people and start a civil war in France. I would rather die."

Cléry relates a touching scene that occurred later that night as he prepared the king for his shave. "Such was my fainting state," Cléry wrote, that "I dared not raise my eyes to my unfortunate master." Yet as he leaned over Louis, their eyes suddenly met, and Cléry found "tears flowed in spite of myself." A paleness spread over the king's face and he blanched suddenly as if the full horror of his plight had only just touched him. They were both being watched. Neither could show their affection for the other, without putting Cléry at risk, too. The king was harboring hopes that Cléry would be able to take care of the dauphin, to give him "all his care in this dreadful place." He didn't want Cléry to expose his deep feelings of loyalty to the royal family. Cléry was certain that his knees were about to give way under him. The king gently took his valet's hands in his and pressed them firmly, murmuring in a low voice, "Come, come, more courage." Later, he told

Cléry that he did not fear death for himself, "but I cannot contemplate without a shudder the cruel fate that I leave behind me for my family, for the queen and my unfortunate children."

At two o'clock in the afternoon of Sunday, January 20, the door of the king's room was suddenly opened. The Minister of Justice and twelve or more officials piled into the tiny room. With due ceremony it was announced that the death penalty would be carried out within twenty-four hours. There was no appeal.

That afternoon, Louis was permitted to see a priest who would hear his confession and give the last rites. The Irish priest, Abbé Edgeworth de Firmont, who was already in danger as a nonjuring priest, had risked his life to come and comfort the dying man. Louis was so overcome to find one man prepared to help him that for the first time, he betrayed his distress. "Forgive me, sir," he said to the priest as he rallied, "a moment's weakness."

Later that day Louis was able to see his family for the first time in six weeks. "We heard the sentence pronounced upon my father on that Sunday, January 20, from the news criers who came to shout it under our windows," said Marie-Thérèse. "At seven in the evening we were permitted to go down to my father. We hurried there and found him greatly changed."

The king was waiting in the small antechamber. He had been pacing up and down, "returning several times to the entrance-door, with signs of the deepest emotion," wrote Cléry. "The queen appeared first, holding her son by the hand; then Madame Royale and Madame Élisabeth; they ran into the arms of the king. A gloomy silence reigned for several minutes, interrupted only by sobs." The queen made a movement to draw the king into his private room, but he explained that he was ordered to see them in the dining room, where they could be watched by the guards through a glazed door. He led them in and closed the door.

Through the glass, Cléry could see that "they were all bending toward him and held him half-embraced. This scene of sorrow lasted almost two hours during which it was impossible to hear anything; we could only see that after each sentence of the king, the sobs of the princesses redoubled, lasting some minutes; then the king would resume what he was saying. It was easy to judge from their motions that the king himself was the first to tell them of his condemnation."

"He wept for our grief, but not for his death," Marie Thérèse wrote later. "He told my mother about his trial, excusing the scoundrels who were bringing about his death." Speaking directly to Louis-Charles, he "told him above all to pardon those who were putting him to death." As if to emphasize the Christian oath that the dauphin was being asked to take, Louis held his son's hand above his head as he repeated the words. He urged him and Marie-Thérèse always to be close friends, to support each other and be obedient to their mother. "He gave his blessing to my brother and myself. My mother desperately wanted us to spend the night with my father. He refused, having need of tranquillity."

As they came out of the dining room, the queen, already thin and weak from months of anxiety, "could barely stand." Louis-Charles was clinging onto both his parents, "in his little hands he clasped the king's right hand and the queen's left, which he kisses and waters with his tears." Marie-Thérèse was "filling the room with the most heartrending cries." The king promised to see them again in the morning at eight. The queen feared that this might be too late and begged to see him earlier. "At seven, then," he agreed.

But as the king said "adieu—" he "uttered this in so expressive a manner that their sobs redoubled," wrote Cléry. Marie-Thérèse suddenly collapsed in a faint at his feet. Cléry and Princess Élisabeth tried to help her up and support her. "The king had the strength to tear himself from their arms. 'Adieu—Adieu,' he said, and reentered his chamber." The guards would not let Cléry help Marie-Thérèse up the stairs. "Though the two doors were shut," he wrote, "we continued to hear the cries and sobs of the princesses on the staircase."

When they returned to their rooms the queen did not have the strength to undress her son and put him to bed. "She threw herself, dressed as she was, upon her bed and we heard her through the night trembling with cold and sorrow," said Marie-Thérèse. The next morning they rose at six and waited in Marie-Antoinette's room, hoping desperately for their last chance to see him. They heard the distant sound of drums and then they realized there were soldiers in the forecourt. Commands were shouted out. They could hear someone approach the door. Louis-Charles was shaking with fear and had his face buried in his mother's lap as the door opened and an official approached. "We thought we were to go with him," said Marie-Thérèse, but he had not come to take them to Louis. Instead, he asked for Madame Tison's prayer book, which was required for Mass in the king's apartment. As he was leaving, Louis-Charles tried to rush past to get to the stairs. The guard restrained him in a rough manner and asked what he was doing. "I'm going to speak to the people," cried the little boy. "I'm going to beg them not to have my father killed. For heaven's sakes do not prevent me from speaking to the people."

It was a cold, foggy winter's morning. The hours passed so slowly time seemed to have stopped. No one came to take them to the king. Doors were opened and slammed shut around the Tower. Raised voices were heard and the shuffling of feet up and down the stairs, followed by the sound of departing horses and carriages. An eerie silence fell on the Temple.

The king had risen at five to dress and hear his last Mass with the Abbé Edgeworth. He had wanted to see his family once more, but the Abbé warned against it, advising "this additional agony" would be too much of a shock for the queen. Solemnly Louis turned to Cléry and entrusted him with his last few treasured mementos to give to Marie-Antoinette after his death. There was his wedding ring. "Tell her that I part from it with pain, and only at the very last moment," he said. There was also a royal seal for Louis-Charles and a little packet on which the king had written, "Hair of my wife, sister and children." "Give her that also," he asked Cléry. He cried as he continued, "say to the queen, to my dear children, to my sister, that although I promised to see them this morning, I wish to spare them the pain of so cruel a separation—how much it costs me to go without receiving their last embraces!" He wiped away his tears. "I charge you to take them my farewell," he said and then immediately turned and reentered his room.

At eight o'clock officials arrived to take the prisoner. Surrounded by over a thousand guards, his closed carriage moved very slowly through the streets. It took nearly two hours to reach the Place de la Révolution. Abbé Edgeworth accompanied him; an unexpected comfort, since Louis thought he would have to endure this alone. He asked the priest for psalms for the dying and the two were absorbed in prayer together all the way to the execution site.

Louis stepped out of the carriage. The square was crammed with twenty thousand people whose minds had only one thought: to see his death and the hated royal mystique crushed utterly. The guillotine, mounted on a platform, dominated the scene. Its two wooden posts rose fifteen feet high, at the top of which hung the steel blade, twelve inches wide. Charles Sanson, the executioner, was waiting.

Louis's arms were tied and his hair roughly cut to reveal his neck. He took the Abbé's arm to mount the steep steps to the scaffold, and then tried to address the crowd. "I die innocent of all the crimes of which I have been charged. I pardon those who have occasioned my death; and I pray to God that the blood that you are about to shed may never be visited on France."

His speech remained unfinished, his voice drowned out by fifteen drummers who were ordered to start up their beat. Louis was seized and strapped to the upright plank, which was swung over, pinning his neck firmly in the wooden brace. As the blade came down, because the king's neck was so large, it took time to slice through before his head fell. A stupendous silence hung in the still, gray air.

One of the guards lifted up his head and strutted around the platform triumphantly showing the crowds their trophy. The stunned silence continued, then, slowly at first, the cries began and were soon resounding almost hysterically around the square and across Paris: *"Vive la République! Vive la Nation!"*

The king's body was put in a basket, his head between his legs, and taken to the cemetery of the Madeleine. It was transferred to a plain pauper's coffin, scattered with quicklime to aid decomposition, and buried ten feet deep.

. . .

Inside the Tower, shortly after 10:20 in the morning, Marie-Antoinette and her children heard the sound of the firing of guns. They had still dared to hope that there was a chance to see the king, wrote Marie-Thérèse, "until the cries of joy of a frenzied populace came to inform us that the crime was consummated." Nearby, the drums of the Temple garrison were beating.

"Nothing was able to calm the anguish of my mother. We could make no hope of any sort enter her heart," said Marie-Thérèse. "She was indifferent to whether she lived or died," almost as if her own lifeblood had drained away. The queen was on the brink of nervous collapse and began to suffer from recurring convulsions. Impassive in her chair in the small, cold room in the Tower, she had aged rapidly; her hair was grey, her skin colorless, her body painfully thin, almost emaciated. She could not even bring herself to leave her prison to sit in the garden. "This obliged her to pass the door of my father's room, and that caused her too much pain."

Over the last months Marie-Antoinette had lived through some terrifying, life-threatening experiences. Friends had been with her then, friendly Swiss guards, her husband. There had always been some small seed of hope. Now there was no hope. All the glory of the royal past had come to this. Everything had been taken from her. Her two remaining children were all that was left in her life of human warmth and goodness. "She looked at us sometimes with a pity that made us shudder," wrote her daughter. Marie-Thérèse herself became severely ill after her father's death. "Happily," said Marie-Thérèse, "grief increased my illness, and that occupied her."

The queen did ask to see Cléry, hoping to learn of any final message that her husband might have left with his loyal valet. Yet Cléry was detained in the Tower and forbidden to see "the widow Capet," as she was now known. They soon learned that Cléry "was in a dreadful state," since he was unable to carry out the king's last wishes. He entrusted the king's treasured mementos, the wedding ring, hair and seal, to one of the officials, in the hope that they would be given to Marie-Antoinette. However, they were taken to the commissioner's room on the ground floor and locked away.

Louis-Charles became the focal point of Marie Antoinette's wretched life. She made a huge effort to rally to console the children after their father's death and to do the things that Louis would have wished. Knowing that the king would have given his son lessons in math, history and geography, she now took on this task. She also encouraged her son to pray, although he told her, "When I pray to God, it's always my father that appears to me." Early in February they held a small ceremony in their room to mourn the king, at which Louis-Charles sang specially composed verses:

Everything is fled for me on this earth
But I am still by my mother's side.

Later that month, fearing that the lack of air in the Tower might be harmful to her children's health, she asked if they could go up on the roof of the Great Tower to walk around the battlements. Louis-Charles, still playful, liked to be lifted up so he could see outside through the gaps in the parapets. Since Marie-Antoinette was thin and weak, a sympathetic guard arranged seating for her in the top turret, so she could watch.

With the death of Louis XVI, for royalists and many émigrés, this lively seven-year-old boy was now the acknowledged king, "Louis XVII," who could still reign with his mother or uncle, Provence, as regent. In early 1793, plots to help the prisoners escape were hatching in Paris, the provinces and overseas. Count Axel Fersen, concerned at news of the queen's desperate situation and failing health, told his sister, "In my social circle we do nothing but grieve and cry over her fate. . . . We speak only of ways of saving her." He devised countless schemes; the difficulty was trying to organize an escape, without taking any steps, which if discovered, could precipitate her trial. He was bold enough to bribe officials in Paris; however, they reneged on any agreement and merely took his money.

Inside the Temple, two of the queen's jailors were also moved to action by her pitiful plight. The once-fanatical François-Adrian Toulan, a hardened veteran of the storming of the Tuileries, put himself at risk by secretly bringing her the king's last mementos. Toulan surreptitiously broke into

Cléry's sealed package in the commissioner's room and arranged his theft to look like a real burglary. Soon he went much further and began to devise an escape plan. He enlisted the help of another guard, Jacques Lepître, who was in charge of passports and passes, and a royalist outside the Temple, the Chevalier de Jarjayes. Their daring idea was simplicity itself: the royal women, disguised as commissioners and with the appropriate passes, would walk straight out through the main gate. Certain guards would be doped with doctored tobacco; Marie-Thérèse and Louis-Charles were to be dressed as lamplighter's children, their faces blackened with oil.

As they planned their escape, fears were growing of royalist counter-revolution, and the control of passports and security at the Temple was stepped up. It became too dangerous to attempt a rescue of the whole family. The Chevalier de Jarjayes was still keen to help the queen escape—without her children. She refused. "We had a beautiful dream, and that is all," she wrote to Jarjayes. "The best interests of my son are my only guide. However happy I might have been to be out of here, I cannot agree to be separated from him. It would be impossible for me to take pleasure in anything if I left my children behind, and I have no regrets about this."

So many people were sympathetic to the plight of the queen that one conspiracy after another was taking shape that spring of 1793. In England, the wealthy aristocrat Charlotte Lady Atkyns, who had lived for a while in France prior to the revolution and was horrified at the queen's downfall, began to contact royalist supporters within France to organize an escape. Meanwhile, the French general François Dumouriez conceived a daring plan to march on Paris and proclaim Louis XVII as king. Jacques-René Hébert fumed in *Le Père Duchesne*, there would be no rest until "the widow Capet . . . and her foul progeny . . . have been destroyed. Little fish grow big," he warned. "Liberty is hanging by only a hair."

The young republic was indeed under threat. Following the death of Louis XVI, European monarchs had formed a coalition joining the Austrians and Prussians against France, including Britain, Spain, Russia, the Netherlands, and Sardinia. French armies were forced to retreat as Austrians overran Belgium, the French position collapsed in the Netherlands, and the Spanish invaded to the south. Within France, in the Vendée, a Catholic region southwest of the Loire, forced conscription to the revolutionary army finally stirred a brutal royalist uprising. Counterrevolutionary centers spread rapidly throughout France, and growing food shortages and inflation prompted street riots in many provincial towns.

In Paris, revolutionary leaders were determined to preserve the gains of the revolution and establish ways of crushing opposition. "Be terrible to dispense the people from being so," urged Georges Danton to the Convention. Danton, who had inspired the insurrection at the Tuileries, now instigated the creation of a special court, with powers to try political prisoners, notably anyone suspected of royalist sympathies. This Revolutionary Tribunal was created on March 10, 1793, and was soon to become a key instrument of the Terror. At the Convention, Robespierre urged that Marie-Antoinette be brought before the Revolutionary Tribunal for "violations against the liberty and security of the State." "The time has come," he declared on March 27, "for patriots to rekindle their vigorous and immortal hatred of those who are called kings."

A week later, on April 6, 1793, a special committee was created with Danton as its head: The Committee of Public Safety. This was charged with the power to raise new armies, organize food supplies and save the republic from its internal and external enemies. Any suspects were to be ruthlessly hunted out and cut down. Within a week, several prominent aristocrats were arrested, including the king's cousin, the Duc d'Orléans, now known as Philippe Égalité. Robespierre then initiated an attack on the moderate republican leaders at the Convention—the Girondins. He blamed them for the treasonable defection of the French general Dumouriez—who had links with the Girondins—to Austria. In the prevailing atmosphere of betrayal and suspicion, there was no hiding place for any "traitors."

The royal family soon faced further restrictions and humiliations. Late in the evening on April 20, they had just gone to bed when Jacques-René Hébert arrived with four other officials from the Commune. "We rose hastily," said Marie-Thérèse. "They read us a decree of the Convention ordering that we be carefully searched, even the mattresses. My poor brother was asleep; they pulled him roughly out of his bed, to search it; my mother held him, shivering with cold." Although the guards searched for hours, until four in the morning, they found just a few last remaining treasures. "An address of a shop my mother always kept, a stick of sealing wax from my aunt, and from me a Sacred Heart of Jesus." Marie-Thérèse thought they seemed "furious to find nothing but trifles." Later they returned to remove a hat from Madame Élisabeth. She insisted that it was the king's hat, but the municipals wanted to take it as "a suspicious object." She begged to keep it "for the love of her brother." It was no use. They carried away the hat.

The strain of their restricted life began to take its toll on Louis-Charles. "The want of air and exercise did him much harm," observed his sister. "Also the sort of life the poor child lived, in the midst of tears and shocks, alarm and continual terrors at just eight years of age." That spring he began to complain repeatedly of a pain in his side, which hurt him when he laughed and "suffocated him when he lay down." By early May, he was suffering from bad headaches and attacks of fever and convulsions, not to mention a worm infestation. His mother anxiously demanded that he see his former royal physician, Dr. Brunier, but the Commune refused. As his condition deteriorated they did permit him see the prison doctor, a Dr. Thierry. Thierry was worried "and had the kindness to go and consult Brunier about my brother's illness," said Marie-Thérèse. Throughout May, Marie-Antoinette and Élisabeth nursed him night and day.

As Louis-Charles recovered in early June, there was a dramatic coup d'état against the moderate Girondins at the National Convention. Twenty-nine leading Girondists were arrested on June 2 and many were subsequently guillotined. With the fall of the Girondins, the Jacobins and Robespierre's extremist Mountain party now dominated the Convention. In the prevailing atmosphere of fear and betrayal, where even well-intentioned leaders could find themselves facing the guillotine, no chances were going to be taken with the royal hostages. Commune officials had already interrogated guards at the Temple for details of any conspiracy. Under pressure from her husband, Madame Tison had repeatedly betrayed the queen. She had claimed that Marie-Antoinette continued a secret correspondence with royalists, and denounced the royal doctor, Brunier, and the guards, Toulan and Lepître, who had been forced to leave. In late June, the Committee of Public Safety learned of yet another plot to rescue the boy king and his mother by force under the leadership of the royalist Baron Jean-Pierre de Batz. Batz's plan was only foiled by the vigilance of Commissioner Antoine Simon, who was alerted to the plot and rushed back to the Temple in a frantic state to check the prisoners.

The Committee of Public Safety soon devised a cruel way of stepping up security. When Madame Tison heard of their pitiless plans, she was tortured with remorse at having betrayed the royal family and became distraught and confused. She repeatedly threw herself at the queen's feet, raving hysterically and begging for pardon; gradually she lost her mind altogether. On July 1, it took eight men to take her forcibly from the Tower to the hospital at the Hôtel Dieu. A guard was placed over her, in case, in her incoherent ramblings, she revealed other secrets.

On the night of July 3 at ten o'clock, the royal family heard the dreaded sounds of a party of municipal officers approaching. The bolts flew back and officers came into Marie-Antoinette's room, disturbing the peaceful scene; she was sewing by candlelight, her son was asleep in bed nearby, with a shawl wrapped over him to shield him from the light. One of the men read out the decree of the Commune: the "Son of Capet" was to be immediately separated from his mother and lodged in a more secure room in the Tower.

Marie-Antoinette was beside herself. Weak and emaciated as she was, she rose to defend her son with determined ferocity. "She was struck down by this cruel order," wrote Marie-Thérèse, and pleaded forcefully with them to let him stay. Louis-Charles woke up, realized what was happening and "flung himself into my mother's arms, imploring not to be taken from her." The idea of parting with her young son and abandoning him to God knows what fate was utter agony for her. The officers became increasingly threatening, but "she would not give up her son," wrote Marie-Thérèse, and blocked the guards from reaching him on the bed behind her. "They were absolutely determined to have him and threatened to employ violence and call up the guard." Marie-Antoinette would not yield. "She told them they would have to kill her before they could tear her child from her," said Marie-Thérèse. Guards were summoned. "An hour passed in resistance on her part, in threats and insults from the municipals, in tears and efforts from all of us."

"At last they threatened my mother so positively to kill him and us also that she had to yield for love of us," wrote Marie-Thérèse. "We rose, my aunt and I, for my poor mother no longer had any strength. After we had dressed him, she took him and gave him into the hands of the municipals herself, bathing him with her tears and overwhelmed with a sense of foreboding that she would never see him again." As for Louis-Charles, "the poor little boy kissed us all very tenderly and went away with the guards, crying his heart out."

The guards pushed the boy along the corridor and down the spiral stairway into a room on the floor below. It was the king's room. Louis-Charles had not been here since that tearful evening when he last saw his father, shortly before his execution. The two heavy security doors closed behind him; the bolts were drawn and the padlocks firmly secured. There was the sound of the guards' footsteps growing fainter as they went away downstairs. He was locked up in the place that held such frightening memories for him, with no father and no mother, terrified of what might happen next. He cried hysterically, quite unable to stop, for two days.

Although Marie-Antoinette could not see him, she could hear his inconsolable sobbing in the room immediately below. For this to happen to her treasured little *chou d'amour* was more than she could bear. She was near collapse, beyond consolation, soaked in grief. She begged the guards incessantly to let her see him. "Why is he crying?" she asked. "What are they doing to him?" It was easy to imagine the worst.

When her sister-in-law exhorted her to try to find strength in her faith, Marie-Antoinette could not. "God himself has forsaken me," she said to Élisabeth. "I no longer dare to pray."

Chapter Five

THE YOUNG
"SANS-CULOTTE"

*The little whelp must lose the recollection of his royalty
. . . and his mother be chopped up like mincemeat . . .*

—JACQUES-RENÉ HÉBERT

*Forgive him, my dear sister. Think of his age and how
easy it is to make a child say what one wishes, and even
what he does not comprehend.*

—MARIE-ANTOINETTE, OCTOBER 1793

Walking down the steep stone steps to the floor below, escorted by six commissioners, the weeping eight-year-old boy was now a pawn in a fast-changing political landscape. He had been recognized as king by many countries, including England, Austria, Portugal, Russia, and the United States of America. Within France, aristocrats, members of the clergy, even some commoners, recognized the child prisoner as monarch. Consequently the child represented a real danger to leaders of the revolution who feared that proroyalists both in France and neighboring countries might rally around the boy king. They were haunted by comparisons with English history; Charles I, like Louis XVI, had been executed, yet his son was eventually restored to the throne. How could France stop history from repeating itself?

A revolution led by high ideals could not openly countenance the outright *murder* of a small boy. Some argued plainly that murdering the boy might stir up public opinion against the revolution. He was too young to be tried and executed like his father. There was also the genuine possibility that he could become a useful bargaining chip to the revolutionary government should France need to negotiate with its enemies. For the moment, Louis-Charles was best kept alive. Consequently, the aim of the Commune was to keep Louis-Charles in prison under close guard, but to "reeducate" him as a good little citizen or *sans-culotte*. He was to understand the evils of the autocratic royal regime that his family had inflicted on France, and to grow up sympathetic to the high ideals of the revolutionary government. Once fully reeducated he would no longer be a threat to the revolution but a committed republican—at least, this was the theory. The man selected for this great honor of serving the revolutionary cause as teacher and guardian to the "son of Capet" was waiting for him in the king's former apartments below. It was none other than the shoemaker, Commissioner Antoine Simon.

In the dimly lit room, Louis-Charles saw an older man who could not present a more stark contrast to his previous governesses, the sensitive Gabrielle de Polignac or the disciplined and dignified Madame de Tourzel. Antoine Simon was fifty-seven years old, with "a square, robust build, tanned complexion and a coarse face, and with black hair coming down to his eyebrows and thick whiskers." He was known for his rough and brutish demeanor; "he had a gruff, short way of talking and insolent gestures." Ironically, the revolution had appointed an almost illiterate man as "tutor" who would later be described by Goret, one of his colleagues at the Temple, as "a poor wretch without education or instruction."

For Antoine Simon, this prestigious appointment represented the high point in his working life. He had a string of failed enterprises behind him. Despite his early training as a master shoemaker, he had been unable to make a living at this trade and had tried running a cheap eating-house near the Seine, which, like almost anything he tackled, ended in disaster. A poor businessman, careless and lazy, he had soon run up debts and lived in abject poverty. He had turned once more to shoemaking, resoling shoes at home, where he lived in a single room with his wife. When she died they were so short of money he had been forced to pawn his wife's clothes to pay for her burial. Later, he had married again, a charwoman called Marie-Jeanne Aladame, who had the considerable attraction of a dowry of one thousand livres, which he soon squandered repaying his debts. Bitter and frustrated about his lack of business success, he increasingly raged at the social order which he saw as based on privilege and patronage to favor a rich elite at the expense of the poor.

Simon seized on the ideas of the revolution. It gave expression to all his deeply held prejudices against authority that he had nursed for so long, and provided him with a much-wanted opportunity to satisfy his ambitions. He rapidly digested all the revolutionary rhetoric and could impress others with his loyalty and commitment to the cause; his patriotic zeal even came to the attention of Robespierre. Simon was one of four commissioners selected to transfer the royal family from the Assembly to the Temple in August 1792. After this, he had been chosen to search the royal prisoners' rooms and remove any writing materials, and later to help supervise general security arrangements at the Temple. His rapid elevation owed much to the patronage of Anaxagoras Chaumette, procurator of the Commune, and his deputy, Jacques-René Hébert. Both knew Simon well and recognized that he was a simple man whom they could easily manipulate and control, a man who would blindly follow their lead. Consequently, beyond Simon's wildest expectations, in July 1793, he found himself appointed as tutor to the son of the former king. His wife soon joined him at the Temple. "I've got a grand position," she told a friend proudly. "They'll take me there in a carriage, and perhaps something better still."

For the first few days, Simon could make no progress. The captive child sat on a chair "in the darkest corner of the room" and wept, "his eyes constantly turned toward the door . . . every time he heard the noise of the bolts and the grating of keys in the locks." Nothing in Louis-Charles's background had prepared him for his new situation. At Versailles, for the first four years of his life he had been accustomed to being treated with deference and respect as a royal prince and had been led to believe that one day he would inherit the throne as the king of all France. Even after the revolution, in the Tuileries and later in the Tower, though aware that his family was in danger, and increasingly puzzled and confused by events, he had been shielded from the worst by his parents and always enjoyed his mother's devoted attention. Now he shared a room with a brutish, illiterate man with a steely expression; "often he remained motionless and tears rolled down his cheeks." Simon could scarcely get a word from him.

Since he was so visibly distressed, Simon did not dare take him outside for a walk on the battlements or in the garden where he might be seen. This fuelled speculation that the boy had indeed escaped. There were "sightings" all over France. Some claimed he had been abducted to a royal palace, perhaps Saint-Cloud, to be proclaimed king; others believed he had been kidnapped by leading members of the Commune who hoped to improve their own political standing. The rumors became so persistent that on July 6, Maximilien Robespierre was obliged to reassure members of the Convention that their royal hostage was indeed safely behind bars. The following day officials from the Committee of Public Safety went to check on the child for themselves.

They found the young boy in his room and immediately led him into the garden so he could be seen by the guards. Despite the obvious importance of the officials, Louis-Charles found the courage to protest at his treatment. "I want to know what law you are using that says I should be separated from my mother," he demanded bravely. "Show me this law. I want to see it!" He was sharply reproved and told to "hold his tongue." The deputation then went to see Marie-Antoinette, where she, in turn, complained "of the cruelty shown in taking her son from her." The officials replied that he was being well attended. Marie-Antoinette persisted. "He has never been away from me. . . . I cannot believe that the convention will fail to see how legitimate are my complaints." However, the deputation dismissed her concerns and left, satisfied that their pawn had not escaped. Orders were given by the Commune that each day Louis-Charles should exercise in the garden, not out of concern for his health, but to ensure that he was seen and help prevent further rumors.

Initially, Simon appears to have treated Louis-Charles reasonably well in that he was fed, washed and his clothes were regularly cleaned. Temple records show he was allowed to play with a collection of toys, including a remarkable aviary retrieved from a royal storehouse, which was "made entirely of silver with molded, gilded garlands . . . chimes and a bird organ." Best of all, every two weeks when clean linens arrived, he was allowed to play with the laundry woman's daughter, a girl called Clouet.

Simon and his wife may well have tried to win the boy's confidence before they embarked on their task of "effacing the stigma of royalty from his brow" and "shading it with a red cap instead of a crown." Yet Simon was under no illusion that the aim of his captors at the Commune was to break the boy's will, to brainwash him and force him to accept their authority and control. Anaxagoras Chaumette, the leader of the Commune, had declared, "I will make him lose the idea of his rank." Although Jacques-René Hébert was Chaumette's deputy, for many he was the real leader of the two, and he expressed their aims even more forcefully. Louis-Charles was nothing more than "a little monkey sired by an ape," whose mother, "the Austrian tigress should be chopped up like mincemeat. . . . The little whelp must lose the recollection of his royalty."

There is evidence that the leaders of the Commune gave their tacit approval for Simon to go much further. On July 3, 1793, Simon questioned his superiors quite bluntly about their aims. "Citizens, what have you decided about the wolf cub? He has been taught to be insolent but I shall know how to tame him. Hard luck if he dies because of it! I will not answer for that. After all, what do you want done with him? To deport him? To kill him? To poison him?" The unequivocal answer from the members of the Commune was, "We want to get rid of him!" Inspired by these men, in the secret, hidden environment of the Tower, a pattern of abuse began to develop, which, unchecked, grew worse and more terrible over time.

Through a narrow opening in the wall, by the toilet stairway—according to a secret note from Princess Élisabeth to Turgy—Marie-Antoinette now spent her days anxiously watching and waiting for a fleeting glimpse of her son. "The sole pleasure my mother had was to see him through that little

[103]

chink as he passed in the distance," wrote her daughter. "She stayed there for hours, watching for the instant when she could see her child; it was her sole hope, her sole occupation." In the days that followed his separation she could hear his distressed cries for her; she could only imagine what he was suffering. "My mother's anguish was at its height when she learned that Simon, the shoemaker, whom she had seen as a municipal, was entrusted with the care of the unfortunate child," wrote Marie-Thérèse. Although Marie-Antoinette repeatedly asked after him, she "rarely heard news of him" and had little idea of what might be going on in the rooms below.

Marie-Antoinette still could not quite bring herself to believe that her family would abandon her and her children. She had, after all, been the instrument of political initiative inspired by her mother to bring Austria and France closer together. However, to the Austrians, Marie-Antoinette had obviously become expendable. The king had been executed, which the Austrians deplored; but to negotiate with the abhorrent revolutionary government for the queen's release was regarded by Austria and her allies as a tactical mistake. As she waited in the Tower, straining for any sight of her son through the crack, Marie-Antoinette was on her own.

Her fate seemed inextricably linked with events beyond her control. During the summer of 1793, the revolutionary government feared a ring of opposition tightening around Paris. To the west, there were royalist uprisings in Normandy, Brittany, and further down the coast in the Vendée. To the south, parts of Provence, the Rhône valley, and Lyon were in rebellion. The Austrian army was threatening Paris from the north, down the valley of the river Oise and the river Marne. On July 26 the important frontier stronghold of Valenciennes, north of Paris, fell into Austrian hands. Extreme threats called for extreme measures and the very next day, Maximilien Robespierre was elected by the National Convention to the Committee of Public Safety, empowered to crush the enemies of the revolution once and for all. Together with his allies, Saint-Just and Couthon, Robespierre now held the balance of power in this committee; the more "conciliatory" Danton had left earlier in the month. Robespierre believed in the power of a political system temporarily backed by terror. "The revolutionary government owes the good citizens complete national protection," he decreed. "It owes only death to the people's enemies." Saint-Just went even further: "The republic consists in the extermination of everything that opposes it." Under the influence of the "Incorruptible," as Robespierre became known, the Reign of Terror was about to begin.

The revolutionary government now lashed out at France's royal past with a renewed fervor determined to whip up hatred of the royal tyrants. Three days after Robespierre joined the Committee of Public Safety, a decree was passed which ordered that "the tombs and mausoleums of the former kings in the church of Saint-Denis and elsewhere . . . be destroyed." In the name of national justice, *sans-culottes* were instructed to storm the ancient tombs, now despised symbols of their royal past, on the anniversary of the insurrection at the Tuileries. Statues and ornaments were stolen, coffins were opened and looted for souvenirs—the shoulder blade of Hugues Capet, the beard of Henry IV—bodies were unceremoniously dumped in two large pits nearby. There were even reports of revolutionaries playing *boules,* using the ancient bones of kings as skittles. According to one account, the remains of kings, once revered for up to twelve centuries, were now no more than "common dust, scattered to the wind."

By the same decree of August 1, 1793, the Committee of Public Safety turned its anger on the royal "she-devil," the "enemy within" who was conspiring to ensure that the Austrian invasion succeeded and the monarchy restored. The widow Capet was to be tried by the newly created Revolutionary Tribunal. She was to be removed from the Tower and taken to another prison where she would be held as a common criminal along with the rising number of political prisoners.

In the small hours of the night of the August 2, 1793, four officers came to Marie-Antoinette's room. They read a decree of the Convention which ordered that she should be taken to the *Conciergerie* in the heart of Paris, in preparation for her trial. "She listened to the reading of the decree without emotion, and without saying a single word," wrote her daughter. "My aunt and I asked immediately to go with my mother, but this mercy was not granted to us." Marie-Antoinette wrapped up a small parcel of clothes and was "obliged even to dress herself before the municipals." The guards emptied her pockets. "They left her only a handkerchief and a smelling bottle in the fear that she might faint."

"After tenderly embracing me and telling me to have courage . . . she then threw herself into my aunt's arms as she commended her children to her," wrote Marie-Thérèse, who found herself quite unable to speak as her mother left. "I could say nothing, so terrified was I at the idea that I saw her for the last time." For her part, Marie-Antoinette "went away without casting her eyes upon us, fearing no doubt that her firmness might abandon her." She was then escorted down the stone staircase of the Tower, passing the door to her son's room, unable to see him and knowing full well she might never see him again. On her way out she accidentally struck her head on the last beam. "Did you hurt yourself?" asked one of the guards. "Oh, no," she replied. "Nothing can hurt me anymore."

The *Conciergerie*, a prison on the Île de la Cité, close to Notre Dame, had become a revolutionary prison. Balzac, in time, would describe its atmosphere of terror as "the antechamber to the scaffold." The "widow Capet" was admitted at three o'clock in the morning as the 280th prisoner of the house, and taken to a small cell on the ground floor. The cell was divided into two equal parts by a simple screen—barely five feet high—over which she was subject to the constant surveillance of two gendarmes, who remained in her cell, drinking, smoking and playing cards. To further reduce any remote chance of a moment's privacy, in the narrow space remaining on her side of the screen she could also be viewed from the main corridor through a small iron grill. For a fee, the prison authorities allowed visitors to observe the former queen in her squalid cell; people were only too eager to see for themselves the former queen's precipitous downfall. From all angles, it seemed, hostile eyes were watching her.

Her part of the cell contained a canvas bed, a crude wooden table and chair, and a bucket. Set high in the wall was a window, which was covered by a thick iron grille, making the room gloomy and airless. This opened onto the *Cour des Femmes*, where other women prisoners could wash their clothes in the fountain; Marie-Antoinette herself was not permitted to leave her cell. Fersen anxiously asked for details from a friend and wrote, "The cell was small, damp and fetid, without a stove or fireplace; there were three beds, one for the queen, another beside it for her woman attendant, the third for the two gendarmes who never left the cell, even when the queen had to satisfy the needs of nature."

An abject political prisoner, a widow separated from her children and desperate for news of them, Marie-Antoinette found that trivial things assumed great significance for her: a bottle of dentifrice and a swansdown puff. A servant in the *Conciergerie*, Rosalie Lamorlière, later described her recollections of the queen's circumstances. "The prison regime did not permit us to give her a mirror," said Rosalie, although Marie-Antoinette requested one every morning. Eventually, the sympathetic concierge, Madame Richard, permitted Rosalie to give the prisoner her own mirror. "I blushed when I offered it to her. That mirror, bought on the quais, had cost me only twenty-five sous." The emperor's daughter who had once seen her reflection in the Hall of Mirrors, repeated endlessly in gleaming polished mirror, gilt and silver, was now presented with a crude object, a red-framed hand mirror with Chinese figures painted on each side. To Rosalie's delight, "The queen accepted this little mirror as if it were something of importance and Her Majesty used it until the last day." On another occasion, Rosalie successfully obtained permission to lend a simple cardboard box to the queen to hold her linens. "She received it with as much satisfaction as if she had been given the most beautiful treasure in the world."

Once Madame Richard, the concierge, was accompanied by her own youngest son, who was an attractive child, "well above his station," said Rosalie, with blond hair and blue eyes. As they went into the queen's cell, the young boy's presence was such a forceful reminder of her own son left behind in the Tower that Marie-Antoinette was overwhelmed. "She took him in her arms, covered him with kisses and caresses, and began to cry as she spoke to us of Monsieur le Dauphin," says Rosalie. "Her own son was about the same age, and she said that she thought of him night and day." Perhaps shocked to have evoked such an emotional response, Madame Richard did not bring her son again.

Madame Richard was anxious not to show any favoritism to her royal prisoner. Even though, Rosalie says, when they went shopping, some merchants pointedly gave the most tender chickens and best fruits "for our Queen" it is doubtful that these reached her. Back in the Temple, Marie-Thérèse and Aunt Élisabeth also made valiant efforts to find ways of sustaining her spirits. Knowing that Marie-Antoinette could not drink the water of the Seine, they begged the municipals to send her that of Ville d'Avray. They also tried to gather any silks and wools "for we knew how she liked to be busy," wrote her daughter. At the Temple, she had just started a pair of stockings for her son. "We collected all we could, but we learned afterwards that nothing had been given to her, fearing, they said, that she might do herself harm with knitting needles." So the queen unpicked the cloth that was draped over the stone walls, so she could continue to weave with the thread.

One day in late August, among the visitors who paid to see the spectacle of the former queen in prison was a royalist sympathizer, the Marquis de Rougeville. While the guards were distracted, he signalled to her and threw a carnation into her cell. As she looked into the petals, there was a secret message hidden, raising the possibility of escape. Marie-Antoinette was able to make her reply by tracing letters with pinpricks: "I am watched. I speak to no one. I trust you. I shall come." However, as arrangements were being made for her escape, one of the guards who had been let in on the secret suddenly lost his nerve. He raised the alarm and foiled the "Carnation Conspiracy."

While Rougeville managed to escape from Paris, following this abortive attempt to flee on September 3, 1793, Marie-Antoinette was interrogated. Over the course of two days she was challenged at enormous length about any possible treasonable activity: her escape plans, loyalty to France, even her knowledge of the news came under scrutiny in the hope she might accidentally incriminate some secret contact. However, she proved remarkably adept under pressure. When she was pushed on whether she was interested in the success of enemy troops, she insisted, "I am interested in the success of the troops of my son's nation; when one is a mother, that is the primary relationship." When pressed still further on her support for the enemy, she answered skillfully that she only regarded as her enemies "all those who would bring harm to my children."

Meanwhile, Madame Richard, her husband, and her oldest son, were imprisoned, and under the tougher regime established by the new concierge the queen was taken to a smaller, more secure cell further from the prison entrance. During this time, she was suffering from chronic hemorrhages and was growing steadily weaker, which Rosalie attributed to "her sorrows, the bad air, and the lack of exercise." When the queen asked Rosalie secretly for some linen, "I immediately cut up one of my chemises and put those strips of cloth under her bolster." Rosalie tried to help her in other ways, such as extending her evening chores so that the queen spent less time alone in the dark of night.

Marie-Antoinette, perhaps partly influenced by the months of captivity with her pious sister-in-law, drew strength from religion. One night, the guards permitted her to see a priest who had not sworn the oath of loyalty to the revolution, the Abbé Magnin. Improvising an altar and chalice in her cell, he held Mass and heard her confession. She received great comfort from this and it helped her prepare for the terrible ordeal that lay ahead, for which, for the sake of her son, she was determined to find the strength to survive.

However, at a secret, all-night meeting of the Committee of Public Safety on September 2, 1793, Marie-Antoinette's enemies had already plotted her death. Hébert was most vociferous in pushing for the queen's head "to be shaved by the national razor," in the words of *Le Père Duchesne*. "I have promised my supporters Antoinette's head. If there is any further delay in giving it to me, I shall go and cut it off myself," he raged. When some equivocated, not out of concern for justice at her trial but for fear that the jury might not find her guilty, or that she was better kept alive as a hostage to bargain with their enemies, Hébert was dismissive. "The *sans-culottes* will kill all our enemies, but their zeal must be kept on the boil," he stormed, "and you can only do that by putting Antoinette to death." After a heated session, it was decided to bring her before the Revolutionary Tribunal.

The public prosecutor, the notorious Antoine Fouquier-Tinville, expressed doubts as to whether there was enough evidence to be sure of the death penalty. Hébert, determined that Marie-Antoinette must be condemned at her trial, hatched an outrageous plan. The French public had grown accustomed to hearing the lurid, pornographic rumors that had circulated about Marie-Antoinette. She was, according to reports, a sexual she-devil whose natural desires were only satisfied in an orgy of sexual encounters in which no boundaries, no moral values contained her lust. Hébert realized that the way to overcome the shortage of hard evidence against her would be to provide "proof" of what was already common currency; that Marie-Antoinette was sexually incontinent. Her son, now a frightened, confused boy surrounded by unfamiliar, hostile men, would become the means by which Hébert's plan would be delivered. A trap was to be set for the boy that would ensnare him and help to destroy his mother.

In the first few weeks of Louis-Charles's "reeducation," he was made to sing revolutionary songs loudly at the window so the guards could hear, much to the despair of his sister and aunt upstairs. "We could hear him every day, singing with Simon, the *Carmagnole*, the air of the *Marseillaise* and other horrors," wrote Marie-Thérèse. "Simon taught him to swear dreadful oaths against God, his family and aristocrats. My mother, happily, did not hear these horrors. Oh! My God, what harm they would have done her!" Marie-Thérèse also heard that "Simon made him eat horribly and forced him to drink much wine, which he detested. All this gave him a fever . . . and his health became totally out of order."

Apart from singing like a revolutionary, he also had to look like one. Simon removed the child's mourning clothes and replaced them with the revolutionary uniform. Louis-Charles had a red jacket made in the *carmagnole* shape—a typical revolutionary-style jacket—trousers and a red cap. To complete the effect, Madame Simon cut off his blond curls, which were deemed to give him an aristocratic air. Just at this point, one of the kitchen staff, Meunier, came in with the dinner. "Oh, why have you hacked off his hair, which so became him," he protested. "Don't you see, we are playing the game of the shaved king!" laughed Madame Simon. Louis-Charles "remained sad," but Simon was well satisfied. "Finally, Capet, you are a *sans-culotte*!" he said with delight to see the red cap on the royal heir.

There were no lessons in this unusual educational regime. Instead, his "tutor" encouraged him to lose his aristocratic demeanor and to sing bawdy songs and use bad language. For Simon and the guards it was amusing to see the son of the deceased king behaving in a common way. Coaxed on with wine, and sometimes even brandy, he was taught to refer to his aunt and sister upstairs as "common whores." This would make the guards roar with laughter. Applauded and encouraged, the confused child, who had always learned to be obedient, would repeat the remarks time and time again. After a while, if he refused to play along, he could be beaten or subdued with a slap. He was also sometimes the defenseless object of his tutor's fury for other reasons. When Simon heard of the defeat of the French at the border town of Condé by the Austrian army, "he threw himself upon him, crying out in his fury: 'D—d wolf cub. You are *half* Austrian, and therefore you deserve to be *half* beaten!' "

Hébert kept a close eye on Simon's progress. According to a report from a spy who was trying to gather information for a royalist, the Comte d'Antraigues, "Hébert and his soldiers . . . only taught him filthy language and blasphemy. He was permitted just the most unspeakable books and every effort was made to corrupt him." Hébert could strike terror into the child's heart even more successfully than Simon. The report continues: "Several times Hébert threatened him with the guillotine and this threat frightened him so horribly that he [Simon] has often seen the child faint from shock." Hébert was not the only one who played on the child's fears of the guillotine. On August 2, Anaxagoras Chaumette sent the child some toys, which included a little model of a guillotine. Fortunately for Louis-Charles, there happened to be a commissioner on duty who recognized how alarming it would be to give him such a potent symbol of his father's death, and the "plaything" never reached him.

There are few witnesses to this period of Louis-Charles's captivity, and apart from information gleaned from official documents, records, and the anecdotes of guards, no one can prove precisely what happened behind the locked doors of the Tower. The first detailed investigation came from the historian Alcide de Beauchesne, who spent twenty years after the Restoration gathering information and was able to interview some of those who had worked at the Temple during the revolution. Although undoubtedly seen from a royalist perspective, the picture that emerges from the records gathered by Beauchesne and others is that, inspired by men like Hébert, the boy was abused, and this abuse became progressively worse over time. To many of the guards in the Temple, including Simon, Louis-Charles was a legitimate target. He was the son of the hated tyrant and his depraved wife who, in their eyes, had selfishly brought famine, poverty and misery to their people and ruthlessly imposed an autocratic, oppressive and unjust rule on France. Their revenge would be simple, local and direct. According to Beauchesne, soon pure sadism prevailed.

There are official documents to back up this view. According to a report written after the revolution by Jean-Baptiste Harmand, an agent of the Committee for General Security, Simon subjected the boy to "atrocious cruelty." Harmand interviewed the guards at the Temple and learned that Simon would waken his prisoner several times a night, shouting out: "Capet! Capet!" Louis-Charles would answer, "Here I am, citizen." "Come near me so I might touch you," Simon would reply. According to Harmand, as the boy approached the shoemaker's bed, "Simon would put one leg out of bed, and with a kick, directed as far as he could reach, he would hurl his victim to the ground, crying, 'Go to bed, wolf cub!'" Harmand added to his report, "The commissaries gave us an account which makes me still shudder." While there is evidence that such scenes were interspersed with more kindly interludes where Simon might coax the child with games of drafts, billiards or new toys, nonetheless, his drinking, brutishness and his unpredictability all served to undermine Louis-Charles. Gradually, the child became increasingly nervous around other adults. Prison staff noticed that Louis-Charles could be frozen with terror at the sight of anyone he did not recognize and would not utter a word to them unless they showed him some act of kindness.

Evidence from minutes of the General Council of the Commune also reveal that those few guards who disliked what they saw became afraid to complain. Sympathy for a member of the royal family might be repaid at the guillotine. On August 19, 1793, a schoolteacher, magistrate and municipal representative known as Commissionaire Leboeuf happened to witness Simon's treatment of the child when he visited the Tower. The young prince was serving Simon, as usual, at the table; Simon was the worse for drink. When Louis-Charles accidentally spilled part of the meal, Simon swung round and struck him forcefully with his napkin, "almost taking out one of his eyes with the blow." Before Leboeuf could protest, Simon was scolding the child. "See here, citizen! How awkward the d—d wolf cub is in waiting at table! They want to make a king of him and he is not fit for a servant!" Simon could never have imagined before the revolution that one day he would be served dinner by the king of France. Like many ordinary men who had advanced under the revolution, he revelled in his elevated status; this was his chance to spit at the system.

However, Leboeuf protested at Simon's brutality. The minutes for the General Council of the Paris Commune reveal that on August 28 Leboeuf was denounced "because he had complained of the too republican kind of education given to little Capet." Leboeuf, who attended the meeting, tried to defend himself. He pointed out that as a schoolmaster he did not like to hear "improper songs" and "repeated obscenities" and that "he wished to see the little Capet receive an education more consistent with good morals." Chaumette was outraged. He accused Leboeuf "of having obtained entrance to the Temple in a manner unworthy of a magistrate, of having found and worshiped an idol there, and of daring to find fault with the educating of the young Capet as a *sans-culotte*." Leboeuf, in turn, was so appalled at Chaumette's "reeducation" that he resigned his post at the Commune. It was not long before the police raided Leboeuf's house and he was imprisoned. Although he was later acquitted, he fled Paris, fearful of his life. After this, no more formal complaints of the boy's treatment are recorded in the General Council minutes.

Simon's wife, Marie-Jeanne, who did not have any children of her own, tried to protect the boy from her husband's roughness and the victimization of the guards, but with little success. Like her husband, she, too, relished the reversal in their fortunes. "The little fellow is a very amiable and charming child," she told a friend. "He cleans and polishes my shoes for me and he brings me my foot-stove to my bedside when I get up!" She made sure that their little royal servant was reasonably well fed and kept clean, but she was a timid woman who was obliged to turn a blind eye to her husband's excesses.

Simon and the guards gradually became bored with their daily routine in the prison. As a result of the perpetual fears that royalists would try to smuggle the boy out of prison, Louis-Charles had to be kept under constant surveillance. They had little to do other than watch over him; with plenty of time on their hands, drinking, bullying and then terrorizing the child became an amusing way of passing the time. One day a doctor was called to treat Madame Simon, who had fallen ill. The doctor, a surgeon from the Hôtel Dieu called Monsieur Naudin, happened to catch Simon trying to make Louis sing a bawdy song. When he refused, Simon lost his temper, punched him and pulled him "off the ground by the hair of his head." "Damned viper!" Simon is reputed to have said. "I have a mind to crush you against the wall." The doctor took in the scene, the abusive tutor, the crying child, looking pale and weak, and was full of indignation. He scolded Simon, who was indifferent and just shrugged his shoulders, but no formal complaint was made. Simon knew that he would face no reprimand for the abusive way he treated the child.

It is perhaps hardly surprising that eventually Louis-Charles succumbed to the regime. In time, he appeared to any who observed him to have inculcated the beliefs and mannerisms of his captors. One visitor to the Temple, Commissioner Daujon, was shocked at a scene he witnessed. "I was playing *boules* with him," Daujon explained. "The room we were in was below his family's apartment and we could hear the sound of chairs being dragged across the floor which created quite a lot of noise. The child then cried out with an impatient gesture, 'Haven't those bloody women been guillotined yet?'" Whether he was echoing his captors to win approval, whether he had no idea of the significance of what he was saying, or whether he really had become confused to a point where he would readily condemn his family is not known. What is known is that Hébert, aware how easily the child was manipulated against his family, seized his opportunity. In late September and early October, in his desire to gather more evidence against Marie-Antoinette, he hatched an outrageous plan to make Louis-Charles testify against his mother.

Hébert knew that whenever her son had been terrified, Marie-Antoinette had protected and comforted the boy in her bed. He himself had repeatedly stoked the belief in *Le Père Duchesne* that Marie-Antoinette was a sexual deviant, promiscuous and immoral. Now he aimed to put these two things together and go one step further.

Historians cannot agree on the means whereby Hébert and his men lured the child into the trap. Some believe that apart from physical abuse, the child also suffered some form of sexual abuse. One piece of evidence for this view comes from the letters of an aristocrat, the Comte d'Antraigues, who set up a network of spies in Paris to obtain information about events at the Temple. D'Antraigues informed the Spanish ambassador: "Simon says that he [Louis XVII] is infected with a venereal disease. . . . Hébert himself used to bring him young prostitutes to spend several hours with the child to pervert his heart and ruin his health." Other historians have cast doubt on this evidence; the count, it seems, was not beyond fabricating stories for the ambassador or repeating gossip in the papers, if his spies had nothing new to report. Nonetheless, such accounts have prompted much speculation.

According to historian Vincent Cronin, writing in 1974, Simon encouraged the child to practice self-abuse, "probably on Hébert's orders. . . . In the course of one of these revolting lessons it seems one of the boy's testicles was hurt and had to be bandaged." The injury was passed off as one he sustained playing with a stick. Gradually these sessions became worse as Simon had the child more and more in his power "and began to turn him against his mother." In order to avoid Simon's anger, and terrified of further beatings, the boy played along with these fantasies until he was unable to distinguish fact from fiction, right from wrong. Eventually, according to Cronin, Hébert "gave orders to Simon that from time to time a prostitute was to be brought to Louis's room. The boy was too young to have intercourse, but the prostitute would sap his strength and eventually perhaps infect him with syphilis."

Even leaving aside the unknown question of whether or not Louis-Charles was subject to sexual abuse, he was still barely eight years old and only too easily influenced. Marie-Antoinette herself had long been aware of his indiscretion and had warned Madame de Tourzel of how readily "he repeats what he has heard, and often without intending to lie, he embellishes imaginary details." Trapped in the Tower away from his one surviving parent and at the mercy of a brutish teacher, within three months he had become easy prey to the abusive, brainwashing treatments of his captors. On Sunday October 6, 1793, Hébert was ready to act.

A deputation of senior leaders including Pache de Montguyon, the mayor of Paris; Chaumette, the leader of the Commune; and several other officials arrived at the Temple and went to see the son of Capet. The child had been plied with more than a little liquor for the occasion. The deputation then proceeded with a cross-examination.

Court records show that Hébert had drafted a confession for the boy to sign. Firstly, Louis-Charles was made to swear that his mother had repeatedly taken part in activities designed to thwart and bring down the revolution. Then Hébert embarked on a second, even more twisted section:

Charles Capet declares that Simon and Simon's wife, who were ordered by the Commune to watch over him, several times found him practising self-abuse in bed, and he told them that he had been taught these pernicious habits by his mother and aunt, and that on several occasions they took pleasure in watching him perform these practices in their sight, and that very often this took place when the women made him sleep between them.

In the highly charged atmosphere, the men manipulated Louis-Charles into providing a written confession that he had had sexual relations with his mother. The child's embarrassment over his regular, observed masturbation, the filthy songs he was taught, the constant stories he had heard about his mother's outrageous behavior, the confusion created by the drink and Hébert's relentless insinuations, and, above all, his anxious desire to please his captors so as to stop the beatings: all this led the young boy to commit a terrible act. He agreed to sign.

Just to be sure the public was left in no doubt, Chaumette then added a footnote to the document. "However the child explained himself, let us understand that once his mother pulled him close to her, which resulted in copulation and which also resulted in swelling of one of his testicles, observed by citizen Simon, on which he is still wearing a bandage and that his mother told him never to tell anyone; and these acts have been repeated *several times* since then."

Armed with this signed statement, the next day these men made the child confront his sister and aunt, who were interrogated about the same accusations.

"At midday we were busy doing up our chamber," wrote Marie-Thérèse, "when members of the Convention arrived with several municipal guards." She was ordered to go down alone with the guards. "My aunt wished to follow me; they refused her." Marie-Thérèse felt very awkward and frightened. "It was the first time I was ever alone with men," she wrote. On entering her brother's room she rushed to embrace him. "I kissed him tenderly; but they snatched him from my arms telling me to pass on into the next room." She was made to sit down and was interrogated by Chaumette and Hébert.

At first, she was questioned about alleged plots to escape. Who was behind them? She was confused and denied any knowledge of them, persisting in her request to be reunited with her mother. "I can do nothing," replied Chaumette. Then, to her horror, she was questioned about an alleged sexual relationship between her mother and her brother. "I was so aghast at such horrors, and so indignant that, in spite of the fear I felt, I could not keep myself from saying that it was an infamy," she wrote. Chaumette persisted for a long time, covering "a great many vile things of which they accused my mother and my aunt." Marie-Thérèse, still only fifteen years old, barely understood all the details of the charges, "but what I did understand was so horrible that I wept with indignation." Louis-Charles was made to repeat what he had said the previous day. She was grilled for three hours and eventually conceded "that it may be possible that her brother had observed things that she had missed as she was busy with her lessons." Marie-Thérèse was distraught as she returned to her room.

After this, it was the turn of Aunt Élisabeth. "She replied with still greater contempt to the vile things about which they questioned her," recorded Marie-Thérèse. However, Louis-Charles, utterly brainwashed by his captors, insisted to his aunt that it was all true. Élisabeth was blunt: "Such infamy is too base, and too far beneath me, to permit me to reply." Her questioning lasted an hour. "The deputies saw they could not intimidate her as they expected to do with one my age," observed Marie-Thérèse. This wretched session was the last time Louis-Charles would ever see members of his family.

Armed with Louis-Charles's "confession," Hébert was ready to launch his strike against Marie-Antoinette. By now, as one of the leaders of the Commune, Hébert wielded immense power and had set his sights on becoming Minister of the Interior. In September 1793, by putting pressure on the Convention with popular demonstrations, he helped to push through the Law of Suspects, which defined those who could be arrested for treasonable activities and was enforced by the Revolutionary Tribunal. He also continued to enjoy widespread popular support through his paper, *Le Père Duchesne*, and was determined to deliver to the people that long awaited prize: the queen's head.

Four days after her son's ordeal, at six in the evening, Marie-Antoinette was taken from her cell and led across the courtyard to the Revolutionary Tribunal for a preliminary examination prior to her full trial. The guards escorted her into a chamber lit by only two candles casting two pools of light in what was otherwise a large, dark space. She could sense the presence of people in the room watching her, but couldn't see them. Immediately before her were her inquisitors: the public prosecutor, Fouquier-Tinville, and the Tribunal President, Armand Martial Herman. In this intimidating atmosphere she had no illusions about what lay ahead; yet even now she maintained her composure and her self-respect. This once-conceited, frivolous, and selfish young woman of Versailles stood before her inquisitors, full of courage and highly articulate.

She was accused of crimes that had circulated many times before as rumors, but were now paraded as solid, indisputable facts. She had sent millions of livres to Austria and squandered huge sums of money on clothes, jewels, and private palaces like the Trianon. She was the one who had constantly preyed on her husband, taking advantage of his weak nature to manipulate him against the people. Had she not persuaded Louis Capet against signing the Assembly's decree on refractory priests? Had she not instigated the flight to Varennes, persecuting Capet into complying with the treason of trying to leave France? Had she not trampled the tricolor cockade underfoot at the banquet in October 1789 and organized a counterrevolution? As they pressed their numerous accusations, Marie-Antoinette could not be caught out. It was an impressive performance, which at times left her examiners frustrated that they could not expose her. "Never for one moment have you ceased wanting to destroy liberty. You wanted to reign at any price and to reascend the throne over the bodies of dead patriots," stormed Herman.

"We never wished for anything but France's happiness" came her dignified reply. When her examiners accused her of plotting with her husband to deceive France, she replied, "Yes, the people, have been deceived. They have been cruelly deceived, but not by my husband or me." Marie-Antoinette was not about to make some last-minute grovelling accommodation with the ideals of the revolution. She had indeed hoped that France's enemies would prevail, crush the revolution and restore the monarchy, but her examiners failed to force an admission. "No doubt you regret that your son has lost a throne which he might have ascended if the people, finally conscious of their rights, had not destroyed that throne?" She replied cleverly, "I shall never regret anything for my son when his country is happy."

At eight o'clock in the morning on Monday, October 14, 1793, Marie-Antoinette was taken back to the *Grande Chambre* for her full trial. This time it was packed with people. As she entered, a proud, frail figure dressed in black, the crowd was shocked at the immense change in her. The so recently charming, much-fêted queen was turned into a haggard old woman. Her dark clothes only served to emphasize her frailty; the widow Capet was almost unrecognizable from the young princess of twenty years ago. Yet here, in the flesh, was the she-devil of the pamphlets and *libelles*, and the public's curiosity was insatiable.

The trial was to take place before five judges and a jury of twelve, all eager patriots of whom Robespierre would approve. The lengthy indictment against her was read out. The Widow Capet was accused of the treason of conspiring with her brother against France, of influencing Louis to veto the decrees of the Assembly, of organizing counterrevolution, of maintaining secret relations and correspondence with the enemy, of numerous conspiracies. To support their case the prosecution relied mainly on the testimony of forty-one "witnesses," all stooges of the revolutionary government.

However, one accusation against the queen was to cause a sensation. This was not a charge levelled by some republican fanatic against a former queen. Marie-Antoinette was about to stand condemned by the evidence of her own son. She was utterly unprepared for what was to follow.

Jacques-René Hébert stepped forward to drop his carefully orchestrated bombshell. Simon, he explained, had caught the young Capet in the act of masturbating. When questioned, the child had admitted that "he owed his familiarity with the fatal habit to his mother and Aunt Élisabeth." Hébert went on to reveal that the boy had made a declaration in the presence of both the Mayor of Paris and the Prosecutor of the Commune that "these two women often made him sleep between them and that acts of the most uncontrolled debauchery were committed there." To ensure that his claim had full impact on the court, Hébert spelled it out clearly: "There is no doubt, from what Capet's son has said, that an act of *incest* was committed between mother and son!"

Hébert, the professional insinuator, who for much of his working life had profited from selling the image of a queen who would stop at nothing to satisfy her monstrous sexual appetites, now distorted her grotesque image one step further. Here was a demon she-devil who would even have sex with her own son if it suited her purposes. He proceeded to explain to the court *why* she chose to have incest with her son. "There is reason to believe that this criminal intercourse was dictated not by pleasure, but by the calculated hope of enervating the child, whom they still like to think of as destined to occupy the throne and whom they wished to be sure of dominating morally." To make his view more persuasive, he added his evidence. "As a result of the efforts he [Capet's son] was forced to make, he suffered a hernia for which a bandage was needed."

The queen was finally brought face to face with the journalist whose web of lies and deceit had for so many years spun the tales of horror that slowly and inexorably brought her to this terrible point. Now like a creature ensnared on the point of death, she hesitated, her mind apparently frozen, reeling from the accusations made against her. It is not known what was passing through her mind: whether she was too appalled and distressed at the idea of what had been happening to her son, or whether she was overwhelmed as she glimpsed the power of this latest lie to sway opinion. Not only was she a scheming, politically motivated, promiscuous wife, but now she was also the worst of mothers.

When she was asked what she had to say about the charges being made by Hébert, which the court heard had been corroborated by a sworn statement signed by her son, she replied that she had no knowledge of them. Her composure began to falter. Overwhelmed by the charges of sexually abusing her own son, she desperately tried to remain calm. She was asked once more about the accusation—by her own son—that she had abused him. Again she replied that she had no knowledge of the charges. She was pressed by the judges to say more. Why was she being so reticent? Was this the reticence of guilt?

Gathering herself to make a measured, dignified stand against these preposterous charges, finally she rose from her chair.

"If I have not answered, it was because Nature refuses to answer such a charge against a mother," she said, her reply charged with emotion. She turned to the audience in the courtroom. "I appeal to all mothers in this room."

For a moment the courtroom wavered. Her dignity and courage inspired interest—even a little sympathy. The charge against the former queen did not seem credible. Such was the disruption that the proceedings were suspended for a few minutes.

However, members of the jury had heard all the stories of her sexual depravity before. The scandal sheets had been full of it for years. Now that her own son had confessed to the most disgusting debauchery, they were ready to believe it to be true. Such was the deep-seated loathing in France for the "Austrian bitch," entrenched by years of unchallenged slander, that her spirited defense was seen as further evidence of her arrogance, pride and utter contempt for the French people.

At around three A.M. in the morning of October 16, the jury retired to deliberate. Outside, a large crowd gathered in the bitter cold, eager for news of the hated queen. As the jury reentered an hour later, a deep silence fell over the courtroom.

By a unanimous vote, Marie-Antoinette was found guilty of all the charges against her. She was asked if she had anything to say. She shook her head. Then the Tribunal President, Herman, announced the verdict: "This tribunal, following the unanimous declaration of the jury . . . condemns the said Marie-Antoinette, known as Lorraine of Austria, the widow of Louis Capet, to the death penalty."

If she was terrified, she did not betray herself. She showed "no sign of fear, indignation or weakness," recorded one of the lawyers, until she was out of the public gaze. The condemned woman almost fell as the guards escorted her back to her cell in the *Conciergerie.*

In the few hours left before her death, she was allowed no visitors and could not see her son and daughter. Instead, she wrote to her sister-in-law, Élisabeth:

16th October, half past four in the morning

It is to you, my sister, that I write for the last time. I have just been condemned, not to a shameful death—death is only shameful for criminals—but to rejoin your brother. Innocent like him, I hope to show the same courage as he, in these last moments. I am quite calm as when one's conscience is clear. I am profoundly grieved to have to quit my poor children. You know that I existed only for them; and you, my good tender sister.

She then wrote at length of her children, hoping that one day they could be happy:

I hope that one day, when they are older, they will be able to rejoin you, and be happy in your affectionate care. Let them both keep in mind what I have continually shown them, that principle, and dedication to duty, form the first basis of life, and that their mutual friendship and confidence will constitute its happiness. Let my daughter feel that because she is older, she should always help her brother with the advice, which her greater experience and her friendship may inspire her with. Let my son, on his part, render to his sister all the attention, all the services that friendship may suggest. Let them both, in a word, feel that in whatever position they may be placed, they will never be truly happy unless they are united . . . for happiness is truly doubled when shared with a friend.

She specifically urged Louis-Charles never to seek revenge for what had happened. "Let my son never forget the last words of his father, which I emphatically repeat: 'that he never seek to avenge our deaths.' "

Although she had been condemned by the testimony of her son, her love for him never faltered. Knowing the pain that Louis-Charles must have caused Élisabeth by his "confession," she urged her sister-in-law to forgive him.

I have to speak to you on a subject which is sorely painful to my heart. I know how much pain this child must have given you. Please forgive him, my dear sister. Think of his age and how easy it is to make a child say what one wishes, and even what he does not comprehend. I only trust a day will come when he appreciates more fully all your goodness and tender affection for both of them.

She paid tribute to her few friends for their support. Of her family and friends she wrote:

The thought that I am about to be separated from them forever, and of their troubles, is one of the deepest regrets that I bear with me in dying. . . . Adieu, my good and loving sister, may this letter reach you! Think always of me; I embrace you with my whole heart, and my poor, dear children. My God, it is agony to leave them. Goodbye. Goodbye . . .

When she had finished, grief overcame her and she broke down, weeping. Rosalie, the servant, came to see her early in the morning. "Entering her cell, I saw that she was all dressed in black, stretched out on her bed. 'Madame,' I said to her, trembling. 'You took nothing to eat last evening, and almost nothing during the day. What do you want to have this morning?' The queen was shedding abundant tears. '*Ma fille*, I no longer need anything. Everything is finished for me.' " The maid persisted, determined to find someway of revitalizing her before she had to face her final ordeal. " 'Madame, I've kept some bouillon and noodles on my oven; you need to sustain yourself,' she insisted. 'Allow me to bring you something.' The queen's tears redoubled and she said to me, 'Rosalie, bring me only some bouillon.' " However, the queen could only manage a few spoonfuls. "I swear to God that her body received no other sustenance and I had reason to believe that she was losing all that blood."

Before the execution, she was ordered to change out of her mourning dress. The officer of the Gendarmerie on duty had been told to keep her under constant guard. She tried to obtain a little privacy to change her bloodstained undergarments with Rosalie standing by her bed, blocking the view of her body. The officer would not have it, and instantly moved to the bed head to watch the queen change. The queen appealed to him: "In the name of decency, Monsieur, allow me to change my linen without a witness."

"I cannot give my consent," the guard replied. "I have orders to keep an eye on all your movements." The queen sighed and tried to change "with all possible precaution and modesty," said Rosalie. She concealed her linens in a chink between the old canvas wall covering and the wall.

A little later, at around ten o'clock, the executioner, Charles Henri Sanson, entered her cell. He tied her hands behind her back and roughly cropped her hair short, exposing her neck. An hour later, she was led across the dark hall, passed cells of other prisoners, to the door of the *Conciergerie* and into the daylight of the *Cour du Mai*, the courtyard where tumbrels waited to take the condemned to their death. Marie-Antoinette's own strength momentarily deserted her when she saw she was to be taken to the guillotine in an open rubbish cart. She asked for the guards to undo her handcuffs and had to face the indignity of relieving herself in the public gaze against the prison wall.

She returned to the cart, which moved slowly through the dense crowd of people that had assembled to see her go to the scaffold. Although it was only a short distance to the Place de la Révolution, now the Place de la Concorde, at the bottom of the Champs-Élysées, it took over an hour for her to reach her final destination. Triumphant crowds had gathered along the route, eager for her death, some hissing or jeering as the she passed. Others were already relishing the latest outrageous *libelles* against her, such as *The Queen's farewells to her Sweethearts, Male and Female.*

In the Place de la Révolution, the stark, angular contours of the guillotine stood out sharply against the sea of faces, all impatient for her death, pressing close to the soldiers for a better view. Marie-Antoinette climbed down from the cart and mounted the steps to the scaffold. Trembling and exhausted, she urged the executioner to hurry, but long minutes had to be endured while Sanson went through the procedure. He tied her to the plank, which then swung forward. The crowd, concentrating on that frail figure, had their reward a few minutes later; the queen of France was dead.

As people rushed forward to soak anything at hand in the blood of the she-devil, Sanson picked up the bleeding head and displayed it for all to see. Elation surged through the crowd and a great cry went up, "Long live the Republic! Long live Liberty! The devil is no more!"

"Frenchmen, Republicans, you have purged the earth of a monster who was its abomination!" wrote one militant journalist in *The Testament of Marie-Antoinette, the Widow Capet*. "That loathsome woman, whom the odious House of Austria sent among us to gratify its hatred and to plunge us into an abyss of calamity, that infernal Fury who only asked to bathe in French blood . . . you have just sent her hurtling into the night of death." For Hébert it was a moment to savor. He would not concede her courage but told his readers that she was "audacious and insolent right to the very end. . . . It was the greatest of all the joys of *Père Duchesne*, having with his own eyes seen the head of the female veto separated from her fucking tart's neck!"

While the queen's body was being carted away and buried without ceremony in an unmarked grave, in her cell at the *Conciergerie* Rosalie gathered together her few remaining possessions, the mirror and the cardboard box, and wrapped them in a cloth. There was also the letter that the queen had left for Élisabeth. Her last words were for her children: "Oh my God, have pity on me. My eyes have no tears left to weep for you, my poor children. Farewell. Farewell." Her note was never allowed to reach Élisabeth.

A mile away at the Temple prison, Louis-Charles was unaware of his mother's death. It is likely that he still imagined that she was in the room above him, where he had last seen her on the night of their separation. The only person who could possibly have saved Louis-Charles from the enveloping abuse and neglect was now dead.

❧ Chapter Six ❧

THE ORPHAN OF THE TEMPLE

*Let this little serpent and his sister be cast on a desert island.
I do not know of any reasonable means of getting rid of
them; and yet we must rid ourselves of them at any price.*
—JACQUES-RENÉ HÉBERT

*The unhappy child had long been accustomed to none but
the worst treatment—for I believe that no research can show
such barbarity to any other child.*
—MARIE-THÉRÈSE, ON HER BROTHER'S TREATMENT

Although we heard the hawkers crying my mother's condemnation in the streets," wrote Marie-Thérèse, "hope, so natural to the unhappy, made us think she had been saved." She steadfastly "refused to believe" that they had been entirely abandoned by Marie-Antoinette's Austrian relatives or other royalists who could have helped them, and remained in ignorance of her death. Among those who guarded them, there was no silent sympathizer who could give her or Élisabeth fragments of news; Cléry had been moved out of the Temple months before. The guards, who were often drunk and rude, says Marie-Thérèse, refused even basic comforts such as an ointment to treat an ulcer on Élisabeth's arm. They searched the small, airless apartment that held the two princesses three times every day. "One search lasted from four in the afternoon until half past eight at night," protested Marie-Thérèse. With fanatical zeal "they carried away mere trifles, such as our hats, cards with kings on them and books in which there were coats of arms." Far from fulfilling Marie-Antoinette's wish, Marie-Thérèse found there was no hope of reuniting with her brother. Even questions about him were greeted with silence, hostility or "insults and oaths." On the floor below, Simon continued to terrorize Louis-Charles. After the death of the queen, he realized he could continue to use his position as "tutor" to his advantage if he was able to elicit more damaging royal secrets. He bullied "Charles Capet" into revealing details about the royal family's life in the Tower before the execution of his father. On October 26, 1793, ten days after the death of his mother, the minutes of the Commune at a meeting at eight o'clock in the evening record that "Citizen Simon came to the Temple council in order to report a conversation he had had with little Capet, by which it appeared that a certain member of the Commune had held some correspondence with his mother."

Commissaries were eagerly dispatched once more to interrogate the eight-year-old. As before, unwittingly, the child became drawn in, revealing guards who had been sympathetic, the means by which secret messages were slipped in and out of the prison and more significantly—since she was still alive—information against his aunt Élisabeth. The Commune heard how she had once managed to post notes to the king by tying them to a piece of string, which she passed through a small gap in the blind at her window and down to his rooms on the floor below. Under interrogation, Louis-Charles was made to reveal "that his mother was afraid of his aunt, and that his aunt was the person who carried out the plots best." Simon pushed him for more information. What other acts of conspiracy were there? What had the former king and queen done to resist the people's revolution? What plans had there been to escape? The propaganda war against the royal family was vital to bolstering the standing of the revolution in the public's eye. Yet Louis-Charles seems to have had little more to say. His signature confirming this latest declaration on his aunt's plots was made in a sprawling, unsteady hand, unlike his former writing from his lessons with his father, in which the letters were well composed.

On November 25, 1793, Chaumette and others in the Commune made recommendations once more to the Convention proposing how to dispose of the "odious remnants of power" that still remained, the royal prisoners in the Temple. For Chaumette, their confinement was "too aristocratic" and exceptional. He argued that Élisabeth should be tried without delay by the Revolutionary Tribunal and the two orphans should be transferred to a state prison and treated like common prisoners. As usual, Hébert went even further. "Let this little serpent and his sister be cast on a desert island. I do not know of any reasonable means of getting rid of them; and yet we must rid ourselves of them at any price." However, the Convention took no action. Ever fearful that the royal children could escape, they balked at the idea of moving them out of the Tower.

The interrogations continued. A week later, on December 3, another report was fabricated with the help of "Charles Capet."

On this day, 13 Frimaire, second year of the Republic, one and indivisible, we commissaries of the Commune on duty at the Temple, on being informed by citizen Simon that Charles Capet had some facts to state which were of importance to the safely of the Republic, repaired at four o'clock in the afternoon to the apartment of the said Charles Capet, who made a declaration as follows: "That for a fortnight or three weeks past, he has heard the prisoners [his sister and aunt] knocking every day consecutively between six and nine o'clock." The moving of the furniture "gives reason for supposing that they are in the habit of hiding something." . . . He thinks it might be false *assignats*, but is not sure of this, and that they might be passing them through the window to someone. . . . Citizen Simon, asked if he knew of the above-mentioned noise, replied that being a little hard of hearing he had perceived nothing of the kind; but his wife confirmed the statement of Charles Capet respecting the noise.

However, the Commune could do little with the trumped-up charge against the princesses of counterfeiting money. In fact, there was an entirely innocent explanation for the noise each evening, as Marie-Thérèse explained. "It was that of our backgammon, which my aunt, wishing to amuse me a little, had been kind enough to teach me. We played it each evening." She was under no illusion that her "poor little brother" had been "forced to sign the declaration" by Simon. Yet despite their best efforts, for the time being, the leaders of the Commune could elicit nothing else to pin on Aunt Élisabeth.

Since it was becoming harder to advance his own position by feeding his superiors with more "secrets," Simon began to feel that his work in the Tower was leading nowhere. With increasing security, he was also concerned to find he was forbidden to leave the Temple. Toward the end of December, Simon asked for permission to go to a fair but this was refused. To his alarm, he found he had to be escorted by two guards just to collect some possessions from his home. In the suspicious, conspiratorial atmosphere that prevailed, he realized he was not entirely trusted. It is plausible that Chaumette feared that Simon would help royalists free the boy king for money and kept him on a tight rein. Simon resented being treated as a virtual prisoner. The position that had once been so flattering to his pride was fast becoming oppressive.

It is possible that he took out his growing frustrations on his prisoner. Early in January 1794, according to a report from one of the guards, Simon found the boy had woken up one night and, still in a dreamlike state, was kneeling by his bedside, repeating the prayers that his mother had taught him. Simon was so exasperated he took a pitcher of water and poured it on the child's head. Louis-Charles, shivering, stretched out on his soaking bed, not daring to say a word. His tutor, however, had not finished. He "flew into a violent passion . . . and armed with his hobnailed shoe, struck him in the face."

By now, Chaumette and others in the Commune were putting pressure on Simon to quit his job at the Temple prison. Chaumette warned members of the Commune of a recent law by which they were not allowed to hold more than one post at any time; he was irritated by the numerous absences from meetings by those who were "occupied in other administrations." Simon found himself having to choose between his membership in the Commune and his post as tutor to Louis-Charles. Chaumette may have had other reasons for wanting to move Simon out of the Tower prison at this point. Some historians have argued that Chaumette and Hébert were themselves plotting to seize Louis-Charles so as to enhance their own political position, either by allying with the monarchists against the revolutionary government, or by ransoming the boy to France's enemies. It would have been easier to do this with Simon out of the way. Whatever their motives, Simon had served his purpose and helped to deliver the queen's head with her son's evidence. Now they put pressure on Simon to leave, and he seems to have had little difficulty making up his mind.

"On January 19, 1794, we heard a great noise in my brother's room, which made us conjecture that they were taking him from the Temple," wrote Marie-Thérèse. "We were convinced of it when, looking through the keyhole, we saw them carrying away packages. The following days as we heard his door open and persons walking in his room we were more than ever convinced that he was gone."

The disturbance was, however, Simon leaving the Tower with his wife. The register of the Temple Council for that day confirms that "Simon and his wife, formerly entrusted with the custody of Charles Capet . . . were released from the guard today." Before they left, the four commissaries on duty made a cursory inspection, confirmed that the boy was "in good health," and duly signed the ledger.

The child, who had for so long suffered at the hands of Chaumette and Hébert, had now fallen totally into their power. No new tutor was appointed; the "reeducation" of the boy, for so long a sham, finally lapsed altogether. With the "son of a tyrant" directly under their control, their overwhelming priority was to ensure that he was securely incarcerated and had absolutely no opportunity to escape. Consequently, although Simon's treatment of the boy had been shameful, what was to follow was even more shocking and cruel. Louis-Charles was to have all semblance of humanity stripped from him and had to face the most nightmarish treatment possible for a young child. As security was greatly increased around him, the child was effectively entombed alive.

The day after Simon's departure, on 1 Pluviôse of the second year in the Republican calendar, Louis-Charles was moved into solitary confinement. He was barricaded in one of the rooms on the second floor of the Great Tower that had been specially converted to detain him—probably the dining room, where he had last seen his father. Surrounded by the phantoms of his previous existence, in a room that held such frightening memories for him, he was confined to a space of about thirteen by eleven feet. Over the next few days, the Temple records show that a number of alterations were made to his room. The door opening onto the antechamber, where he used to play with Cléry, was double-locked and strengthened from top to bottom with iron bars. To further secure him, a stove was installed against the partition between this room and antechamber. Above the height of the stove, an opening was made, barred with a heavy grille. This was to serve as a wicket through which to shove meals to the child, or to provide an opening to allow in a little heat from the stove.

The room was cold and damp and had virtually no natural light. The window, which was inset into walls that were ten feet thick, was almost completely boarded up, save for a lower part of three latticed panes. Even if he were able to get close to this window, he would see nothing outside because of a hood over it. A gloomy half-light that could penetrate the grille or the gap in the shutter, or an occasional weak lantern was all the light in his cell during the day. No lantern was allowed after dusk and Louis-Charles spent his nights in complete darkness, which at first terrified him. In this cell, with little ventilation or daylight, he was effectively walled up.

There was no question of any amusements or diversions; he had no books or playthings of any kind. No one was even permitted to enter the cell to provide Louis-Charles with basic support, such as clean clothes, or to sweep or ventilate the room. His food was minimal, a frugal diet consisting of two bowls of soup each day with a hunk of bread and perhaps a portion of boiled meat. This meager fare was slid into his room through the small wicket; he did not see the face, even the hand of his captors. Guards would peer in through the grille to ensure he was still there. There was nothing to break the loneliness or the monotony of his day except the arrival of meals or the inspection of a commissioner.

The brief human contact that served to punctuate his existence only added to his wretchedness. Apart from putting food through the wicket twice a day, late in the evening the commissaries on duty would peer into the boy's room through the grille and shout out, "Capet, where are you? Are you asleep? Get up!" The child, pale and anxious, would have to show himself at the aperture so that he could be seen. This done, he was sent smartly back to bed accompanied by a tirade of insults: "viper's race" or "son of a tyrant." The commissary would then sign a ledger to confirm that Louis-Charles was secure. Sometimes this procedure could be repeated several times a night if the guards coming on duty did not arrive at the same time.

Marie-Thérèse managed to find out about her brother through some of the prison staff, such as Caron, who sometimes delivered his meals, and Gagnié, the cook. She was outraged. "They had the cruelty to leave my brother alone; unheard of barbarity which has surely no other example! That of abandoning a poor child, only eight years old, already ill, and keeping him locked and bolted in, with no succor but a bell, which he did not ring, so afraid was he of the persons it would call; he preferred to want for all, rather than ask anything of his persecutors."

To complete his descent into abject squalor, it would seem from the records that no sanitary facilities were provided. Louis-Charles had to urinate and defecate in his own room. He was too frightened and disorientated to complain or ask for help and became passive and withdrawn. As the weeks passed, he ceased to make any attempt to clean his room or to take proper care of himself. His bed was left unmade for months; bugs and fleas covered it, and latched onto his body, covering it in bloody sores. Little by little he succumbed to the misery and spent many hours just curled up on the bed. His energy waned and his resistance to infection began to fail.

The prince who had been brought up in the splendor of Versailles and who was due to inherit the greatness that was France now lived a life more wretched than a pauper's. There was no family or friends to encourage him, no kindly contact, no chance even to breathe the fresh air of day. In time, his excrement accumulated on the floor and a foul smell filled the room. His dark cell became infested with rats and mice. "Everything is alive in the room," Caron was to report later. According to Caron, the child sometimes left his meals out uneaten to distract the vermin so that he could try to sleep.

Gradually, his once indomitable spirit, so happy and full of joy, surrendered to the utter hopelessness of his existence. One witness who saw Louis-Charles around this time was shocked by "the face of the victim, formerly so smiling, which showed well the imprint of a deep melancholy; his fresh and rosy complexion had become mat and yellow; the pure lines of his features were altered and his back was beginning to stoop insensibly, as if bent under the heavy weight of the time."

Marie-Thérèse heard reports of her brother and wrote, "He lay in a bed, which had not been made for more than six months, and he now had no strength to make it. Fleas and bugs covered him, his linen and person were full of them. His shirt and stockings had not been changed for more than a year. His excrements remained in the room; no one had removed them during all that time. His window, the bars of which were secured by a padlock, was never opened. It was impossible to stay in his chamber on account of the foul odor. It is true that my brother neglected himself. He might have taken rather more care of his person; he could at least have washed himself, because they gave him a pitcher of water. But the unhappy child was half dead from fear, so much had Simon and others terrorized him. He spent the day in doing nothing. They gave him no light; this condition did as much to harm him morally as it did physically. It is not surprising that he lapsed into a fearful marasmus."

Certainly there were many in the revolutionary government who had always wanted to see the son of Capet disposed of, murdered if necessary, so as to prevent this former heir to the throne from ever restoring the monarchy in France. His future continued to hang in the balance. The pale shadow of a child, clinging to life in the Temple cell, only survived at all since he remained a useful potential bargaining chip with France's enemies. It was rumored that there were plans to smuggle him to southern France as a hostage should the enemy threaten Paris itself. For the time being, he was suspended in this shadowy twilight world, somewhere between life and death.

The appalling treatment of the boy mirrored the growing brutality in the rest of France as the Terror was increasing its grip. The Committee of Public Safety had unrestricted powers to search out and arrest enemies of the revolution; any traitors could be brought before special courts and might face the guillotine the next day. Police measures were also introduced by the Committee for General Security, which used vigilant local committees to ferret out suspects. Robespierre was a mesmerizing speaker in defense of these tactics. He easily persuaded his admirers that the Terror was right and necessary, even praiseworthy; only by ruthlessly crushing the enemy would the republic survive. Under Robespierre, the number of executions increased each month; there were 21 in September 1793, rising to 68 in December and over 120 by March the following year. The counterrevolutionary revolt in the Vendée was brutally crushed and tens of thousands were arrested. In Paris, Danton and Robespierre disagreed over the use of terror tactics to enforce control; Danton wanted to end the Terror, but for Robespierre it was a legitimate means of establishing the republic while it was under threat. Robespierre gained the upper hand over Danton and accused him of favoring a reactionary policy.

As the Terror swept through France, in a remarkable twist, Louis-Charles's own jailors suddenly became caught up in the wholesale butchery. Hébert's increasing control over the Commune through his supporters, the Hébertistes, seemed a threat to the power of Robespierre and provoked his hostility. Gradually Hébert found himself blackened by less extreme republicans. "Is there anything more disgusting and execrable than *Le Père Duchesne?*" mocked Camille Desmoulins in his journal, the *Vieux Cordelier*, launched in December 1793. Desmoulins ridiculed Hébert's coarse ways and "language of the charnel house," accusing him of merely posing as a revolutionary when in fact he had managed to acquire large sums of money for his journal from aristocratic contacts.

In early 1794, schisms opened between the Hébertistes and the Dantonistes, each accusing the other of ever more outrageous plots and counterplots. Incredible as it may seem, given Hébert's role in savoring the destruction and torment of the royal family, he and his supporters were charged with forming a royalist conspiracy. It was claimed that he had accepted funds from royalists to arrange the escape of the royal prisoners. Speakers railed against him and other Hébertistes at the Convention: "They have attempted to deliver to the Temple, to the children of Capet, a letter, a package of fifty golden Louis; the aim of this delivery is to facilitate the escape of the son of Capet. Because the conspirators have formed the aim of establishing a Regency Council, the presence of the child was necessary to install a Regent. I hope they are trembling, these villains who wanted to give the French a master. Their hour is approaching. They must *die*!" stormed one of Robespierre's men, Couthon. As the threat to Hébert grew, even Chaumette denounced him as he struggled to distance himself from his former ally.

On March 24, 1794, barely five months after forcing Louis-Charles to testify against his mother, Hébert and eighteen of his supporters were led to the Place de la Révolution. A huge crowd had gathered to watch their downfall. "They died liked cowards without balls," reported one jeering witness. Hébert, the great brutalizer, whose ugly journal *Le Père Duchesne* had done so much to incite violence, found his courage failed him as the wheel turned full circle and it was his turn to feel that sharp steel on his neck. Three weeks later, Chaumette, too, "went to hold the hot hand," convicted, like Hébert, of royal conspiracy. It was alleged that he wanted to "place the young Capet on the throne." Georges Danton and his allies also found themselves facing trumped-up charges of conspiracy and were sent to the scaffold.

However, even as the revolution devoured its own creators, this did nothing to ease the plight of the victims in the Tower. "On May 9, just as we were going to bed, the bolts were withdrawn and someone knocked at our door," wrote Marie-Thérèse. Élisabeth insisted on dressing before they entered, but "they rapped so hard that we thought the door would burst in." When the guards entered, they turned to Élisabeth. "Citoyenne, will you please come down," they demanded brusquely. Élisabeth tried to reassure her worried niece that she would return, only to be sharply corrected. "No, citoyenne, you will not return," they announced. "Take your cap and come down." According to Marie-Thérèse, they "loaded her with insults and coarse speeches." Élisabeth, for her part, was concerned about leaving her niece when she had been expressly charged to act as her second mother by Marie-Antoinette. She embraced her and told her "to have courage, to practise the good principles of religion given me by my parents, and to hope in God."

Marie-Thérèse was devastated. "I remained in greatest desolation when I was parted from my aunt. I did not know what had become of her, and no one would tell me. I passed a very cruel night." Alone for the first time in the Tower, she was terrified.

In the pouring rain, Élisabeth was led across the garden and courtyard of the Temple and taken in a coach to the *Conciergerie*. Later that same evening, she was led before the Revolutionary Tribunal and examined by the prosecutor, Fouquier-Tinville, and two others. Afterward she was returned to her cell. Élisabeth was under no illusion about what lay ahead; this would be a trial with no defense and no appeal. She was deeply religious but she knew any request to seek the help of a Catholic priest would be refused. Kneeling in her cell she "offered direct to God the sacrifice of her life."

The next day she was tried, along with twenty-four other prisoners. The public prosecutor read out the names of those that had been denounced to the Tribunal: "First, Marie Élisabeth Capet, sister of Louis Capet, the last tyrant of the French, aged thirty and born at Versailles. . . . It is to the family of the Capets that the French people owe all the evils under the weight of which they have groaned for so many centuries. . . . The crimes of all kinds, the guilty deeds of Capet, of the Messalina Antoinette, of the two brothers

Capet, and of Élisabeth are too well known to make it necessary here to repaint the horrible picture." The prosecutor proceeded to outline how this "detestable family" had subjugated the great nation "to the despotism and fury of a few individuals" and that Élisabeth "had cooperated in all the plots, and conspiracies."

The jury took only a few minutes to decide that she was guilty as an accomplice in these plots, and she was condemned to death. At the *Conciergerie*, she asked to be taken to the common cell to join the others who would die with her tomorrow, who were "in different stages of agony and fear." According to two witnesses who were in the room that night, but were not condemned, she tried to inspire them with her own courage: "She seemed to regard them all as friends about to accompany her to heaven. . . . Soon the serenity of her look, the tranquillity of her mind subdued their anguish." One woman, Madame de Montmorin, who had lost nearly all her family, was inconsolable, not because of her own death, but because of her son, who was doomed to die with her. "I am willing to die," she cried, "but I cannot see him die." Madame Élisabeth replied, "You love your son, and yet you do not wish him to accompany you; you are going yourself to all the joys of heaven and you want him to stay on earth, where all is now torture and sorrow." Inspired by these words, Madame de Montmorin "rose to a species of ecstasy." Weeping, she embraced her son. "Yes, yes," she cried, "we will go together."

The next day, on May 10, 1794, Élisabeth was taken by cart to the Place de la Révolution. "At the foot of the scaffold was a long bench on which the victims were told to sit. By a refinement of cruelty, Madame Élisabeth was placed nearest the steps to the scaffold, but she was the last of the twenty-five called to ascend them; she was to see and hear the killing of all of them before her turn should come. According to one witness, during that time she never ceased saying the *De profundis*. Each of the women, when called, turned and kissed the princess before they ascended the scaffold; each of the men bowed low." However, in another report, it would appear that even Élisabeth could not cope with the ordeal and fainted. Whatever the reality, after her execution, there were no cries of *"Vive la Révolution."* The crowd scattered silently. The bodies were flung onto one cart, the heads were flung in a basket. The clothes of the victims were taken, "because they were a prerequisite of the State."

Unknown to the two captives in the Tower, they had now lost their second mother. "When I asked the municipals where she was, they said she had gone to take the air," Marie-Thérèse was told, contemptuously. "I renewed my request to be taken to my mother, as I was parted from my aunt; they replied that they would speak of it." She repeated her requests frequently but was told that she needed no one, and she heard no news of her relatives. The guards, she wrote, "redoubled their severity." Searches were frequent; knives, which had been returned to them, were again removed and on another occasion, her tinderbox, which had enabled her to warm the stove. Silently, the teenage girl endured the terrifying uncertainties that surrounded her.

"My brother was still wallowing in filth," she wrote. "No one entered his room except at mealtimes; no one had pity on that unfortunate child. There was but one guard whose manners were civil enough to induce me to commend my poor brother to him. He dared to speak of the harshness shown to the child, and he was dismissed the next day." Marie-Thérèse, who had learned from the endurance of her family, now found new reserves of courage to keep her sanity and her will to live, unlike her brother. She carried out simple routines in her room with great dedication, as though her life depended on it. "At least I could keep myself clean," she wrote. "I had soap and water. I swept the room every day. . . . I had no light, but when the days were long I suffered less from that privation. They would no longer give me books. I had none but those of piety and travels, which I had read a hundred times."

The children were never taken out into the gardens or up on the battlements. There was an empty, eerie atmosphere in the Tower that now held only a sick young boy and his desperate sister, both of whom were kept out of sight of most of the prison staff. Apart from the guards responsible for checking the presence of the prisoners or taking up food, few of the staff at work in the Temple even saw the children. Some were reported later to say that they wondered what they were keeping watch on, "precious stones or something?" Without any sighting of the children, staff began to wonder whether the prison was in fact empty and the royal children had escaped or been secretly moved. This helped to feed the many rumors. It was widely believed that a switch had taken place and that the boy now held in the Tower was not the son of the former king at all. Many Parisians thought he had secretly escaped and was being protected by royalist sympathizers either in England, Prussia or Austria. No sooner was this denied than the rumors started up again.

On the May 11, 1794, the day after Élisabeth's execution, Maximilien Robespierre himself came to the Temple prison to check on the two children. The Grand Pontiff of the Supreme Being—as he was now known behind his back—wanted to assure himself that they were securely detained. "The municipals showed great respect for him," recalled Marie-Thérèse. "His visit was secret to all persons in the Tower, who either did not know who he was, or would not tell me. He looked at me insolently and cast his eyes over my books." Marie-Thérèse gave him a note. "My brother is ill. I have written to the Convention for permission to take care of him. The Convention has not yet replied to me, so I am asking again." However, the girl's concerns for her brother were once more greeted with a mocking silence. Although there is no formal record of it, Robespierre almost certainly inspected Louis-Charles, perhaps just by peering through the grille. He could see for himself the conditions in which the boy was held, and, it seems, was quite satisfied with what he saw. No orders were given to clean the cell, provide new clothes or alleviate his suffering.

Louis-Charles was now paying the price for this calculated neglect. He had visibly outgrown the filthy rags that passed for clothes, emphasizing the fact that his arms and legs seemed disproportionately long. Large swellings on his knees made any movement a painful process, and his skin, once so clear and fresh, was covered in various scabs and pustules, giving him no peace. He spent the day in silence, curled up motionless on the bed or the floor, absorbed in his misery. According to Gagnié, the cook, the boy had to be shouted at just to draw his attention to a plate of food slid through the wicket. On one occasion, he noticed that the boy had not touched his food for three days. Gagnié obtained permission to go into the child's cell to talk to him. He asked Louis-Charles why he wouldn't eat. "Well, what would you do, my friend?" came the reply. "I want to die!"

In the room above, Marie-Thérèse's requests to take care of her brother or obtain news of her mother or her aunt were constantly ignored. Not knowing what might happen next, or whether she too would meet her end, Marie-Thérèse gained some kind of solace from scratching a permanent record of her suffering on the walls of her room:

Marie-Thérèse is the most unhappy creature in the world. She can obtain no news of her mother; nor be reunited with her, though she has asked it a thousand times.

Live, my good mother! Whom I love so well, but of whom I can hear no tidings.

Oh, father. Watch over me from Heaven above. Oh my God, forgive those who have made my family die.

The revolution had been inspired by the ideals of liberty, equality, and fraternity. Yet by the late spring of 1794, Robespierre's apparently decisive, strong leadership was now being exposed as criminal madness. In the name of the "Supreme Being" and the "Goddess of Reason" he had become a ruthless murderer. Originally only aristocrats and clergy were persecuted, but now quite ordinary people became fearful of arrest on trivial charges under the Law of Suspects. Although since Robespierre had been in power, the enemy had been entirely driven from France and pushed back beyond the Alps and the Pyrenees, and royalist rebellions in the Vendée and at Lyon had been suppressed, the Terror continued to intensify. The more blood that flowed, the more Robespierre became obsessed with purging the State of traitors. Executions increased sharply during the spring: 258 in April and

345 in May. In June, when the Revolutionary Tribunal was given still more powers, that figure rose to almost 700. During this "Great Terror," no one felt safe at the National Convention; the fear that they might be next forced their hand.

There were many now who hated Robespierre, especially the more moderate members of the Convention and followers of Georges Danton, and they wanted above all to see Robespierre dead and Danton avenged. In July, delegates at the Convention conspired with Robespierre's enemies on the Committees of Public Safety and General Security. The once-powerful dictator now found himself rapidly outflanked as events moved swiftly against him.

Heedless of the warning signs, in a lengthy and radical speech on July 26, Robespierre insisted that more blood must be shed to rid the government of traitors; even the all-powerful committees should be purged. The following day he was greeted with shouts of abuse, derision and "Down with the tyrant" in the National Convention while trying to defend his policies. Finally, the National Convention issued a writ against Robespierre and many of his supporters, such as Couthon, declaring them outlaws—*hors la loi*. As outlaws, they could be guillotined without trial on mere proof of identity by the Revolutionary Tribunal.

Seeking refuge in the Hôtel de Ville, Robespierre and his allies in a panic-stricken frenzy may have tried to kill themselves before they were taken prisoner. A member of the Convention, General Paul-François Barras, was appointed head of the troops to capture the outlaw.

As his troops closed in on them, Augustin Robespierre, Maximilien's brother, fell from an upper story. Couthon appeared to have fallen down a flight of stone steps and was collapsed on the floor with a head wound. Robespierre himself was lying on the table of the Committee of Public Safety in agony. Covered with his own blood, his jaw shot away, and his face distorted in gruesome pain, it seemed he had tried, and failed, to kill himself.

The next day, Robespierre was taken through crowded streets, people pursuing the tumbrel to curse him. The Supreme Being who was always so neat and well presented now made a hideous spectacle. According to one account, "He was covered with blood and dirt, his jaw was shattered, one eye was out of its socket and hanging on his cheek." One of the spectators pushed through the crowds, seized hold of one of the bars of the cart and contemplated this awful sight for a moment in silence, and then said to the dying man in a solemn voice, "Yes, there *is* a God."

At the Place de la Révolution, Robespierre was tied to the plank in readiness for death. Far from being able to display silent, dignified courage to the end, when Sanson pulled away the makeshift bandage binding his jaw, he could not stop himself from screaming in terrible agony which, as the crowding onlookers saw, was only silenced by death.

Among the batch of twenty-two victims who would die with Robespierre that day, the report of the execution reveals, number 13 was "Antoine Simon, shoemaker, aged fifty-eight years, a native of Troyes, department of Aube, residing at Paris, no. 32 Rue Marat."

Simon's political ambitions—which he had hoped would release him from poverty and obscurity—had brought him nothing but a bloody end. In the days that followed, three hundred of Robespierre's supporters throughout France were rounded up and sent to the scaffold.

At dawn, the day after Robespierre's death, Marie-Thérèse "heard a frightful noise in the Temple; drums beat, gates were open and shut." She was very uneasy at the uproar and soon found out that it was caused by a visit from members of the National Convention, "who came to assure themselves that everything was secure." This delegation was led by Barras, who had just been made Commander General of the army and was also appointed by the Committee of Public Safety to guard the "tyrant's children." Given the secrecy surrounding the captivity of the royal orphans and the very few people who had actually seen them in the last few months, Barras wanted to satisfy himself that there had been no conspiracy to spirit the royal orphans out of the Temple prison.

Upstairs, Marie-Thérèse heard the sound of heavy footsteps on the stairway and "the bolts of my brother's door drawn back." She flung herself out of bed and hurriedly dressed before anyone could enter her room.

On the floor below, General Barras was coming face to face with the cruelty of Louis-Charles's captivity and was apparently taken aback at what he saw. As he entered the foul-smelling, dark room, covered in filth and excrement, he was struck to find the child was curled up in a small cot, shaped like a cradle, in the middle of his room and not in the bed close by. The cot was much too small for him and had no sheets or blankets, only a mattress. He lay motionless, dressed in dirty, tattered clothes. Barras assumed he was asleep, but as he drew nearer he could see that the child's eyes were open, watching him. The general asked him why he was lying in this small cot: "The child, without moving at all, answered that he was in less pain in this cot than in his bed."

The general then asked whether he was ill and where the pain was. "The child, instead of speaking, pointed to his head and his knees. Barras asked him to get up. He didn't move at all, so he asked the officers to raise the child up carefully and to stand him on the floor so that he could watch him walk. The child resigned himself to the care that was taken to stand him up. No sooner was he on his feet than he collapsed against his cot, resting his head first." Was this debilitated child who could barely stand or talk really the offspring of the famous Bourbon dynasty?

"Barras again ordered them to attempt to stand him on his feet by lifting him by the arms. As the child took the first step, he appeared to be suffering from such pain that he was allowed to sit down." Noticing the boy's tight clothing, Barras had the trousers cut open. He saw at once that the child's knees were "terribly swollen and a ghastly color, as well as his ankles and hands. His face was puffed and pale." When he questioned the guards, "he learned the child neither slept nor ate."

General Barras then went to see Marie-Thérèse. She reports, "He spoke to me, called me by name and seemed surprised to find me risen." After a brief visit, she then heard the delegation leaving. "They harangued the guards and exhorted them to be faithful to the National Convention. There were many cries of *Vive la République! Vive la Convention!*" Then as the sounds receded into the distance, a deep silence once more invaded the Tower.

According to Barras's account given years later, he took action to help Louis-Charles. "I gave orders to the Commissioners and scolded them for the neglected state of the room. . . . I proceeded to the Committee of Public Safety and informed it that order has not been troubled at the Temple, but the prince was dangerously ill. I gave the order that he should be taken for a walk and summoned Monsieur Dessault [a doctor]. . . . I gave the order that other doctors be consulted and that they examine his condition." Despite these claims, nothing happened and there is no confirmation in the Temple ledger of the arrival of a doctor.

General Barras's interest in the boy appears to have been a fleeting one. Caught up in political concerns, he seems to have made little effort to ensure that his orders were carried out. As far as the child was concerned, Barras's primary concern, like others before him, was security at the prison. He wanted to ensure that members of the Commune did not try to take charge of the children again and use them as a political weapon. After his visit he gave orders that the garrison at the Temple be strengthened still further; according to Marie-Thérèse, the guard was doubled! Although Barras asked that the boy's room be cleaned and that he be given fresh clothes, the prison staff were loath to carry out these orders. There are several possible reasons for this. The guards may have been unimpressed by Barras's apparent show of sympathy for the son of the despised king and queen, and were reluctant to improve the conditions of the boy. Cleaning out his cell was a filthy job and they may have regarded such work as beneath them. More significant still, although Robespierre was dead, the mood in France was still uneasy and fearful. No one in the prison dared to take a lead and lay themselves open to the charge that they were helping the royal family. They had already seen committed republicans go to their deaths on trumped-up charges of royal sympathies. Weeks later, the child's room and clothes were as filthy as they had been on Barras's visit.

Three commissioners were notionally appointed to oversee the boy's care, including his education. These commissioners seemed to have done very little; no schooling was provided and no doctor was summoned to investigate any illness. However, Barras did make some headway. He succeeded in having a guardian, Jean-Jacques Christophe Laurent, appointed to provide personal care for Louis-Charles. This may have been more out of a wish to have someone he could trust to keep a close eye on the boy to make sure that he did not escape, rather than out of a desire to improve his plight. Jean-Jacques Laurent was, however, quite unlike Louis-Charles's previous "guardian," the cobbler, Simon.

Marie-Thérèse was struck by the difference when she first met him. Laurent was a young, educated Creole from Martinque, with a gentle personality and an air of respect for the prisoners. "He asked me politely if I wanted anything. He came daily three times to see me, always with civility, and did not 'thee and thou' me. He never searched my bureaus and closets," she wrote with relief. Although Laurent was a committed republican, this did not blind him to the cruelty being inflicted on the nine-year-old boy in the Temple. He was horrified by what he saw when he entered his cell for the first time.

As he approached the dark room he was aware of an overwhelming stench coming through the grille. The bolts were drawn back and he entered, holding his candle high, to find the floor was covered in vermin and excrement. With a sense of shock Laurent caught his first glimpse of the child. He was lying so still and silent, he was almost inanimate. His clothes were foul smelling and torn, his hair was "stuck fast by scurf, like pitch." Appalled at this, Laurent challenged the prison guards about why no action had yet been taken to clean the boy and his room. He also made a full report about what he saw and what should be done. It may well be that his sympathy for the boy was also tempered by his concern that if the boy should die in his care he might be held responsible. He immediately set about protecting his interests and insisted on a formal inquiry into the child's condition and circumstances. Consequently, several officials from the Commune came to check on Laurent's claims. Their reports confirmed what Barras had seen; an emaciated boy in great pain, his head and neck fretted with sores, his shoulders stooped, his limbs unusually long and thin, and blue and yellow tumors on his wrists and knees.

Despite the official interest, weeks passed after Barras's visit and the prison staff still refused to carry out the foul and disgusting task of cleaning Louis-Charles's room. Laurent was determined to break the impasse and finally, on August 31, he obtained the necessary permissions. "I have been authorized by the representatives of the people to let two *trusted* men enter junior Capet's room," he recorded, "to clean it and to attempt to get rid of the vermin that are encouraged by the dirtiness" [his italics].

The next day, September 1, 1794, eight months after the commencement of his solitary confinement, Louis-Charles's cell, at last, was cleaned out. He had his first feeble glimpse of daylight as a small section of the shutter was removed. The grille was taken down separating his room and the antechamber. Laurent himself removed the boy's "sordid garments, swarming all over with vermin" and bathed his sores with lukewarm water. "His toenails and fingernails were as long as the claws of a wild animal . . . and as hard as horn." These were now clipped. His hair was cut and washed and a doctor came to dress his wounds. "Laurent took down a little bed that was in my room," wrote Marie-Thérèse, "because the one he had was full of bugs; and he removed the vermin with which he was covered."

Apart from being clean, he also had an identity. He was no longer dehumanized as simply "Capet" or "wolf cub." Laurent referred to him politely as "Monsieur Charles" and encouraged other keepers to do the same. Perhaps not surprisingly, it was difficult for the child to adapt to this new treatment. He was suspicious and asked Laurent, "Why are you taking care of me? I thought you didn't like me." And even under this improved regime he was still isolated. Laurent was only permitted to enter his room at mealtimes, and then under the close scrutiny of a guard. Marie-Thérèse wrote with concern that for most of the time, "they still left him alone in his room." He became frightened to speak and withdrew from the adult world. The child who was once outgoing and sunny-natured "had become almost entirely silent." His eyes were languid, his expression fixed and disinterested. "Solitude was completing the work that ill-usage had begun."

The day before Louis-Charles's room was cleaned, there was a massive explosion at a powder factory in Grenelle. Royalist sympathizers were thought to be behind the disaster and, fearing an upsurge in proroyalist activity, the Committee of General Security ordered a fresh inspection of security at the Tower. In September, the authorities panicked about a suspected royalist plot to seize the dauphin. There were rumors of English involvement in a complex plot masterminded by the exiled French princes to rescue Louis XVII. So intense was the speculation that by October, the Committee of General Security again sent two deputies to the Tower to check on Louis-Charles and his sister. Security was tightened still more. Unbelievably, the entire guard for the sick boy and his teenage sister now exceeded five hundred men.

Laurent, concerned for the boy's health, had, without success, repeatedly asked for an assistant to help him. In October, following reports from spies in London that an attempt to free the dauphin from prison was imminent, it was finally agreed that Laurent should have support. The Committee of General Safety appointed Jean-Baptiste Gomin, the son of an upholsterer. At first, Gomin was so alarmed by the plight of the boy that he resisted taking on such a position. Laurent persuaded him to stay on. "Gomin took extreme care of my brother," writes Marie-Thérèse. "For a long time my brother had been without lights; he was dying of fear. Gomin obtained permission that he might have them. . . . He spoke to the committee and asked that he might be taken down to the garden for exercise." Marie-Thérèse understood, presumably from Gomin himself, that "Louis-Charles soon perceived Gomin's attentions, was touched by them and attached himself to him. The unhappy child had long been accustomed to none but the worst treatment—for I believe that no research can show such barbarity to any other child."

No one had told Louis-Charles about the fate of his mother. With the greater freedom he now had to move around the prison, he was able to walk past the locked door of his mother's former room, where he had been separated from her over a year previously. According to one account, once when he went for a walk to the top of the Tower he saw some yellow flowers clinging to some crumbling stonework in the parapet wall. He picked them, and on his way down he left them outside her room on the third floor, in the wild hope that she was still near him. To his young mind, it might only be a matter of time before they were reunited.

Marie-Thérèse still had no contact with her brother. She constantly begged to be able to see him but her requests were always refused. "She was continually questioning the keepers and commissaries, without being able to obtain anything from them but vague words, which though intended to reassure her, only alarmed her the more. Her entreaties to see her brother and to be allowed to nurse him were always refused." Both children were now permitted to walk outside under guard—but never together. It had been expressly forbidden to allow any meeting to take place between the two children. Deputies of the Committee for General Security had insisted on this "prohibition in the most formal manner." Consequently, although Laurent was at pains to reassure her that her brother's nightmare was over and that he was now in good care, he would go no further to reunite them.

The official reason for their separation was to prevent any collusion between them that might help an escape plan or undermine the security of their imprisonment in any way. However, historians have suggested a more sinister reason for keeping them apart. The real motive for their enforced separation could be that the sickly and uncommunicative child held captive in the Tower was not Louis-Charles at all, but a substitute child. If Marie-Thérèse were to find out that her brother had escaped and tell the guards, rumors could spread, precipitating a political crisis. Consequently, the kindly Laurent was forced to keep the children apart. It was entirely possible that the young boy, guarded like precious stones in the keep, was no longer the royal prince.

By late 1794, the mood in France was slowly beginning to change. In this slightly more open atmosphere, news of Louis-Charles's shameful treatment in prison began to leak out. On November 26, 1794, journalists for the newspaper *Le Courrier Universel* dared to publish the following piece, which openly acknowledged some of the horror:

The son of Louis XVI should also benefit from the Revolution of the 9th Thermidor. It is well known that this child was abandoned to the care of Simon, the shoemaker, a favored acolyte of Robespierre whose punishment he shared. The Committee for General Security, being of the opinion that a human being ought not to be degraded below the level of humanity, just because he happens to be born the son of a king, has appointed three commissaries, men of sound judgment and intelligence, to replace the late Simon. Two are responsible for the education of the orphan. The third should ensure that he is not deprived of the necessities of life, as he was in the past.

The journalists were promptly arrested and brought before the Convention. Their article caused such a stir that Mathieu, a member of the Committee for General Security, was forced to give a formal denial to the "calumnious and royalist" article in the *Courrier.* In his statement before the Convention, to reassure the many citizens who wanted no pity shown to the offspring of the hated tyrants, he explained that the boy was treated as a common prisoner and "that any idea of bettering the condition of Capet's children or giving them tutors was completely foreign to their intentions."

Although Robespierre was dead, France was not yet ready to make peace with its royal family. Many still wanted to purge France of every last vestige of royalty. Toward the end of 1794, there were repeated calls for the son of Capet to be banished from France forever. Others argued that to deport him would simply deliver him up to France's enemies who would rally royalists and threaten the republic. Many republicans continued to be haunted by the fear that while Louis XVI's son was still alive, the return of the monarchy remained a possibility. Even though his wretched conditions in the Temple were becoming more widely known, few dared to intervene, fearful of being branded royalist traitors. Members of the Convention were increasingly making a cynical calculation. If Louis-Charles were to die in prison, this would solve the problem of what to do with the boy at a stroke.

European diplomacy to secure the release of Louis-Charles had come to a standstill; in truth, he had been all but abandoned. By early 1795, Spanish ministers tried to bring an end to their two-year war with France. They offered to recognize the French Republic on the condition that Louis-Charles was handed over. Sensing that Spain had no stomach for a fight over the issue, the French refused.

In February 1795, a report was secretly passed to the Committee for General Security stating that there was "imminent danger that the prisoner's life was slipping away." The committee heard that he had swellings in all his joints and "that it was impossible to extract a word from him." Yet the son of Capet's final agonies evoked little sympathy from those around him and no doctor was summoned. Years later, Gomin reported a comment of one guard who saw the ill child, covered in tumors and barely able to move: "Well, there are plenty of children worth as much as he who are far more ill. And many die who are far more useful!"

For many at the Convention, it would be only too convenient if the boy were to die. On February 26 the Committee for General Security ordered a team of three to make a full report on his health. Jean-Baptiste Harmand later wrote an account of this visit in which, to his astonishment, he found a completely mute child.

The prince was sitting beside a little square table on which were scattered a good many playing cards. . . . He was busy with these cards when we went in and did not cease his occupation. . . . I approached the prince. Our movements did not appear to make any impression on him. I told him that the government was too late appraised of the bad state of his health and of his refusal to take air and exercise, or to answer any questions . . . and had sent us to him to find out the facts.

Harmand then claims that he tried to encourage the prince to talk by offering inducements. He told the prince that they were authorized to find ways of extending his walks, or procuring "any objects of amusement or diversion" that he might wish.

While he was speaking, however "the boy looked fearfully at me, without changing his position and listened, apparently with the greatest attention, but not one word did he reply."

Harmand says he then offered even more attractive delights: "a horse, a dog, some birds, playthings of any kind, one or more companions your own age. . . . In vain did I repeat everything that I could think of as agreeable to his age. I received not one word in reply, not even a sign or a gesture, although his head was turned toward me, and he was looking at me with a strange fixedness in his eyes which expressed the utmost indifference."

Harmand persevered for more than an hour, but could not elicit a single word. "I was in despair and so were my colleagues; indeed, that look had such an expression of resignation and indifference that it seemed to say, "What is it to me? Complete the sacrifice. Finish off your victim!"

Harmand wrote his report during the Restoration, at a time when there was considerable interest in the fate of Louis XVII by a public now appalled at the cruelty he suffered. Consequently Harmand cast himself in a favorable light, when according to Gomin, the offers of toys, pets, or other inducements were never made. Nonetheless, there seems no doubt that the child would not speak, although the delegation tried hard even to extract a simple yes or no. Officials could not be entirely sure that the sick, dumb child was really the royal prince. Was it possible that royalists had somehow substituted a sickly child in his place? And if this was the prince, what degradations had brought him to this tragic point? Harmand writes that they debated the moral and physical condition of the prince at length in the antechamber once they had left him: "I asked them in the anteroom whether this silence did really date from the day on which the child had been forced, by the most barbarous violence, to sign that odious and absurd deposition."

Almost three more months were to elapse before the apparently mute child was permitted to see a doctor. On May 6, 1795, the authorities finally agreed to appoint a Dr. Pierre-Joseph Desault, head surgeon at the Hôpital d'Humanité and a leading practitioner in Paris. Desault was authorized to examine the boy only in the presence of the guards. He soon arrived and once he had signed his name in the register, he was taken to see the young prince.

Desault was shocked and did not hesitate to state his opinion. He reported that he "encountered a child who is mad, dying, a victim of the most abject misery and of the greatest abandonment, a being who has been brutalized by the cruellest of treatments and who it is impossible for me to bring back to life. . . . What a crime!" Desault gave instructions for lotions to be applied to the tumors and rubbed into the child's knees and wrists to ease the pain. He pointed out that there had been far too great a delay in sending him to the child and he proposed "his immediate removal to the country in the hope that the healthy air might succeed in prolonging his life." Needless to say, the committees were not impressed and no action was taken.

Desault, however, returned at nine every morning to see the patient and see that his instructions were being carried out. He made sure that the child was at least carried out onto the roof of the Tower for some fresh air. Desault gently asked Louis-Charles if "he wished to breathe, to see a garden, birds or flowers, to possess a few toys." It was useless. "The child looked at me sadly and bent his head without answering." According to Beauchesne, gradually the child responded to the keen interest of the physician, and "ended by placing his entire confidence in him." Although he rarely spoke, "the kind treatment restored his speech. . . . He found the words to express his thanks."

Aware of the child's gratitude, Dr. Desault tried to prolong his morning visits as long as the officers of the municipality would allow. When the guards announced the end of the visit, the child, not daring to ask for a longer time, "held back Monsieur Desault by the skirt of his coat," hardly able to bear the departure of this man who showed genuine concern. "Twice when he had left the Temple, the good and kindhearted Desault was obliged to retire to his own house, so much was he hurt by the affecting sight of the deserted child, whom he could not tend, whom he could not cure, and yet who seemed, as it were, crying to *him* for help!"

On one visit, as Desault was leaving the Tower, one of the guards asked the doctor whether the boy was dying. "I am afraid so," Desault replied. "But perhaps there are people in the world who hope so." However, in an unexpected twist, it was the doctor who died before the child.

Having submitted his first report on the condition of the child, Desault was invited to a public dinner on May 29 as a guest of the Convention. After this, he suddenly fell ill, suffering from severe abdominal pain and vomiting. His condition became worse and he died in agony three days later. Many suspected poisoning was a likely cause. To add to the mystery, within a few days, Choppart and Doublet, two of Desault's assistants, also died suddenly. Did Desault discover something about the boy that had to be kept secret and for which he was murdered? On inspecting the boy, did he believe that this was not the son of Louis XVI but some impostor placed there by royalists? Was he too outspoken in his criticism of the Convention? His premature death at the age of forty-nine was formally announced in the *Moniteur*: "France and all of Europe have just lost citizen Desault. . . . Such was the superiority of this great surgeon that posterity will certainly call him a great man . . . . He had been persecuted by our former tyrants and his death was caused by their last accomplices."

Not knowing of his death, at the Temple the child waited eagerly for his arrival at nine o'clock every morning. When he failed to come for a second time, "the little invalid was much distressed by it." On the second of June, he was finally told, "You must not expect to see him anymore. He died yesterday." A week was to elapse in which the dying child received no medical attention at all before the Committee for General Security found a suitable doctor. On June 6, 1795, the new surgeon in chief of the Hôpital d'Humanité, Dr. Philippe-Jean Pellatan, was told his presence at the child's bed "was urgently needed."

Philippe-Jean Pellatan visited the child immediately and saw a boy covered in scabies and ulcers. His head drooped, his face and limbs were wasted, his stomach was enlarged and he was suffering chronic diarrhea. Shocked at his condition, Pellatan treated the boy as best he could. Observing that the child seemed very sensitive to noise, he gave instructions that "the sound of bolts and locks that seems to afflict the child . . . be muffled." He even went so far as to blame the officers "for not having removed the blind, which obstructed the light, and the numerous bolts . . . that caused him to shudder. The prisoner, he advised, should to be taken to the keeper's lodge overlooking the garden where he could at least breathe fresh air in the hope "that he would find more consolation there."

For the first time in over a year the prisoner found himself in an airy room, with a large window free from bars and obstructions, "decorated with large white curtains beyond which he could see the sun and the sky." According to his guardians, the child responded immediately to these unexpected delights. When he returned later that day, Pellatan found that the patient "seemed a little better and took more interest in the care that was being taken of him." He realized, however, that Louis-Charles was in a poor state and that he could do very little for him. Pellatan was later to report that "unfortunately, all assistance was too late. . . . No hope was to be entertained."

By now, Laurent had left the Temple, having been posted elsewhere some weeks previously, understandably relieved to be out of the oppressive atmosphere of the Tower prison. Gomin had taken over responsibility for the boy's immediate care, assisted by a man called Étienne Lasne. According to interviews carried out twenty years later, after the restoration of the monarchy, Gomin and Lasne claimed they were genuinely distressed by the boy's final suffering. Lasne says he tried to divert the invalid by playing cards and singing songs while Gomin accompanied them on the violin. These scenes are not entirely credible, as Lasne also admits that three weeks into his appointment, "he was not able to extract a single word from the dauphin" and the child, who was always "grave and sad in his presence, inspired a mixture of pity and disgust."

Dr. Pellatan visited the prisoner again on June 7 and found "the child's weakness was excessive and he had had a fainting fit." Later that evening the boy's condition suddenly deteriorated and an urgent message was sent to Pellatan recalling him to the Temple. Pellatan sent instructions to give him some medicine and visited the boy again the next day. Louis-Charles was sitting up but still very weak. Pellatan "expressed astonishment at the solitary state in which the child was left during the night and part of the day . . . and strongly insisted on giving the poor little Capet a nurse." He wrote to the Committee for General Security, "We found Capet's son with a weak pulse, and an abdomen distended and painful. During the night and again in the morning he had several green and bilious evacuations. His condition appearing to us to be very serious, we have decided to see the child again this evening. . . . It is essential to have an intelligent female nurse by his side."

When interviewed by Beauchesne years later, Gomin claims that when he went to see the invalid that evening, the boy was crying. Gomin "asked him kindly what was the matter." Louis-Charles replied that he was "always alone," and that "his mother was not here to help him." He believed his mother was in one of the other towers and desperately wanted to see her, unable to understand why she could not come.

Once more he passed a night in solitude. On June 8, 1795, Lasne was alone with Louis-Charles while Gomin went to the committee to ask for a nurse; but it was too late. During the afternoon, the child began to slip into unconsciousness. He was given a spoonful of the potion that Dr. Pellatan has prescribed. To no avail; he began to sweat profusely. There was the sound of a rattle "followed by the most violent crisis." At around three o'clock, Lasne found the child was having great difficulty breathing. To try to ease this problem he lifted him up and placed the frail arms around his neck, but the enormous problem of breathing that the boy was having soon ended in a long-drawn-out sigh. His arms, his whole body, went limp. There was no more help required. The orphan of the Temple was dead.

Such was the sensitivity of this news that it was not immediately publicly announced. While a sheet was placed over the little corpse, his guardians continued to behave as though all were well. They asked for medicines and soup and maintained the usual routine. Gomin hurried to the Committee for General Security to let key officials know the news. The following day, arrangements were made for an autopsy to establish the cause of death. Dr. Pellatan arrived shortly after eleven with three other doctors: Jean Baptiste

Dumangin, head physician of the Grand Hôpital de l'Unité, and professors Pierre Lassus and Nicolas Jeanroy.

Stretched out on a table, the child who had been so neglected in life, as a corpse was anatomized in meticulous detail for over five hours. "Before proceeding to open the body, we noted that there was general emaciation due to wasting," Pellatan observed. "The stomach was very distended and swollen. On the inner side of the right knee, we found a tumor . . . and another small tumor on the radial bone, near the left wrist. The tumor on the knee contained nearly two ounces of greyish matter which was full of pus and lymphatic . . . the one on the wrist contained the same type of matter, but thicker."

His hair was shaved, and the skin removed from his scalp. Then Pellatan proceeded to saw through the boy's skull "on a level with the sockets." Professor Jeanroy observed "that in more than forty years' exercise of his art, he had never seen the brain so well developed in a child that age." The child's brain, considered the learned gentlemen, "was in most perfect completeness." However, when they cut open the body to examine the internal organs, there were abnormalities. "When the stomach was opened there escaped more than a pint of turbulent serum, yellowish and very fetid. The intestines were also swollen and adhering to each other and the abdominal cavity." Bit by bit, part by part, his liver, spleen, pancreas, gall bladder, every inch of his body was subjected to the close scrutiny of the four men.

Although they concluded that, for the most part, the child's organs were "very healthy," they did find a number of tumors and growths of various sizes throughout the intestines and near the lungs. These, they thought, were the result of a "scrofulous tendency [tuberculosis], which had been in existence for some time, and to which we should attribute the death of this child." At the time, Pellatan did not speculate on the cause of this disease, but in a statement written nearly twenty years later, he said that it was almost certainly due "to the terrible treatment, body and soul, that the infant had endured for so long."

On completing the autopsy, Pellatan replaced the scalp on the skull and, turning back the strips of loose skin, sewed his face back together. The head was then wrapped in a cloth which was firmly fixed beneath the nape of the neck. The boy's light brown curls, once so much admired, lay on the floor. Damont, the commissioner on duty, was permitted to gather them up and keep them.

Pellatan then began to draft a report. With due scientific caution, he could not positively assert that this was the son of Louis XVI and had no proof that the boy he had been treating for the past few days was indeed the dauphin. Lasne and Gomin assured him that he was, even though they had not known Louis-Charles before his solitary confinement in the Tower. If the royal prince had escaped during the Terror and a substitute had been put in his place, they would not have been able to detect the fraud themselves. A cautious, intelligent doctor, Pellatan did not want to be sucked into the political aftermath of the boy's death and clearly balked at the idea of personally verifying the identity of the dead boy. Instead, he wrote, "We found in the bed the dead body of a child who appeared to us to be about ten, which the commissaries told us was that of the deceased Capet and which two of us have recognized as being the child they had been taking care of for a few days."

It was indeed a baffling task for the authorities to secretly confirm the identity of the dead child. He had been locked away in such seclusion for so long that, even after the Terror, few of the guards had seen him. On the day of his death, one of the secretaries of the Committee for General Security, a man named Bourguignon, came to the Tower to see the dead child for himself. Early the next morning, four more officials from the committee arrived. Later that night, when the autopsy had been completed and some thirty hours after the child had died, the president of the Committee for General Security, known as Bergoeing, finally arrived. Anxious to ensure that there could be no doubt about the child's identity, he ordered twelve people on duty at the Temple to sign a declaration confirming that this was the son of Louis XVI. Yet, like Gomin and Lasne, it is unlikely that any of these officials knew the dauphin before his imprisonment. Even those who had known the dauphin earlier would have been hard pressed to identify the boy, since the trauma of his maltreatment and illness had greatly altered his appearance. One commissary, a man called Guérin, claimed he had seen the dauphin at the Tuileries palace. He had not seen the boy for at least four years, but as he peered in the candlelight at the face, now swollen, mutilated by a scalpel, darkened by putrefaction and wrapped in a bandage, he thought he could recognize the once-royal features.

The only person who could have reliably confirmed the death of the dauphin was just a few feet away in the room above. Yet Marie-Thérèse had no idea her brother was dead and remained in ignorance of this for many weeks. No one came to tell her that the last little member of her immediate family had died. No one asked her to identify his body. The officials at the Temple had no authority to override the Committee's order that the children be kept apart at all times—even in death. Locked in her room on the third floor, she was unaware of the gruesome scene under way in the room below.

Preparations were being made to dispose quietly of her brother's body in a common grave. Officials at the Committee for General Security gave permission for the decomposing son of the tyrant to be buried. The caretaker at Sainte-Marguerite cemetery provided a child's pinewood coffin, five feet long. Étienne Voisin, the funeral director, transferred the body into the coffin. He did not nail down the lid right away, since he said later, "That would have moved the bowels of the august princess." Instead, the coffin was taken down the stone steps to the ground floor out of earshot. Civil commissaries arrived from the town hall to sign the death certificate:

Register of the decease of Louis-Charles Capet, on the 20 Prairial at three o'clock P.M. aged ten years and two months, native of Versailles, residing at Paris in the Temple tower, son of Louis Capet, last king of the French, and of Marie-Antoinette-Josèphe-Jeanne of Austria.

As darkness fell late in the evening of June 10, 1795, the child finally left the Temple prison in a coffin held by four bearers. It was a modest procession that progressed uneventfully along the Parisian streets across the

Faubourg Saint-Antoine and into the cemetery. There was no family to mourn him, just a few officials, including Lasne and Gomin, and two detachments of soldiers to serve as an escort. At Sainte-Marguerite the gravedigger, Pierre Bertrancourt, was waiting and, without the delay of a blessing or a simple prayer, the cheap coffin was lowered unceremoniously into a common grave for the poor. The gravedigger's wife, Gabrielle Bertrancourt, who described the scene years later, said, "There were very few people. He was put into the common grave, which was the grave for everyone, children and adults, the rich and the poor. Everybody went into it, because, so to speak, everybody was *equal*." Afterward, two sentinels were posted at the cemetery to prevent anyone from trying to steal the body.

In a macabre twist, unknown to the authorities, a small part of the child was not buried in the common grave. During the autopsy, a crucial event took place that remained a secret for many years. Taking advantage of a moment when the other doctors were distracted, perhaps discussing notes or looking out of the window, on impulse, Dr. Philippe-Jean Pellatan had stolen the child's heart. He hurriedly wrapped it in a handkerchief and placed it in his pocket.

His motive for stealing Louis-Charles's heart is not stated in any of the records. However, Pellatan was convinced the dead boy on the table before him was indeed the prospective king of France. For centuries, it had been a tradition for the heart of a king to be embalmed and placed in the crypt of Saint-Denis. It seems likely that Pellatan wanted to conserve this important relic of what he believed would be the last little king of France—after all, Louis XVI had been beheaded, his brothers had fled and the republic was established. Pellatan was by no means an ardent royalist; indeed, he had served well under the revolution, yet some instinct urged him to preserve a small token from this historic scene. He said later he felt it was important to have "this sad and mournful relic of the child-king to convey to the royal family."

Wrapped in a handkerchief and concealed in Pellatan's coat pocket, the heart of the ten-year-old boy was smuggled out of the Temple. Once at home, Pellatan placed it in a jar and covered it with distilled wine alcohol to preserve the precious contents. Hidden on the top shelf of his bookcase, it was gradually forgotten. After a few years, the alcohol evaporated and the child's heart went dry.

PART II

🍂 *Chapter Seven* 🍂

FARCE AND FRAUD

My dearly beloved sister, forgive me if, rejecting all court etiquette, the tenderness of a brother who has never forgotten you dictates these lines. For I declare it to you, I am living, I myself, your own brother. . . . Doubt no longer of my existence!

—LETTER ADDRESSED TO MARIE-THÉRÈSE FROM
HER OWN "BROTHER," DATED 1815

Although the orphan of the Temple had been seriously ill for some time, this had been reported only to the Committee for General Security. The public, even deputies at the Convention, were not aware of the child's precarious state of health. Consequently, news of his sudden death was greeted with astonishment and aroused the deepest suspicions.

Rumors began to circulate about the true story of the ill-fated prince. "Some contend that this death means nothing; that the young child is in fact full of life and that it is a very long time since he was at the Temple," reported the newspaper, *Le Courrier Universel* on June 13, 1795, giving voice to the widely held view that there had been a cover-up. For many, the death and burial was a farce played by the revolutionary government to conceal the fact that the real dauphin had escaped months ago with the help of royalists who had bribed the prison guards. Others believed the burial was of a substitute child, the dauphin having been murdered months previously, at the height of the Terror. As speculation spread, government assurances that the son of Capet was indeed dead and buried on June 10, 1795, merely added to the sense of confusion and conspiracy. The young prince was surely alive and well, hiding in a foreign country. It would only be a matter of time before he returned to France to claim his throne.

As the news reached foreign courts, they too were cynical. "There is no real and legal certainty that the son of Louis XVI *is dead*," declared the Austrian minister, Baron Franz Thugut. "His death, up to now, has no other proof than the announcement in the *Moniteur*, along with a report drawn up on the orders of the brigands of the Convention and by people whose deposition is based on the fact that they were presented with the body of a dead child who they were told was the son of Louis Capet." He went on to argue their motives for claiming the son of Louis XVI was dead. "The leaders of the villains" considered it in their interests to announce his death, "whilst retaining this precious prize in a secure and unknown location . . . in the event that a change in circumstances could threaten them."

However, in Verona, the younger brother of Louis XVI, the Comte de Provence, did not express any doubts over his nephew's death or attempt to investigate the details. He had his own reasons to accept the announcement. Eagerly waiting in exile to claim his own right of succession as Louis XVIII, he did so, for some, with unseemly haste, in a proclamation on June 24, 1795.

The only person, it seemed, as yet unaware of the news of the death was his sister, Marie-Thérèse, still confined above his now-empty room in the Temple and still persistently inquiring after her brother's health. That June, reports of Louis-Charles's death began to focus public attention on the princess's plight. Articles were written portraying Marie-Antoinette's daughter as the very symbol of some of the worst excesses of the revolution. On June 18, 1795, a delegation from the City of Orléans was bold enough to appear before the Convention to petition for her "speedy release" in the strongest possible terms: "The daughter of Louis XVI is languishing within a horrible prison . . . deprived of every comfort and support and condemned to ceaseless weeping." If she were released, "all Europe would applaud your decision."

Aware of the changing mood France, the guards, at last, began to request better food and clothing for their prisoner. According to Jean-Baptiste Gomin, Marie-Thérèse "was extremely reserved in expressing her wishes," and did not dare to ask for anything but the barest minimum. In spite of her refusals, a record, dated the third of Messidor in the republican calendar—June 20, 1795—from the Commission of Public Relief to the guards at the Temple reveals that the following articles were procured for her:

Two morning dresses of colored taffeta.
Two morning dresses of nankeen and cotton, lined with Florence taffeta.
Six pairs of colored silk stockings.
Six pairs of shoes.
A green silk dress.

The sixteen-year-old "Charlotte Capet," as she is referred to in the documents—from her third name, Marie-Thérèse-Charlotte—who had been denied even a pencil for the last two years, was suddenly in possession of a wardrobe. Although she makes no reference to it, Gomin observed later, "Madame seemed so glad to leave off the old puce dress which she had been mending up since the time of Robespierre. Her toilet was now very suitable." After all the years during which she had discovered that to be invisible and to ask for nothing had become second nature, now suddenly her bare and shrivelled world was offering hope. Soon she was to be supplied with books. For thirteen months she had had only *La Harpe's Travels*, which she had perused over and over again. Now she was given two other books: *Historie de France* by Velly and *Mondes* by Fontanelle. The record shows that "to this parcel were added some pencils, paper, India ink and brushes."

Later in June, the Committee of Public Safety decreed that a woman should be appointed as her companion, and they selected Citizeness Madeleine Bocquet de Chantereine. Madame de Chantereine soon realized that Marie-Thérèse did not yet know about the death of her family. Details were given to her "amid tears and sobs; and thus at a single stroke, Madame learned of the loss of all that she loved best. . . . The wounds of her heart now formed one great wound and all her griefs merged into one general grief. . . . She knew now that she was alone upon the earth."

The two women were permitted to walk freely in the garden. As the word spread, royalists anxious to catch sight of the daughter of Louis XVI would wait in the houses of the Rue des Cordeliers, where the top windows overlooked the Tower wall. Monsieur François Hüe, the king's former Gentleman of the Bedchamber, who had not seen her since the day he was removed from the Tower in 1793, rented a house on this street and made a point of waving to her to provide encouragement. It is even said that Madame Hüe, who could play the harp, would arrange small concerts at the hour that the princess took her walk; a ballad was specially composed to give her hope:

> *Be calm, unhappy one,*
> *These doors will open soon;*
> *Soon from thy chains set free,*
> *'Neath radiant skies thou'lt be . . .*

After weeks of negotiation, on September 3, 1795, her former governess, the Marquise de Tourzel, and her daughter, Pauline, finally obtained permission to visit Madame Royale. "Madame came to meet us, embraced us tenderly and led us to her room, where we mingled our tears for all the objects of her regret," wrote the marquise. The two women were amazed at the change in Marie-Thérèse. "We had left Madame, frail and delicate looking. Now after three years of captivity, we were astonished to find her beautiful, tall and strong and with that air of nobility which is a marked characteristic of her appearance." Nonetheless, the marquise was keenly aware of her state of mind. "Madame betrayed not the faintest touch of bitterness . . . yet she added such touching remarks concerning the slight account in which she held her life, that it was impossible to hear her without our being deeply affected." Determined to raise her spirits, the marquise and her daughter came to see her as often as possible.

On one of these visits, Marie-Thérèse offered to take her guests to see the different rooms of the Tower. As they went down to the second floor, the

Marquise de Tourzel stopped at the threshold and could not bring herself to enter, knowing full well that these were the rooms where her young charge, Louis-Charles, had suffered so greatly. Pauline and Marie-Thérèse went into his room together. The only remaining trace of his sad little presence were some words etched in charcoal on the wall of his cell: *"Maman, je vous pr—"* The message to his mother was unfinished. For whatever reason—whether stopped by Simon or other guards—he had never been able to complete the sentence. On another wall there was a child's drawing of a flower.

However, on October 5, 1795, growing dissatisfaction with the government led to a pro-royalist insurrection in Paris. The marquise and Pauline de Tourzel were with Marie-Thérèse when they heard shots fired and cannon booming near the Tuileries. They delayed their departure, unwilling to leave her alone. When they eventually left, "silently and in great anxiety," the women found "crossing the bridge was terrible; we could see the smoke and flame of the cannon incessantly discharged."

A twenty-six-year-old gunnery officer from Corsica was in charge of the cannons: Napoleon Bonaparte. His exploits on that day would signal his striking debut on the political arena and turn the relatively unknown *Little Corporal* into a name that was on everyone's lips. By this time, Napoleon had over fifteen years of military experience, having entered the royal military college of Brienne at the age of nine. In 1784, he had trained at the prestigious École Militaire in Paris, and later, had been stationed at Valence and Auxonne and distinguished himself at the siege of Toulon, earning promotion to brigadier general. Faced with the insurrection of the crowd against the Convention in October 1795, Napoleon made a plan that was bold and decisive. Although vastly outnumbered, anticipating that the crowds would advance up the Rue Saint-Honoré, he had placed cannon strategically on the steps of the Church of Saint-Roch. The rebellion was suppressed by a "whiff of grapeshot." Napoleon was heralded as a hero of the revolution, welcomed into Parisian society and soon appointed to command the Army of the Interior.

Within a few weeks of the insurrection in Paris, negotiations were hurriedly completed to dispatch the last living symbol of the royal family from the republic to avoid the risk of her presence stirring further royalist sentiment. Marie-Thérèse was to be exchanged for French prisoners held by the Austrian government. Before leaving her prison, Marie-Thérèse was most anxious to acquire any mementos of her family that had been removed during their captivity; she was only too aware of certain personal possessions "removed from my mother soon after our arrival at the Temple." Gomin knew these were locked in a sealed chest of drawers in the lower room of the Tower. Various officials came to break the seals and form an inventory. However, she was not allowed even to see these personal reminders of her parents and their former lives together. Nor was she allowed to have the companion of her choice to escort her to Vienna. After the royalist uprising, the Marquise de Tourzel was arrested once more, interrogated, and imprisoned.

Toward the end of 1795, arrangements were finally completed for her journey. Marie-Thérèse travelled incognito, under the name Sophie. "I left the Temple at eleven o'clock on the night of the 18th December," she wrote, "without being seen by anyone." Waiting for her at the outer gate was the minister of the interior, Benezech, and his assistant. She took his arm and walked down the deserted street of the Temple to his carriage: "We made several turns about the streets until we reached the boulevards in front of the Opera House where we found a travelling carriage." She could hardly believe that she was out in the streets of Paris at last, in the chill December air, unnoticed by passersby, just another anonymous Parisian but one hardly able to contain the huge prospect of freedom ahead. "At the gates of Paris our passports were demanded," she recalled, and then they set off at speed into the night. It was her seventeenth birthday.

In a curious reversal of her mother's journey as a hopeful young princess twenty-five years earlier, Marie-Thérèse made her way across France to the border and toward Austria. According to the minister, at the frontier her eyes filled with tears: "I leave France with much regret," she said. "I will always regard it as my country." At Basel, officials arranged the transfer of the prisoners—to much cheering and shouting of *"Vive la République"* as the French prisoners were released. By a strange coincidence, one of them was Jean-Baptiste Drouet, the sharp-eyed postmaster who had proved so instrumental in the arrest of the royal family on their flight to Varennes.

It was January 9, 1796, before her carriage finally turned into the entrance drive of her mother's childhood home, the Hofburg in Vienna. She knew of it from her mother, and suddenly here it was, hope turned into solid bricks and mortar, and with all the pleasant associations of her mother's childhood. Although in exile, the young princess now had her freedom, and "all the charm of early youth," according to her former guardian, Gomin. "Her features, which had been extremely delicate in childhood, had formed into beauty; her eyes were large, and her hair had turned chestnut color. . . . She kept hers long and wore it without powder in a knot behind her."

However, according to the French literary historian Charles-Augustin Sainte-Beuve, the young princess who arrived in Vienna was irrevocably scarred by her experiences in the Temple Tower. She had been imprisoned at the age of fourteen, "and it was in that long series of terrors, enigmas, and painful nightmares that the years and dreams of girlhood, usually so lighthearted, had passed." Now, despite her youthful appearance, he considered "her very soul had been attacked." Indeed, "the young slip of a girl" was so blighted by her early experience that, Sainte-Beuve wrote, "it seems to me that on leaving the Temple, both the life and the soul of Madame Royale were finished. They were closed to the future; all their sources, all their roots were henceforth in the past." Such was the horror of the scenes that had been impressed on her mind that she now seemed quite incapable of finding happiness. "In order to understand her," he wrote, "we must never cease to remember that all that calls itself springtide joy and bloom . . . was suppressed and blighted in her. Her soul, scarcely in its first dawn, was suddenly reduced and worn to the barest thread . . . and could no longer change." Even in her freedom, her prison was still with her as she solemnly retreated within herself. "Indeed, she did not retreat," adds Sainte-Beuve, "for she lived there."

And as this blighted young princess, alone in a foreign court, struggled to adjust to life, she was soon shaken by startling news of her brother.

In 1797, a young man was discovered wandering aimlessly in the countryside near Châlons-sur-Marne in northeast France. In local records he was described as having "long and naturally curly hair, an artless smile, a persuasive tone of voice, and in addition, an air of great dignity and candor." He attracted attention since he was well dressed, had "more than an ordinary education" and possessed the confident air and manner of a young gentleman from an aristocratic family. This was puzzling. Why was such a charming young man, looking as though he had just stepped out of a chateau with self-evidently blue-blooded credentials, scrounging about the countryside like a vagrant? Eventually, in May 1798, he was brought before the local magistrate at Cernon, near Châlons, and ordered to explain who he was. The young man politely declined to answer any questions and so the magistrate ordered that he be held in custody pending further inquiries.

News that the son of an aristocrat was imprisoned in Châlons soon spread around the neighborhood. People had heard stories before of children from noble families orphaned during the revolution and left to wander the land in search of food and shelter. As speculation grew as to which great house he must belong to, many people came to see the apparently high-born prisoner to try to resolve the mystery. Although he stubbornly refused to reveal his identity, it was obvious to one and all that for some mysterious reason, he was merely visiting them from the sublime and lofty heights of the aristocracy. Deeply touched by his misfortune, the local community organized collections to help him. He was permitted out around the town with visitors. Fine clothes and gifts were brought for him, even a handsome silver service on which to dine; soon his cell was exquisitely furnished.

Local police had placed notices in the papers about their unusual prisoner, hoping to obtain more information, but to no avail. Apart from revealing his age—thirteen years—the authorities had no other clues. Yet the more he impressed his visitors with his charming modesty, gentility and refinement, the more the conviction grew that he was no ordinary aristocrat: this was the young son of a truly great line. As word spread around the entire region, quite suddenly, under mounting pressure, the prisoner declared dramatically that he was ready to reveal all.

He was none other than Louis-Antoine-Joseph-Frédéric de Longueville, son of the late Marquis de Longueville. His mother's name was Sainte-Emilie and the family seat was in Normandy, at Beuzeville. Local people were overjoyed, doubtless convinced their friend would be heir to a fortune, and wrote to inform the mayor of Beuzeville of the wonderful news. To their amazement they received an unexpected reply. The authorities in Normandy regretted that they had no knowledge of the House of Longueville, or for that matter, the family of Sainte-Emilie or the town of Beuzeville. However, this information did not deter the good people of Châlons. Clearly, he must be hiding an even more illustrious name. Indeed, it did not take the fascinated locals long to work out who he was when they pondered the names he had given—Louis, Antoine, Joseph—all names from the late royal family: this had to be the lost dauphin. Villagers rushed to see the young man and put it to him that he was Louis XVII. Summoning an air of great modesty, the stranger finally admitted that he was indeed none other than the lost boy king.

For a country that had been ruled for generations by royal Bourbon kings, the romance of finding that the prisoner was none other than the prospective king of France proved irresistible. This tallied neatly with the widespread belief that the prince had indeed escaped from the Tower. It was known that at the height of the Terror, Louis-Charles had been detained in solitary confinement in a darkened cell. Other than the handful of guards who checked on the boy by peering through the grille, few prison staff saw him at all during this period. Those who did validate the ledger only had to see a small figure of a boy lying down inside. It would have been only too easy to make a switch with a sickly boy of the same size as Louis-Charles during this period. Later, as the child's conditions slowly improved, it was noticeable that those appointed as his guardians, such as Laurent and Gomin, had not met the dauphin earlier, and would not have realized if the boy was an impostor. Even if any guard had realized the truth, surely they would have been handsomely bribed by wealthy royalists to keep the secret? To many, the escape of the royal prince seemed only too plausible.

Now that the "prince" had finally resurfaced in Châlons-sur-Marne, there was cause for celebration. Although still in prison, he was treated as a king, his cell luxuriously reappointed as a "little palace" and a small "court" organized with due pomp and ceremony. His "courtiers" expressed their deepest sympathies for the terrible traumas he had had to suffer as a child; presents and money were lavished on him. Local people were immensely proud that "Louis XVII" had surfaced in their district, and he attracted many visitors, some even who had known him as a child. It was quite amazing how much he remembered of those days, how overcome he was at the mention of his mother's death, how heartbreakingly sensitive he was at any reference to his father. All were agreed: he was the lost dauphin.

It was not long before a former Temple guard who had met the "son of Capet" in the Tower heard the news that he had reappeared in Châlons and decided to go there to see him for himself. He was shown into the royal lodgings, where the young "prince" was surrounded by his admirers. "Here is a gentleman who knows me," declared the prisoner at once, "and who will say so if he has the courage." The guard, at first unsure, was then reminded by the "prince" of an incident at the Temple. He immediately bowed before him. "You are indeed the son of the unfortunate king," he declared.

By late 1798, rumors that Louis XVII was alive were spreading across France. The minister of police in Paris, alarmed that this might lead to royalist disturbances, decided it was time to act. "I should have thought," he wrote ominously to the local authorities, "that it ought not to have been difficult to make a young boy speak." The minister began his own detailed investigation and, according to some historical reports, Napoleon Bonaparte himself was informed. By now, Napoleon wielded tremendous power in France. His prestige had grown in line with the triumphant movement of his armies abroad as he had achieved decisive victories over the Italians, Austrians and Sardinians. When he returned to Paris, the twenty-eight-year-old general was triumphantly heralded as the new savior of France and he now set his sights on total power.

Marie-Antoinette by Elisabeth Vigée Le Brun, 1783

The Palace of Versailles by Pierre Denis Martin c. 1722

The elegant *Galerie des Glaces*, or Hall of Mirrors, at Versailles

Louis XVI looking authoritative in his robes of state,
which belied his intrinsic lack of confidence

The Princesse de Lamballe became a close friend of Marie-Antoinette in her early years at Versailles.

Madame Élisabeth, sister of Louis XVI

The queen with her family in 1787: Marie-Thérèse,
Louis-Joseph, and the youngest, Louis-Charles

The glamorous Count Axel Fersen, the queen's favorite

The young Marie-Thérèse, nicknamed Mousseline la Sérieuse by her mother

Many *libelles* and prints damaged the queen's reputation. LEFT: The *Essai Historique* portrayed the queen as an "adulterous wife, soiled with debauchery." RIGHT: The queen takes the scepter from the king, who has collapsed on the throne.

The queen as Harpy

The destruction of the Bastille in 1789

Maximilien Robespierre

10 August 1792. The royal family fled as the Tuileries came under attack.

The tower of the Temple where the royal family
was imprisoned in 1792

Louis XVI shortly before his execution

EXECUTION DE LOUIS CAPET XVI. DU NOM, LE 21 JANVIER 1793.

The execution of Louis XVI

Marie-Antoinette visibly declined during her imprisonment.

Marie-Antoinette being led from the Conciergerie to her execution

Sketch of Marie-Antoinette being taken to the guillotine in an open cart, by Jacques Louis David

Robespierre's arrest. He was found with his jaw shattered, collapsed on the table of the Committee of Public Safety.

A. View of THE TEMPLE at Paris B. National Guard, C. People in tumult, with the Head of Princess Lamballe the 1st of Sept. 1792.

The head of the Princesse de Lamballe was paraded around the Temple prison to show her friend the queen.

The youthful Marie-Thérèse was irrevocably scarred
by her experiences in the Temple Tower.

Curiously, soon after the Paris authorities became involved, a tailor called René Hervagault, from Saint-Lô in Normandy, came forward and declared that the royal "prince" was none other than his runaway son. Under questioning, the "prince" finally admitted that he was indeed Jean-Marie Hervagault, the missing son of the tailor.

However, the "court" at Châlons greeted this new evidence with disbelief. No one could accept that the young man would have such aristocratic credentials and so positively ooze charm if he were merely the son of a tailor. There were rumors that the tailor's wife, formerly Nicole Bigot, a lacemaker at Versailles, had been seduced by an aristocrat, the Duc de Valentinois, who, it appeared, when nature took its usual course in these matters and Nicole Bigot's delightful figure displayed unwanted bulk, had conveniently married her to his valet, Hervagault. Yet people were still not satisfied. The birth certificate provided by the tailor showed that his son, the real Jean-Marie Hervagault, was now eighteen, but the prisoner appeared no more than thirteen—the same age as the dauphin. At a time when conspiracies abounded, people became convinced that the police, on instructions from higher authorities in Paris, had deliberately sought to conceal the truth in order to crush the rumors that Louis XVII was alive. Why, for example, had it taken so long for the tailor, Hervagault, to identify his son? And why did he step forward so conveniently just at the moment required by the Paris police?

The bemused police now found that his followers were more sure than ever that the prisoner was Louis XVII. They could quite understand, after everything that his family had been through, that he did not want to face further persecution from the authorities and consequently he had fallen in with their claim that he was a tailor's son. Some even speculated that the tailor from Saint-Lô may indeed have known the prisoner; he could have been the very man selected to look after Louis-Charles when he had escaped from the Tower. In a delightful twist, his courtiers now respected their "king's" wishes to *pretend* to be the son of the tailor. Presents of food, clothes and money were showered with even more generosity than before.

When the prisoner was finally released from jail, the police gave instructions that he must move away from the area. The young "prince" made his farewells to his distraught subjects in Châlons and, having no definite plan or destination, he was soon involved yet again with the police, and this culminated in the summer of 1799 in a two-year prison sentence. By chance, while in prison a book was published which appeared to lend some plausibility to his claims: *The Cemetery of the Madeleine*. This was a popular fictionalized account of the escape of Louis XVII from the Tower. According to the author, Regnault-Warin, a substitute child was brought into the Tower in a wooden horse, heavily drugged with opium, while Louis-Charles was smuggled out in a dirty laundry basket. Later, the substitute child was poisoned and passed off as the dead "son of Capet." Although the police tried to suppress the book—the author was even temporarily imprisoned—secret editions were widespread and many people believed it was true.

When the "prince" was due for release once more, he was met by his devoted supporters who escorted him back to Châlons. His "court" was soon reestablished and now he was prepared to recount his extraordinary adventures in full. As in *The Cemetery of the Madeleine*, he claimed he had indeed escaped from the Tower in May 1795, in a wicker basket. And he could reveal to his astonished subjects that the unfortunate substitute child who had taken his place in the cell was none other than the *real* Jean-Marie Hervagault. The unscrupulous tailor had consented to sell his own dying son for a large sum. Once he was free, royalist supporters had eventually smuggled him out of France to England where his uncles, who evidently thought his escape would thwart their plans to reascend the throne, were far from welcoming—he claimed the Comte d'Artois even tried to poison him. However, George III provided him with a ship and he fled to Europe, finally returning to France in 1797.

Amazed by his compelling odyssey, one of his followers generously put his mansion at Vitry at the disposal of the young prince, where he convincingly held court in a most royal manner with lavish banquets and charming guests: a Versailles in miniature. Naturally, to avoid further harassment from the police, he made use of his false name, Jean-Marie Hervagault, when necessary. His followers thought it a good protection against the inhumanity that the authorities had shown to the royal family.

Inevitably, all this was greeted with dismay by the authorities. By chance, one of the officials in Vitry, Commissioner Batelier, was a zealous revolutionary who had voted for the king's death in 1793. Now a leading member of the Criminal Tribunal at Vitry, he disliked this outpouring of royalist sentimentality. He undertook to make a full report to the notorious new chief of police in Paris, Joseph Fouché. This "king" in his little "Versailles" would be exposed, once and for all.

As rumors of Louis XVII's miraculous survival spread beyond France, Marie-Thérèse was shaken. She believed that her brother had died in the Temple prison, as the authorities had claimed. Even though she had not been able to see him in the Tower, she had learned of his illness, as well as the conditions in which he was held, and guardians she trusted, such as Gomin, had eventually confirmed his death. At the time, she seemed to be under no illusion as to the cause of his death. His life was shortened, she wrote in her memoirs, by "uncleanness, joined to the horrible treatment, the unexampled harshness and cruelty exercised on him." Yet in 1798, while in exile in Vienna, she learned from a priest, the Abbot of La Trappe known as Père de Lestrange, that a man claiming to be her brother had been found in France. From the evidence of her memoirs, it had not crossed her mind that the authorities might have been lying to her about his death. This would make sense of the numerous occasions when she had begged to see her brother and was denied.

Even if the claimant was fraudulent, the rumors reopened other harrowing wounds. The last time she had seen her brother alive was when, as a terrified fourteen-year-old, she had been interrogated by officials in the Tower about the claim that their mother and aunt had sexually abused him. She was only too aware how vehement Louis-Charles had seemed in his damning accusations. Marie-Thérèse had had plenty of time to replay the disbelieving horror of that scene many times. In her eyes he had been a significant witness to their condemnation and deaths. How was she to feel about him now? Despite these feelings of antagonism, she had promised her mother that she would always look after her little brother.

Faced with this dilemma, she declined to meet the pretender. The memories of the past were too painful and, in any case, her advisors convinced her that "the tailor's son" was almost certainly a fraud. She wrote in 1778 to inform her uncle, Provence, who, as Louis XVIII, was in exile in Russia, stating her opinion that the story was "an idle fancy" which "according to everything I know thereon, is in no way probable." Provence wrote to reassure her from Mitau, "If, against all probability, the statement were true, the person who was most interested in it [that is himself] would experience sincere joy and believe that he had found his son again."

At this stage, Provence was keen to demonstrate to his niece that he had her best interests at heart since he was most anxious to persuade her to marry his nephew, the Duc d'Angoulême. Provence himself had no children, and consequently, the Duc d'Angoulême, as the oldest son of Comte d'Artois, was the Bourbon heir in the next generation in the event of a restoration. Provence was only too aware that at the court in Vienna, Emperor Francis II was also considering a match for Marie-Thérèse, to his younger brother, the handsome Archduke Charles. Louis XVIII pressured Marie-Thérèse to accept the Duc d'Angoulême by telling her that this match had been her parents' wish. Unknown to Marie-Thérèse, his newfound concern for his niece was more than a little tempered by a strong measure of self-interest.

While she saw in Provence a long-lost father figure, he saw in his niece only political advantage, as his letter to Monsieur d'Azara, the Spanish ambassador to the Holy See, makes transparent: "My niece's prolonged period of suffering, her courage, and her virtues have directed toward her a degree of interest and devotion from the French people which it is essential that I should profit from . . . by marrying her to my natural heir." Even though she had not met the Duc d'Angoulême since her childhood in Versailles, with no advisors to help her, Marie-Thérèse fell for her uncle's warm, persuasive letters and committed herself. "I am much touched by your kindness in arranging a marriage for me," she wrote full of optimism to her uncle. "As you have selected Cousin Angoulême for my husband, I joyfully consent with all my heart." On May 3, 1799, Marie-Thérèse left Vienna to join Provence in exile. Her uncles were not wealthy and were reliant on hospitality from foreign courts. Napoleon's successes had driven Provence out of Italy to Russia where he was dependent on Czar Paul I, who had provided him with a home in the small provincial town of Mitau, now in Latvia. When Marie-Thérèse arrived a month later, on June 4, she found Provence had conveniently failed to provide her with a full description of her prospective spouse. If she had been expecting a younger version of Artois, a good-looking and agreeable companion, she was soon to be disillusioned. Unlike his father, the Duc d'Angoulême had inherited the weak and sickly health of the Bourbons: "He is small, ugly and awkwardly built," observed a friend of the royal family, the Costa de Beauregard. "He has very little brains and speaks in an uneducated manner." Whatever Marie-Thérèse may have felt, she was committed by her own pledge and Provence gave her no time to change her mind. They were married six days later.

Marie-Thérèse was soon deeply unhappy. "Her marriage with the prince was a bitter disappointment to the princess—a hollow fraud," said one court observer, Monsieur de Vaulabille. She no longer joked about "her lover" as she had occasionally done in lighthearted moments with her ladies in Vienna. There were rumors that the marriage was not even consummated. Facing the chill of the Baltic winters in her dreary existence with the royal exiles, she had few comforts in her small circle, save the presence of some of her father's most faithful servants—Hanet Cléry and François Hüe, his former valets, and his last confessor, Abbé Edgeworth.

Any phantom prospects of a throne were rapidly diminishing. Napoleon was unstoppable. After decisive victories over the Italians and the Austrians, the Corsican general took Malta in June 1798 and moved into Egypt, winning the Battle of the Pyramids. Although the French fleet was almost wiped out by the English under Admiral Horatio Nelson at Aboukir Bay, when he returned to Paris, Napoleon was triumphantly heralded as a savior. Faced with the incompetent government of the Directory, he seized his opportunity for a successful coup d'état in early November 1799. A Consulate was established and Napoleon soon became First Consul of France, with near-absolute powers. The republic was now in the hands of its most famous young warrior, a legend at thirty, promising glory where there had been chaos. In ten stormy years, France had passed from autocracy to a constitutional monarchy to a constitutional republic and now to military despotism. It was a foretaste of what was to follow.

Despite the Duchesse d'Angoulême's apparent lack of interest in the man many believed to be her brother, the claims of the "tailor's son" in the early years of the new century continued to gain momentum. Wherever he went, he elaborated his story in ever more convincing detail: his bold escape, the tragic fate of the real Jean-Marie Hervagault who had died in his place, his meeting with the pope and twenty cardinals in Rome. . . . His story all seemed most believable and he could now count among his followers leading members of the community, from businessmen to bishops. Even prominent republicans, including the former bishop of Viviers, Charles Lafont-Savine, became converts to his cause. The ex-bishop had been so concerned at the rumors from Vitry that he took the trouble of tracking down some of the doctors who had performed the autopsy on the child who died in the Temple, only to find that "they had not recognized that child to be the son of the former King Louis XVI." Since the bishop had met the dauphin at Versailles, he travelled to Vitry and recognized his sovereign at once. He urged him, for his own safety, to maintain the bluff of being the tailor's son: "Monseigneur, you are Hervagault, or you will die!" begged the former bishop. With great solemnity, he undertook to prepare the prospective "king" for ascending the throne, with personal tuition in a wide range of suitable subjects. So convinced was he of the young man's veracity that he spread the word throughout the churches that Louis XVII was alive and well. People flocked to Vitry to catch a glimpse of their "king."

In royalist circles it was widely believed that before returning to France, the real dauphin had travelled to Rome to see the pope. After crowning the royal exile as king, Pope Pius VI had taken action to ensure that, in the future, there would never be any doubt over his identity, and an emblem of France had been branded on his right leg. To test this, at one banquet in the "king's" honor, some of the more sceptical guests challenged him to show them this mark made by the pope. With great theatrical pomp, "the king" rose and slowly undid his buckle, rolled down his stocking and gently lifted his leg into view. To the delight of the crowd, there on his leg was an imprint of the shield and lilies of France. There were gasps of amazement. This was nothing less than "the holy mark placed by the infallible hand of the Vicar of God!"

By September 1801, Joseph Fouché, Napoleon's chief of police in Paris, had had enough. Concerned at the increasingly strange reports that he was receiving from Batelier, showing how the affair was growing out of control, he issued a warrant for the arrest of Jean-Marie Hervagault. The police tracked down the "king" one evening dining in style with his following. The guests were shocked, but "Louis XVII" remained calmly dignified and had the officers wait while he ordered his courtiers to fetch his coat, pack his clothes and find his spectacles. Prominent members of the local community could be seen weeping, bowing and kissing his hand. In all the excitement and disarray eventually the arrest was made, but as the police marched the "tailor's son" through the town, his supporters followed in stately procession, bearing all the glittering paraphernalia of the court. The banquet, with tables and chairs for everyone, continued in prison and the young "king," by the light of the candles in the silver candelebra, once more held court. The police were baffled by this apparent "epidemic of gullibility" and in frustration they arrested some of the faithful courtiers for complicity. The prefect of police even debated whether all these "eccentric persons" should be "sent to a lunatic asylum."

It took five months for the prosecution to bring Hervagault's case to trial in February 1802. The prosecutors had some difficulty in laying a charge on him—after all, none of his supporters had complained about him. In his defense, it was argued that his followers had been informed that he was a "tailor's son" but nonetheless chose to treat him with great honor and

[181]

dignity. The citizens of Vitry and Châlons were perfectly at liberty to treat a tailor's son in this way: there was no law against it. The judge did not agree. With apparent pressure from Paris, the court decided that Jean-Marie Hervagault should be severely punished. The prosecution maintained he had deliberately misled people into giving money and other gifts under false pretenses. He was sentenced to four years' imprisonment.

There was uproar. There was no previous case of a person being imprisoned for swindling when there was not one complaint against him! Quite the reverse. The swindled persons begged for permission to bring him more gifts; a collection was immediately organized on his behalf. The situation became so inflamed that some historians have argued that the authorities even considered exploiting Jean-Marie Hervagault's claims for their political advantage. According to Alphonse de Beauchamp, author of *Histoire des deux faux Dauphins* in 1818, Fouché, the chief of police in Paris, recommended to Napoleon that he should formally recognize the prisoner as the son of Louis XVI, but then force him to renounce his right to the throne as a condition of his release; Napoleon is said to have rejected the plan. Whatever the veracity of this unlikely claim, there is little doubt that the authorities took no chances. The prisoner soon found himself moved well away from his supporters to the grim Paris prison of Bicêtre. In time, interest in the pretender languishing in jail declined as all eyes in France were focused on Napoleon's meteoric rise.

Appointed consul for life in 1802 and crowned emperor in 1804, Napoleon I provided the dynamic stable leadership that France had lacked as he put an end to the persecutions, reformed local and national government, revitalized France's education system, and established the Code Napoleon which standardized civil law throughout the country. Abroad, despite his naval defeat at Cape Trafalgar in 1805 by the English under Nelson, the French Revolutionary Army forced its way across Europe in a dazzling series of military campaigns. In 1805, Napoleon defeated the Austrians and Russians at Austerlitz; the following year the Prussians at Jena, then the Russians at Friedland—at every turn forcing the great Continental powers to make peace on his terms. By 1810, Napoleon was effectively the emperor of Europe whose territory extended from the Atlantic Ocean to Rome and northern Germany to the Pyrenees. Paris, the center of this vital new empire, was soon to be suitably arrayed to impress with statues, columns and triumphal arches.

It is hardly surprising that, with the success of the empire, the "King of Vitry" on his release was unable to repeat his earlier recognition. Now older, and in declining health, he was less able to pass himself off as the charming prince. The authorities were on his trail and moved him on whenever he became troublesome; local people seemed disinclined to accept his story; even his "father" the tailor seemed to have lost interest in his errant "son." Apart from a brief spell in the army, he survived by a life of petty crime and was repeatedly in prison. By early May 1812, he was back at Bicêtre and became gravely ill. The prison chaplain implored the dying man to confess all and renounce his claim to be Louis XVII. Unrepentant, the tailor's son remained true to his story and insisted to the priest that he was indeed the son of Louis XVI. On May 6, 1812, he died and was buried in a common grave. In the list of deaths in the jail book he is identified simply as "Jean-Marie Hervagault, aged thirty, son of . . . and of . . ." The rest of the details are left blank.

By 1812, however, Napoleon's campaign was faltering. He embarked on an invasion of Russia where the country's terrible winter soon took its toll. Napoleon's Grande Armée was beaten back by the flames of Moscow or swallowed up in snow; those who could, retreated to Paris. Meanwhile the Russians formed an alliance with the Prussians against France; the Austrians soon joined them. The Duke of Wellington moved north through the Pyrenees to meet the Allies. By January 1814, France was under attack from all directions.

As Napoleon's grip on political power ebbed away, the prospect that the Bourbon monarchy would be restored in France resurfaced. Rumors about the fate of the lost dauphin during the revolution started up yet again, but the context of all these claims had changed dramatically. Reports about the fate of Louis XVII could no longer be simply dismissed as fanciful tales of little consequence.

"Dauphins" began to surface in several provinces in France; the young prince was sited in Brittany, Normandy, the Auvergne and Alsace. Although the tailor's son remained the most famous during the Empire, there were others, such as the "boy with tattoos," one of many unidentifiable young men who emerged with the mark of the pope—in this case the Bourbon *fleur-de-lys*, on his leg. There were also one or two "dauphins" in the army such as "Louis dauphin" whose ancestry turned out to be far from illustrious when his father, a Parisian clockmaker, was traced. While some of these pretenders were utterly bizarre, and they vanished almost as soon as they made their claim, others successfully recruited many followers. These reports now had potentially serious political ramifications. If someone could prove himself to be Louis XVII, he should, by rights, take the place of Provence as the prospective king of France.

The pretenders' claims were made all the more compelling by testimony from Marie-Jeanne Simon, the wife of Simon, the shoemaker, who had helped her husband as "tutor" to the royal prince. Not long after the death of her husband on the scaffold she had been admitted to the Hôpital des Incurables, in Paris. Years were to elapse before she could bring herself to speak of the orphan of the Temple and the events of the Terror to her carers, the Sisters of St.-Vincent-de-Paul. However, one day, the elderly widow unburdened herself of a terrible secret, confessing for the first time the true story of "her little prince."

According to Madame Simon, on January 19, 1794, the last day the Simons worked at the Temple, she and her husband had helped Louis-Charles to escape. She claimed members of the prison staff had smuggled into the Great Tower "a wickerwork hamper with a double bottom, a wooden horse and several toys" for Louis-Charles. Hidden in the wooden horse was a substitute child of the same age as the dauphin. The prince himself was wrapped "in dirty linen and loaded onto a cart with the hamper." As they left, the guards demanded to see the contents but "Simon flew into a rage and declared it was his own linen and the guards let him pass." Madame Simon said she had no idea where the dauphin was taken but was "convinced that he was living and would one day wear the crown." Once she had given away her secret, the old woman repeated it frequently, and her startling revelations leaked out. It was difficult to dismiss the evidence of a firsthand witness with an authentic-sounding story.

The continued uncertainty over her brother was a terrible burden to Marie-Thérèse. As the Duchesse d'Angoulême, she had followed her uncle, loyally enduring years of exile in Russia and then Poland. An engraving of her leaving Russia, walking with her uncle through a snowstorm, helped to confirm her status as a living legend, "a French Antigone." Napoleon ordered all copies to be banned. Later she returned to Russia, but in 1807, with Napoleon's army less than two hundred miles away, they were forced to flee the continent to seek safety in England.

In time, the exiles settled at Hartwell House, near Aylesbury, Buckinghamshire, where the years passed uneventfully. They heard of Napoleon's endless exploits and his divorce from his wife, Joséphine. In 1810, le Corse— as they referred to him disparagingly—married into the distinguished Habsburg family, to Marie-Thérèse's own cousin, Marie-Louise, the young daughter of Francis II of Austria. For Marie-Thérèse it was an appalling irony—in view of the fate of her own mother—that another Austrian archduchess should made to seal a political alliance as consort of the ruler of France. Later that year they heard of the brutal murder of Marie-Antoinette's devoted friend, Count Fersen, by protesters in Stockholm in June—the sort of news that would remind Marie-Thérèse that life could be dangerous and painful.

In all her years of exile, "the life of the Temple was there like a background" and the Duchesse d'Angoulême lived as though always on guard, "amid the habit of pain." As the disappointment of her marriage removed all last hopes of happiness, she seemed to others to have "a stiffness and apparent hardness of character." Often she would appear in public "with a redness about the eyes," as though she had been crying for hours. This continued grieving took its toll. "In her twenty-year-old freshness she was gifted with a beauty of which she afterward lost every trace," observed one courtier, the Baron de Maricourt. Stoic endurance and rigid self-control had become such a habit that only occasionally, in her privacy with close friends, "would she let herself go" and adjust to a little gaiety. In those rare moments, "a certain pleasantry did not frighten her."

Just as she was beginning to find some peace of mind she began to receive disturbing letters—from her brother: "It is the companion of your misfortunes, my sister, who writes to you," he began. "You inhabit the abode of honors and veneration; your brother laments in the place destined for crime, destitute of everything and without any other consolation than that which comes from God." It was not long before she would learn from her most trusted advisors that Louis-Charles was in fact still alive, and desperate to see her.

Meanwhile, the heart stolen from the orphan of the Temple was still hidden in Dr. Philippe-Jean Pellatan's house in the Rue de Touraine in Paris. Since the spirit vinegar had evaporated, the relic had become hard and solid, like a small, dark rock. The doctor removed it from his medical cabinet and placed it in a drawer in his desk. "Constantly opening my drawer, I went scarcely a day without seeing the heart, which I hadn't even wrapped for fear of making it appear suspicious," he recorded in a statement years later. However, he found himself unable to keep his strange possession completely secret. "I was imprudent enough to show the heart—along with the other specimens contained in my drawer—to Mr. Tillos, my special pupil and resident secretary."

One day, to his alarm, when he opened the drawer of his desk, he suddenly realized the heart was missing. Pellatan searched everywhere, without success. To his great dismay, it became evident that the child's heart had been stolen. Faced with the growing likelihood that the monarchy might be restored in France, Pellatan began to have some qualms about what he had done and felt he should have taken greater care of the heart. Given the growing number of pretenders, he considered it his duty, if the monarchy was restored, to return the relic to the royal family as a memorial to the dead prince.

The doctor was certain that one of his students had stolen the heart. He strongly suspected Jean-Henri Tillos but could prove nothing. The child's heart had vanished.

Chapter Eight

RETURN OF THE LILIES

If the pretended dauphin should be the true one, his claims should not prevail; reasons of State prescribe silence, and it is time to cover with an eternal veil an intrigue in which unappeased factions find such dangerous sustenance.

—ARCHIVES, MINISTRY OF POLICE, 1817

After years of revolution and war, France now turned to the monarchy it had swept aside over twenty years ago. On Holy Thursday, March 25, 1814, at Hartwell in England, Mass for the royal family was interrupted by news that a carriage, festooned with white cockades and white banners, was winding its way up the drive. Tears and laughter were mixed together in total delight as Provence and the Duchesse d'Angoulême greeted the deputies from Bordeaux who came to recognize their prospective king, and brought news of the swiftly changing political scene in France. Over the next two weeks, the allied troops entered Paris, Napoleon was forced to abdicate to the island of Elba near Corsica, and Provence was formally proclaimed the king of France as Louis XVIII.

Following twenty long years of dreary exile, the emotional journey back home to Paris for the royal family was nothing short of extraordinary. As they entered London and made their way down the length of Hyde Park, Park Lane and Piccadilly, the streets were crammed with exuberant crowds, enthusiastically cheering them on and crying out that all was now well.

Previously on the fringes of society, they suddenly found themselves fêted at the very heart of it in magnificent celebrations led by the prince regent in the "great galleries of Carlton House which shone with gilding and lights." Eventually they set sail from Dover on the *Royal Sovereign* and as they approached Calais, Louis XVIII and the Duchesse d'Angoulême could see an immense crowd, "the shouts, exultation, the enthusiasm of the people on the pier at first overcame them and tears flowed down their cheeks." Finally, they set foot on French soil and, in all the delirious excitement, the royal carriage was unhorsed and pulled triumphantly though the streets by hand, with people running alongside, crying with joy.

They entered Paris through the Porte Saint-Denis on May 3, 1814, in an open carriage drawn by eight white horses to deafening cheers of *"Vive le Roi."* "The crowd was very great, and most of the windows were decorated with white flags," recalled one eyewitness, the Comtesse de Boigne. People had much sympathy for Marie-Thérèse, who had become a symbol of all the suffering of France. "For everyone, the Duchesse d'Angoulême was *the* orphan of the Temple." The last time she had been seen in public in Paris was in 1793 with her father, mother and brother as they were taken through jeering crowds to the prison tower, from which all her family were to leave for the scaffold or the grave. Whether such memories overwhelmed her, or whether it was just not in her nature, Marie-Thérèse disappointed many who came to see her that day, by her unsmiling, sad face and tense manner, partially concealed behind her open parasol. "I must own that the people in the open carriage did not correspond to my hopes," continued the Comtesse de Boigne, a view that became widely held.

While Marie-Thérèse was indeed unresponsive and ill at ease as she reentered Paris, everywhere along the cheering route her eyes met reminders of a previous journey with her parents when violence and hatred could hardly keep their hands off her. On reaching Notre Dame, she lost her composure completely and collapsed on her prayer stool, "face in hands, shaking with sobs." Later as they passed the *Conciergerie*—with its inevitable association with the last days of her mother—and approached the Chateau of the Tuileries, she almost fainted. It was hard for her not to feel that if there was any justice at all, it should have been her charming young brother at her side, instead of ghostly memories of his unloved fate.

Yet many did want to make peace with the haunting recollection of the revolution and its aftermath. On May 14, a Requiem Mass was sung in Paris churches for Louis XVII, his mother, father and aunt. At Notre Dame, the Abbé Legris-Duval captured the royalist sentiment when he paid homage to the *Enfant-Roi:* "This mortal angel . . . we are weeping for you, sweet offspring of our kings, who knew only the bitterness and pains of life." On June 8, the anniversary of his death, funeral ceremonies were held across France in memory of "the little king and martyr." To complete the honoring of his brother's family, Louis XVIII gave orders for the bodies of Louis XVI and Marie-Antoinette to be exhumed from their common graves in the Madeleine cemetery and officially reburied in the royal crypt at Saint-Denis.

However, although bodies that were thought to be those of Louis XVI and Marie-Antoinette were found, it proved much harder to locate Louis-Charles. There were no official records to show the exact position of his grave at the Sainte Marguerite cemetery. Louis XVIII was concerned that unless his body was found and the fate of Louis XVII resolved beyond all reasonable doubt, speculation that the boy king was still alive would inevitably continue. As he set about the enormous task of establishing a parliamentary monarchy after years of military despotism, creating order in a country that was impoverished by revolution and war, and even restoring Versailles, Louis *"Le Désiré"* still had enemies who could potentially exploit the uncertainty about his nephew to undermine his position. Consequently, in January 1815, Louis XVIII instructed his minister of the interior the Comte de Vaublanc, to conduct a full inquiry into the fate of Louis XVII.

From the outset, the inquiry was severely hampered by the secrecy surrounding the detention of the boy in the Temple prison and the lack of documentary evidence. To add to the difficulties, years had elapsed since Louis-Charles had been incarcerated, and many of those who had been present in the Tower between 1793 and 1795 had since died. Louis-Charles's death certificate—signed in 1795 by those on duty at the Temple—was available, but to those who believed that the real prince had been spirited out of the Temple this proved nothing.

Some witnesses, however, did come forward. The staff at Sainte-Marguerite cemetery confirmed that the gravedigger himself was a man called Pierre Bertrancourt. Although Bertrancourt had died in 1809, his widow, Gabrielle Bertrancourt, was still alive. In January 1815, she was granted an audience with Louis XVIII to reveal anything she might know about his nephew's burial.

In her intriguing testimony, Gabrielle Bertrancourt explained that before her husband had died, he had confessed to her that he had secretly moved the prince's coffin. Initially, Louis-Charles had been buried in a common pit in the Sainte-Marguerite cemetery. However, under cover of darkness, on the third night when there were no sentries, Betrancourt had crept back, reopened the common pit and found the child's coffin, which he had distinguished with chalk. To be completely sure, he had even prized opened one of the planks and glimpsed the boy's head, now with growing signs of putrefaction, the scalp shaven and showing gruesome signs of the surgeon's work. Carefully, he removed the coffin and carried it some distance before reburying it partly under the wall of the church on the left side of the chapel. According to his wife, he hoped to benefit if ever a search was made for the royal child. "One day you will receive something handsome and be happy," he told her a few hours before he died. "When they find the dauphin again, they will reward you for me!" Bertrancourt had also confided his remarkable secret to his close friend, Découflet.

Meanwhile, not waiting for the results of the official inquiry, the Duchesse d'Angoulême took matters into her own hands. She had, by now, heard of the story of the shoemaker's widow, Marie-Jeanne Simon. At the Hôpital des Incurables, the Lady Superior of the Community had tried to verify Madame Simon's account. She had interviewed four of the nuns who saw Madame Simon on an almost daily basis: Sister Lucie Jonnis, Sister Euphrasie Benoit, Sister Catherine Mauliot, and Sister Marianne Scribes. The Lady Superior noted that in all details their versions were identical; evidently Madame Simon was consistent from day to day. Furthermore, the nuns confirmed that Madame Simon was far from infirm: "She was sincere, possessed good sense and a good heart. She was clean and had never been seen drunk." Perhaps most convincing of all, "nobody could have influenced her . . . since she never saw anybody; yet she had never erred or varied in her statements." Madame Simon's testimony troubled the duchesse d'Angoulême. The old woman's story matched her own suspicions formed at the time, while captive in the room above her brother, and a small seed of doubt now began to grow. She was only too aware that the Simons had had continuous contact with Louis-Charles, until their departure from the Temple in January 1794. Around this time, she herself had heard a great deal of noise and had conjectured that her brother must be leaving the Temple. She had even seen packages and linen baskets being removed— could one of these be the very same linen basket in which Madame Simon claimed her brother had escaped? She knew only too well that after the departure of the Simons, she no longer heard her brother singing or crying on the floor below.

On Tuesday, December 13, 1814, as part of her tour of hospitals and charities, the Duchesse d'Angoulême made a point of visiting the Hôpital des Incurables. Records show that she was accompanied by two others, the Comte de Pastoret and Vicomte de Montmorency. If she was hoping to see Madame Simon, she was to be disappointed. To avoid causing her any distress, orders were given at the hospital that Madame Simon was to be locked up for the duration of the duchess's visit. Madame Simon was furious. "I had a great secret to tell her," she cried. It seems likely that the Duchesse d'Angoulême was also disappointed. According to an anecdote reported by the historian Georges Lenôtre, she was determined to meet Madame Simon and took the compromising step of returning once more to the hospital.

She was clearly anxious not to start rumors flying or to appear to give weight to Madame Simon's testimony merely by her presence, for she dressed incognito. She was wearing simple clothes and was accompanied by a lady of honor and a friend, the Comte de Montmaur, as they walked through the hospital searching for "Mère Simon." The old woman, dressed in the regulation clothes of a skirt of grey duffel with a black tulle cap, was only too keen to relate her story of his escape in full. She went on to tantalize the princess, adding that "her Charles" had returned to see her in 1802. When pressed about how she could recognize him after so many years, she added, "Well, I recognize you quite well, not withstanding your disguise, Madame Marie-Thérèse." The Duchesse d'Angoulême was so distressed—both at the story, and, perhaps, at being recognized—that she hurried away immediately.

At around the same time, Jean-Baptiste Harmand, who twenty years previously had been asked by the Committee for General Security to investigate the dauphin's health, wrote a report of his findings for Louis XVIII's inquiry into his nephew. Harmand had found in February 1795 that the sickly child in the Tower would not speak—no matter what tantalizing inducement was offered. At the time, he had assumed that the boy's silence might be the result of the trauma that he had already endured in prison. However, when his account became more widely known in 1815, others put a different interpretation on the boy's silence. For many, this appeared to confirm Madame Simon's version that the real Louis-Charles had already been smuggled out of the Temple. The impostor was surely a mute boy deliberately chosen so that he could not reveal his true identity. The reason why the boy did not answer any of Harmand's questions was quite simple: the substitute was deaf and dumb.

There was little chance to pursue these lines of inquiry before the investigation was brought to an abrupt halt. In February 1815, Napoleon set sail from his exile in Elba with a few hundred men and prepared to march on Paris. The Duchesse d'Angoulême was in Bordeaux when she heard the news and immediately set about organizing resistance, striving to "electrify the soldiers" as she went through the barracks; to no avail. Louis XVIII was forced into an ignominious flight from Paris as Napoleon swept to power yet again on a tide of popular enthusiasm. On March 20, 1815, the newspaper *Moniteur* made a short and discreet announcement: "The king and the princes left in the night. H. M. the emperor arrived this evening at eight o'clock in his palace of the Tuileries, at the head of the same troops which had been sent to block his route this morning."

As the news reached foreign governments, the allies would not tolerate the reinstatement of the emperor and united against France. British, Dutch, Belgian and Hanoverian troops under the Duke of Wellington met the French near the village of Waterloo in Belgium. Joined during the battle by the Prussians, Wellington staged an outstanding victory on June 18, 1815. It was Napoleon's final defeat, ending in the rout of his Grand Army and his second abdication. Taking no chances, this time the allies sent the unsuspecting former emperor to the remote, rocky island of St. Helena in the South Atlantic. On July 8, as Louis XVIII reentered Paris, he was greeted even more enthusiastically than the previous year.

Once again he had to restore order and reestablish his government, and consequently, nearly a year elapsed before he was able to resume his inquiries into the fate of his nephew. It was February 21, 1816, when his minister of the interior, the Comte de Vaublanc, reopened his files on Louis XVII and two police commissaries, Messieurs Petit and Simon, were appointed to find his body. They already knew of two burial sites: in a common grave at Sainte-Marguerite according to the official record or, if the gravedigger's wife was to be believed, near the chapel wall. To try to clarify the matter, Petit and Simon tracked down the very man who had been in charge of the dauphin's funeral arrangements: Étienne Voisin.

At seventy-five, Voisin was now an inmate of the Hospice de Bicêtre, and apparently had become an ardent royalist. With great emotion as he recalled the boy's burial, he contradicted the evidence of the gravedigger's widow and claimed that he himself had dug the grave. According to Voisin, "The grave was at least six feet deep and the coffin about five feet long; the young king was tall for his age." The frail old man spoke tearfully with such conviction that a carriage was duly arranged and he returned with Petit and Simon to the cemetery. He was able to identify the very space of ground, between the church and the common pit, below which the young king would be found. The baffled investigators now faced three possible burial sites at Sainte-Marguerite for the orphan of the Temple.

It was not long, however, before other witnesses came forward who confirmed the testimony of the gravedigger's wife. It seemed that the gravedigger, Bertrancourt, had unburdened his secret to the parish priest at Sainte-Marguerite, one Abbé Dubois, and to his good friend, Découflet, who was now a beadle in another parish. Découflet could vividly remember a day in 1802 when he had been with Bertrancourt in the cemetery, digging a grave close to the church wall. Their excavations had revealed a large stone in the foundations, which was marked with a cross. "You see this place?" Bertrancourt had said to his friend. "One day there will be a monument here, for beneath lies the coffin of the dauphin!"

In spite of Voisin's contradictory evidence, the police commissaries Petit and Simon wrote up their conclusions for the minister of police in March 1816, recommending that they should start excavations "in the place pointed out by Decouflet and the widow Bertrancourt." An announcement was made in the local press and a date was duly set for the exhumation on June 12, the anniversary of Louis-Charles's alleged burial.

On that day, a large crowd gathered at the cemetery to witness the opening of the grave, led by a number of clergy with incense and candles. They made a solemn gathering, some holding crucifixes, others with prayer books to bless the child. "We were all there at the appointed hour, with alb, and stole and surplice, and the cross at our head, waiting for the representative of the minister of police who should have presided over the exhumation," recalled Abbot Raynaud, who worked at the parish of Sainte-Marguerite. "He never came. After several hours of waiting we received a message that the exhumation had been postponed." Eventually, the police arrived and told them to disperse. There would be no exhumation.

Unknown to the crowd, there had been an unexpected last-minute testimony. Louis Antoine Charpentier, head gardener of the Luxembourg Palace, hearing that there was to be an exhumation, went to the police on the June 11 with a strange story that was to cast doubt on all their evidence. Charpentier claimed that five days after Louis-Charles's alleged death in 1795, revolutionary officials from the Luxembourg section had approached him with a most unusual request. He was to return "that same night at ten o'clock and bring two of my workmen with me, with a pick axe and shovel." When it was dark, they were taken by hackney coach to the end of the Rue du Jardin des Plantes. Without any explanation, they were led to the cemetery of Clamart and ordered to dig a grave a few paces from the main gate. "When we had reached a depth of about six or eight feet, we heard the sound of a carriage approaching," recalled Charpentier. Three members of the revolutionary committee unloaded a small coffin and lowered it into the grave. Charpentier and his men had to refill the grave and stamp down the earth "with all our might"—evidently there was to be no trace of the child's burial. Charpentier understood that the coffin they had buried had been secretly removed from the Sainte-Marguerite cemetery. They were sworn to secrecy and his assistants were given ten francs each. He too was promised a reward, but he did not claim it when he heard one of the officials say with a laugh, "Little Capet will have to go a long way to find his family again!"

In the light of this conflicting testimony, the authorities were faced with a dilemma. They now had four possible burial sites: the common grave, by the chapel wall, the site indicated by Voisin, or some new location in the cemetery of Clamart. If the exhumation revealed an empty grave or another person's body, this was bound to fuel fresh rumors about the fate of Louis XVII. Yet news that the exhumation had been cancelled at the last minute served to kindle the very kind of speculation that the authorities had been determined to suppress. It was said that Louis XVIII had suddenly discovered that the grave was empty and an exhumation would be an embarrassment to the government.

In an attempt to try to draw a line under the affair, the king decided that at the very least there should be a Requiem Mass at Saint-Denis for the soul of his nephew. Arrangements were under way when the king received unwelcome news from the clergy of Saint-Denis. A Requiem Mass could be held in the Basilica *only* for royalty who were buried in the vaults below. With no body, there could be no Mass.

Louis XVIII and his minister of the interior were becoming increasingly frustrated. Far from resolving the matter as they had hoped, their investigation had merely served to highlight a whole series of contradictions and unanswered questions lending weight to the view that Louis XVII was still alive. The king's advisors recommended that the inquiry should be stopped as quickly as possible. They argued, with some reason, that it was, at best, leading nowhere, but at worst could potentially raise serious doubts of the legitimacy of the current king and lead to a political and constitutional crisis. In the period immediately after the Restoration, the monarchy still had many enemies; anything that might undermine it could be disastrous. Quite suddenly, an order was given to bring the inquiry to an end. The authorities closed rank around the official line: Louis XVII was dead and he had died in the Temple prison on June 8, 1795.

However, questions about the fate of Louis XVII simply would not die down. There were still obvious gaps in the official report and important witnesses had not been called—such as the boy's guardians, Lasne and Gomin, the Commissioner Damont, or Dr. Pellatan himself. All these men were alive, so why did they not give evidence? Why was there no Mass in Saint-Denis? Above all, where was Louis-Charles's body? The authorities were forced to concede that the precise spot where he had been buried was still a mystery. And without a body, there was no proof that Louis XVII was really dead. People increasingly suspected a cover-up. A possible motive for this seemed only too clear. The current king, and all those who depended for their position on his patronage and favor, had too much to lose if the truth came out.

Soon after the battle of Waterloo, in September 1815, a distinctly scruffy gentleman of about thirty years of age disembarked at Saint-Malo claiming to have travelled from New Orleans. His interesting face, which had a certain rugged charm, was heavily scarred and had missing teeth, suggesting an eventful life, but not one in which refinement and education had figured heavily. In spite of this, and other small misfortunes such as no luggage, no shoes, no money, he was more than redeemed by a spirit of enterprise and confidence that made small troubles disappear. He made friends easily and soon fell in love with a local widow, named Phélippeaux; but if he thought that he had landed on his feet, he was mistaken.

One day he was arrested in Saint-Malo for drunkenness and vagrancy and, as he had no passport or papers to identify himself, the police detained him. When he was brought before a magistrate he declared, casually, that he had burnt his passport. Faced with the growing hostility of officials, he eventually revealed that he was a baker: "Charles de Navarre of New Orleans." The magistrate was not impressed. The coarse vagrant before him had no papers to prove this and he was pressed to explain why. Yet still he could give no proper account of himself. The magistrate grew irritable and demanded a full answer.

Changing his tone, the stranger declared that he was about to make an extremely important announcement. He had the court's full attention as he asked everyone to remain calm until he had finished his statement. There were very good reasons why he had no papers, he said, imploring them to understand his very delicate situation: he was none other than the son of Louis XVI and Marie-Antoinette.

In a generous gesture, he went on to emphasize that he would renounce his claim to the throne as long as his beloved uncle, Louis XVIII, was alive; he wished to "serve him faithfully," and wanted nothing more than recognition. The bemused magistrate, convinced the man was nothing more than a drunken tramp making a fool out of him, began to express his doubts in no uncertain terms. At this point, "Louis-Charles" flew into a rage. In a forceful scene, he insisted that he should be taken to the Palace of the Tuileries in Paris where the truth of his claim would be obvious. The magistrate was dumbfounded. He ordered that the man should be held in prison, pending further investigations.

News of the extraordinary proceedings in the Breton courtroom spread quickly, and, within days, crowds gathered outside the prison clamoring for his release. Brittany was suddenly on fire with the news that the dauphin had indeed returned. For many, the timing of "Louis XVII's" return seemed right and entirely appropriate. Napoleon had just been defeated and the monarchy had only recently been restored. Royalists who were convinced that Louis had escaped from the Temple prison were elated that the "lost dauphin" had finally been found. His agony could now be put to an end and France would prostrate itself before him. The romance and poignancy of the story proved utterly irresistible. "Charles de Navarre" was soon to find that his supporters grew almost overnight from a handful of people in Saint-Malo to a well-organized movement across France.

From prison, "Louis-Charles" seized his moment to correspond with the great and the good. Since he himself was illiterate, he appointed secretaries from his supporters in prison to draft the letters for him, starting with the king of France. "Your Majesty, I beg to inform you that the dauphin, son of Louis XVI, is imprisoned in Saint-Malo and begs your Majesty to enable him to reach you. . . . I have had the honor to write to you fourteen times without having received any reply. . . . If you bring me before you, you will see whether I am deceiving you, and thenceforth I abandon myself to the severity of the law." This letter, sent in December 1815, was signed, "Daufin Bourbon." He also wrote to his "sister," Marie-Thérèse, signing himself as "her brother, the king." The governor of Guernsey was soon to receive a letter urging him "to bring this matter to the notice of the king of England." Concerned at developments, the police thought it best to move him on. "Louis-Charles" was transferred first to Rennes and then, in January 1816, to the prison workhouse at Rouen in Normandy.

Despite the authorities' increasingly desperate attempts to deny that their prisoner was Louis XVII, he became even more widely acknowledged than Hervagault. The success of the "Daufin Bourbon" was all the more extraordinary when so much about him lacked credibility. Unlike Hervagault's polished charm and aristocratic demeanor, this man was definitely from the lower orders and usually the worse for drink, encouraged by the prison keeper, Libois, who made money from sales of alcohol to visitors coming to see the famous prisoner. Yet among his increasingly large following, this did not appear to undermine his claims to be the son of Louis XVI and Marie-Antoinette—quite the contrary. There was a simple explanation. His tutor, Simon, had deliberately trained Louis-Charles as a boy to behave in this way, swearing and drinking to excess like a good *sans-culotte*. The process of erasing any last vestiges of royalty had been completed in America, where he had lived among cutthroats and beggars.

The hysteria surrounding the Hervagault case, over fifteen years before, soon repeated itself on an even larger scale. Fine gifts, clothes, linens and money made their way to his prison cell and the once scruffy vagrant began to appear suitably royal. "Courtiers" were appointed and the obsequious bowing, scraping and kissing of hands started up all over again in the prison setting.

The claims of the famous prisoner in Rouen inevitably gained credence from the testimony of Marie-Jeanne Simon in the Hôpital des Incurables. The widow's insistence that she had helped her prince to escape from the Tower in a laundry basket was a key piece of evidence for those who believed that Louis-Charles was still alive. Sceptics suggested that she had deliberately rewritten history to avoid the shame of the Simons' terrible treatment of the young prince; this she vehemently denied. Although now old and frail, she was an entirely credible witness and her account could not be readily dismissed. People began to ask, why not take the old widow to Rouen to identify the prisoner and settle the matter once and for all? Consequently, on November 16, 1816, the police took the matter in hand.

Madame Simon was taken by carriage to the ministry of police. She found herself in such a large and lavishly furnished room that she imagined she was in the Tuileries Palace. According to a report in the National Archives, as before, she embarked on her account of Louis-Charles's escape in a dirty linen basket. However, when the police interrogated her, pressing her on details of her story, she felt threatened and became frightened. How could she be spreading so subversive a tale, asked the police, completely at odds with the official account, "the whole circumstances of which had been so minutely ascertained?" Under pressure, she became flustered and eventually did concede in her signed declaration that she had not actually *seen* the dauphin being placed in a laundry basket and removed from the Temple with her own eyes. Nonetheless, "her conviction [that the dauphin did not die in the Tower] was so innate that nothing could dissuade her of it." She also claimed that the dauphin had visited her some twelve years ago and she had recognized him immediately by his mannerisms and features. Madame Simon was prepared to go to Rouen to identify the prisoner. The police decided that this could be too risky.

When the minister for police heard of this he concluded, somewhat conveniently, that Madame Simon was mad. He wanted to have her certified; after all, who would listen to the ramblings of an old woman in a lunatic asylum? His colleagues advised against this. The nuns who were caring for Madame Simon had consistently maintained that she was of sound mind and might contest any move to certify her. Whatever transpired that day in the police office, Madame Simon became terrified to relate her story of the little prince. "My life is at stake," she told the sisters. They noticed that she now seemed distressed and thought that the police "had sought to intimidate her." Some believed that she was silenced, under threat of the "severest punishment."

All this was an insoluble puzzle to Marie-Thérèse, who was shocked by the claims that her "brother" had appeared in Saint-Malo, and she followed the prisoner's case with interest. After the second restoration, the failure of her uncle's inquiry to determine the exact fate of her brother had almost certainly helped to cast doubt on her conviction that he was really dead. She had always been aware that she had no grounds to place any particular trust in the statements by the revolutionary government in 1795 about Louis-Charles's death. In her eyes, they had murdered her father and mother. Why should she believe their account of what had happened to her brother?

The endless question of her brother's fate had become a backdrop to her life. Marie-Thérèse had always been able to keep her emotions under control and was not inclined to reach overhasty conclusions. Nonetheless, the evidence suggests that she had agonizing doubts over this continuing problem. Worse still, she was obliged to hide these nagging uncertainties, especially from her uncle, who had specifically closed the matter and called an end to the inquiry. Could this new claimant really be her brother? It was impossible to go to Rouen to see the prisoner without appearing to mistrust her uncle, and add still more credibility to the prisoner's claims. Yet if it *was* her brother languishing in jail, she might be cruelly spurning him at the very time he needed her support. Finally, on the advice of her courtiers, she refused to meet the prisoner in Rouen. Some now began openly to condemn Marie-Thérèse for having "disowned her own brother who she knew was living." Rather cruelly, this earned her the name among his royalist supporters as "Duchess Cain."

However, "Duchess Cain" did send her trusted friend the Marquis de Montmaur to meet discreetly with the prisoner in Rouen. The marquis had accompanied Marie-Thérèse when she had heard Madame Simon's testimony and was only too aware of her concerns. He agreed to find out what he could about the prisoner. According to testimony from the concierge, Libois, on March 15, 1817, "two gentlemen in plain clothes and without decorations" asked if they could visit the "supposed Dauphin of France," on behalf of the Duchesse d'Angoulême. He saw from their passports that one was the Comte de Montmaur, the other his friend the Duc de Medini. Libois took them to the prisoner's room. Charles de Navarre immediately asked if they had a letter from his "sister." To his evident disappointment, the gentlemen merely produced the letter he had sent her as proof of their authority. Libois brought a bottle of Madeira, and the count and his friend talked to the prisoner for an hour and a half. Later that day, the gentlemen returned for a further three hours. According to Libois, at some stage he overheard the Comte de Montmaur reveal that the Duchesse d'Angoulême had a "secret presentiment of her brother's existence." Indeed, the count himself apparently did not dismiss the prisoner's claims, for when he reported back to Marie-Thérèse in Paris, she continued to have anxieties over the prisoner's identity and began to formulate a secret plan for taking her own inquiries a stage further.

Needless to say, news of such important visitors soon spread among the prisoner's followers and appeared to lend credence to his case. In spite of repeated attempts by the authorities to scotch the idea that the man in prison in Rouen was Louis XVII, soon the whole country was talking about the dauphin. There were even rumors of dethroning the usurper Louis XVIII. To add still more weight to his claims, the prisoner allegedly received another eminent and unexpected visitor. It was none other than his former governess: the Duchesse de Tourzel.

The Duchesse de Tourzel had not seen Louis-Charles for over twenty years. The last occasion was on the night of August 19, 1792, when she had left her affectionate seven-year-old charge as she and the Princesse de Lamballe were ordered to leave the Tower. The duchess had deep feelings of loyalty toward the royal family and had never ceased to serve their interests during the trauma of the revolution. She had been present at key moments: their eviction from Versailles, the Tuileries, and their incarceration in the Tower. She and her daughter had even risked death for them, and the king and Marie-Antoinette had always held her in high regard. However, there in the cell in Rouen in March 1817, according to Libois and another witness, Branzon, something extraordinary happened.

As the Duchesse de Tourzel spoke with the prisoner she became more and more convinced that he was indeed Louis-Charles. She spent some time with him and when Libois came into the room he found her in tears, embracing the prisoner. The duchess was apparently convinced that in the features of this man she could see the young boy she had nurtured at Versailles and the Tuileries. For the prisoner, this was a memorable experience. He had apparently been identified by his own former governess as Louis XVII, the legitimate king of France.

Libois was making money as visitors flocked from all over France to have an audience with the "supposed Dauphin" and it was in his interests to build up the prisoner's status. With no other evidence it is difficult to confirm the veracity of his story, and certainly the whole scene seems entirely out of character for the restrained and cautious Duchesse de Tourzel. Nonetheless, soon after this improbable occurrence, documents in the National Archives do reveal that Marie-Thérèse was still worried about the true identity of the prisoner and tried, yet again, to resolve the matter. This time she enlisted the help of her first valet de chambre, the Chevalier de Turgy. It was Turgy who had once served as a waiter for the royal family and had loyally followed Marie-Thérèse in many of her exiles. She advised Turgy of a specific list of questions for the prisoner in Rouen about their life in the Tower. Only her true brother could possibly know the right answers to all of them:

1. What happened on January 21st when the firing of cannon was heard? What did your aunt say then and what did they do for you out of the ordinary?
2. Where did you gather together my correspondence? In what room?
3. What did you do to me on New Year's Day and how, in what room?

There were seven very specific questions in all. Turgy dispatched the correspondence and Marie-Thérèse waited eagerly for a reply. Unknown to her, the letter was intercepted and classified by the police. This lends weight to the view that Louis XVIII's government was keen to suppress any inquiries that could add to the status of the prisoner, or lead to his identification as Louis XVII.

Meanwhile, the "dauphin" was busy forming his own inimitable alternative government in prison and living in some style. Plans for a return to Paris, preferably in triumph, were discussed with his "ministers" who were chosen from his admirers; his portrait, as a gallant cavalry officer, looked down on the proceedings, which were always kept lighthearted with the right amount of Libois's wine. With the help of his secretaries, he produced his definitive memoirs: *Historical Account of the Life of Louis XVII*. Much of his story, like Hervagault's before him, bore striking similarities to Regnault-Warin's fictionalized account of the escape of Louis XVII. He too had been branded by the pope and was prepared to show this mark to anyone who showed the slightest interest. There was information which he insisted only the real dauphin could possibly know, for example, secret hiding places in the Tuileries where his father placed his private papers. He also provided a colorful description of life in the Tower, his escape, and his heroic exploits in the American army. Encouraged by their "sovereign's" persuasive memoirs, his eager supporters planned to abduct him, and arrange his restoration.

By April 1817, the authorities were forced to act. Enemies of Louis XVIII were now openly using the situation against him, and politically the case of the "martyr king" had become very sensitive. There were almost daily reports from the police in Rouen to the ministry of police in Paris. On April 29, under cover of darkness, the prisoner was escorted by a heavily armed guard to the prison of the Palais de Justice. "Daufin Bourbon" was to face trial.

There was just the outstanding problem of proving exactly who the unknown prisoner might be, and this was becoming a matter of some urgency. A number of witnesses came forward, all equally convincing. The widow Phélippeaux, who had provided generous hospitality when he had first arrived in Saint-Malo, tearfully identified him as her long lost son. Another witness, the respected Vicomtesse de Turpin, declared she had met the prisoner years previously, as one "Mathurin Bruneau," the son of a village cobbler from Vezins in Brittany. Bruneau had been orphaned and since his sister could not keep him he had turned to a life of vagrancy. The sister was duly summoned and she, too, made a positive identification. However, another witness was quite sure the man in question was not Bruneau as his ears were not pierced; she knew beyond doubt that Bruneau's ears were pierced. Just to add to the confusion, there were others who maintained that the prisoner was none other than Hervagault. Far from dying in prison, he had made a brilliant escape, leaving the inevitable substitute "on point of death" in his place.

Desperate for a conviction, the police brought the case to court in Rouen on February 11, 1818. The trial was a sensation. For months, investigators had done their utmost to refute the prisoner's claims and cast him as a fraud. In a matter of days, with no help from anyone, the man the authorities now referred to as "Mathurin Bruneau" totally destroyed his own credibility.

From the beginning of his trial, he burst into the courtroom like some caged animal. Ignoring the ladies, and without any pretence at maintaining the due dignity of a "dauphin," he swore like a trooper, ranted and raved and was for the most part completely incoherent. The trial quickly degenerated into farce. According to one report, "He insulted the presiding judge, the government minister, his guards, the witnesses and the whole court, sneering, feverish, agitated and brutal with intentional vulgarity and deliberate audacity." Although many in the court were initially sympathetic to his claims, his coarse and drunken performance was so unconvincing that the king's advisors were laughing. His supporters were dumbfounded. In prison, "the hope of the lilies" had been only too believable. Some claimed that he had been deliberately drugged with narcotics or was dangerously drunk. Others clung to the belief that Simon was responsible for making him so uncouth. Alternatively it was argued he had suffered some kind of nervous breakdown locked up in solitary confinement with the strain of the past nine months, or even perhaps that he, too, had been swapped for an "imbecile." Whatever the excuse, his case visibly collapsed.

His rapidly dwindling band of supporters all but disappeared as he was found guilty of swindling and impersonating Louis XVII. On February 19, 1818, he was sentenced to seven years' imprisonment and a fine of three thousand francs. In 1822, after serving four years, he died, alone and quite mad, in a dungeon at Mont-Saint-Michel, his royal pretentions a distant memory.

The conviction and imprisonment of "Daufin Bourbon" dealt a severe blow to all those who believed that Louis-Charles was still alive. Yet it was difficult to stamp out the continuing conviction that the dauphin lived; new "evidence" of his death always lacked certainty. Intriguingly, around the time of his trial, another key witness was discovered. A former cook at the Temple prison, a man called Gagnié, was still alive and could vividly recall his life in the Great Tower. Although he was unable to shed any light on where Louis XVII was buried, he claimed he had seen Louis-Charles at the Temple in the year of his death. Since Gagnié had also been employed by the royal family at the Tuileries Palace, he had known the dauphin for some time and was convinced that he could recognize him correctly. He firmly believed that Louis XVII had not escaped from the Temple but had died there.

In his badly written document, Gagnié conjured up a pitiful scene that he witnessed early in 1795: "I declare that on entering [the cell] I saw the young prince doubled up and crouching down, with his arms wrapped around him. He had a tumor on his knee and his arm; his neck was covered

[205]

with scabies." The child was in pain and wanted to die. In his statement, the former royal cook confirmed that this unfortunate child "really was the child of Louis XVI who I had served at the Tuileries; the same child that I had seen brought to the Temple with the king and walking in the garden in the presence of all his family. . . . I swear that my declaration is indeed the truth and I would swear this again before God."

There was, however, a crucial flaw in his testimony. Gagnié claimed that he saw the sick prince at the beginning of 1795, but the Temple records revealed that he had in fact stopped working at the prison the previous September. When questioned, Gagnié conceded that he may be confused about dates. It was, after all, over twenty years since these events had occurred. Yet if he was confused about dates, could he also be confused about the boy he saw? Did he not simply presume that the sick, curled-up child was the prince? Since the cell was so dark, how could he be sure? And even if he had seen the prince, could the child have been substituted after Gagnié had left the Temple?

For all the growing number of files piling up in the police archives, the fate of the unfortunate prince was still far from resolved.

While claims and counterclaims about the dauphin were emerging throughout France, the heart removed from the orphan of the Temple continued its strange odyssey.

For years, Philippe-Jean Pellatan had assumed that the precious relic in the crystal urn was irretrievably lost. However, one evening a stranger knocked on the door of his house in Paris. He introduced himself as the father-in-law of Pellatan's former assistant, Jean-Henri Tillos, and explained how Tillos had stolen the heart from Pellatan's desk in 1810. The unfortunate Tillos had succumbed to tuberculosis at a young age. The theft had evidently preyed on his mind, for when he was close to death, he had repented and revealed his shameful secret to his father-in-law. "I immediately went to see widow Tillos," wrote Pellatan, "who gave me the heart in a small bag, in the presence of all her family. Naturally, I recognized it, having seen and touched it a thousand times." To spare her feelings, he added, "I did not say anything about the treachery of my young pupil."

Philippe-Jean Pellatan was now able to follow his conscience and return the heart to the royal family. He took a carriage to the Tuileries Palace, where he was advised to speak to the captain of the bodyguard. The doctor explained the whole saga and expressed his wish to return the heart to Louis XVIII. However, it was soon clear that there was a veritable civil service of officials to be encountered: the Grand Master of the Wardrobe, the Premier Doctor to the King, the Grand Chaplain . . . "I made twelve to fifteen fruitless visits," said Pellatan, before he was advised that the king "was persuaded that Louis XVII had been poisoned and the autopsy report was a pack of lies!" Louis XVIII declined the relic and Pellatan was dismissed.

He was, however, summoned for a police interview about the matter. The eminent doctor confessed to the prefect of police that he had indeed stolen the boy's heart during the autopsy and had also given permission for the guard on duty, Damont, to take the child's hair that was lying on the floor. He confirmed that the child in the Temple had shown signs of tuberculosis and provided details of the autopsy, which he hoped might help the police identify the right body. Pellatan was asked to draft a full statement, confirming all this in writing, which he duly did, adding that he was very perplexed that the king would not accept his nephew's heart. "There can only be an obscure intrigue which would delay the results of my endeavors," he wrote suspiciously.

Frustrated by his failure to return the heart to Louis XVIII, Dr. Pellatan felt it was his duty to pass on the memento to the duchesse d'Angoulême herself. This was arranged with the help of her ministers, the Viscounts Montmorency and Chateaubriand. The duchess came to visit the hospital Hôtel Dieu, where Pellatan worked as chief surgeon. "She greeted me kindly," Pellatan wrote, "and asked me if in reality I had attended her brother and if it was true that I could recognize his body by the section of the skull I had made. I replied in the affirmative and her Royal Highness moved away from me." The next day, he received a letter inviting him once more to visit Marie-Thérèse. "Her Royal Highness thanked me for the care I had given her sick brother and inquired into the means I had employed to abstract the heart." Marie-Thérèse, it seems, was prepared to consider that her brother had indeed died in the Temple as this distinguished doctor claimed. She told Pellatan that she would try to make arrangements for him to see the king. Curiously, this meeting never took place and he heard nothing more from the duchess.

It is possible that her change of mind could have arisen because in the meanwhile, she had also heard from the former commissioner, Damont. He had had a special chest made to store the locks of brown hair that he had taken from the orphan of the Temple. Carefully displayed on white velvet embroidered with gold lilies, the hair, which in life had been so matted and neglected, in death was now truly prized. He sent it as a gift to the Duchesse d'Angoulême.

However, she refused this token of her "brother." She informed Damont that she well remembered that Louis-Charles's hair was definitely a much lighter color: these locks could not be from her brother. There was now real doubt in her mind. Who was the child that they had dissected in June 1795 in the room below her in the Great Tower? If it wasn't her brother, surely there was a real possibility that he was still alive?

Chapter Nine

THE SHADOW KING

*"Your eyes is lookin' at this very moment on the pore disap-
peared Dauphin, Looy the Seventeen, son of Looy the Sixteen
and Marry Antonette . . . Yes, Gentlemen, you see before you,
in blue jeans and misery, the wanderin', exiled, trampled-
on, and sufferin' rightful King of France." . . . He {the old
man} said it often made him feel easier and better for a while
if people . . . got down on one knee to speak to him, and always called him "Your Majesty," and waited on him first
at meals, and didn't set down in his presence till he asked
them . . . So Jim and me set to majestying him . . . This done
him heaps of good, and so he got cheerful and comfortable.*

—MARK TWAIN, ADVENTURES OF HUCKLEBERRY FINN, 1885

After the death of Mathurin Bruneau in the 1820s, potential "lost
dauphins" began to come forward all over France. Louis-Charles's
tragic story had captured the public imagination; sightings and confessions
became commonplace. Many a blue-eyed, fair-haired adventurer suddenly
found an overwhelming need to unburden himself and admit to his blue-
blooded descent. And some dark-eyed swarthier claimants were equally sure
of their pedigree; their talents and manifestations of royalty were all equally
diverse.

In time, Louis XVIII's staff at the Tuileries in Paris became expert in
dispatching the various "Louis XVIIs" who were bold enough to present
themselves at the palace gates requiring to see their "uncle," the king. They

usually had the required tattoo and just wanted to reassure their uncle that they were not laying claim to the throne; a meal and a bed for the night would suffice. The Paris asylum, too, seemed to have the monopoly of lost dauphins for a while. Once, one of the inmates, bearing the royal banner and not much else, rather dramatically proclaimed his "rights" on the Champs-Élysées. Another, determined on life as a "royal," was renowned for removing his trousers with great enthusiasm in order to reveal those private parts of his anatomy that bore the appropriate moles. They came from all walks of life; there was a certain army captain with a head wound who miraculously remembered his life as the prince. And so the list went on, with the "dauphin epidemic" spreading to London, where one hopeful Louis XVII bore such a striking resemblance to Artois that his claim was hard to doubt.

The United States became a favored location for many pretenders. One of the most intriguing claims to be Louis XVII came from a man called Eleazer Williams who was a half-caste with a native Indian mother who lived near the Great Lakes in America. This ancestry apparently proved no impediment to the credibility of his tale, which began with Indians adopting him when he had arrived in New York with French refugees after his escape from the Tower. "Indian Williams" caused a sensation in his local community when he announced that he was Louis XVII. "His person was as pleasing as his manners," enthused one supporter. "His complexion was fair, his hair brown, his eyes hazel, and not a feature betrayed any trace of his Indian lineage." The doubt about his paternity could perhaps be better understood when it was discovered that Williams received money from a certain French nobleman. As news of his survival spread to France, Eleazer Williams claimed that he agreed to abdicate in favor of the king of France in return for a rich settlement.

Eventually the tragedy of Louis-Charles's story spread worldwide, and lost dauphins—not necessarily of French origin or even French-speaking— surfaced in all corners of the globe; there was even a "Monsieur Louis" in the Seychelles archipelago who held court beneath the shade of palm trees. From France, England, Denmark, Canada, America, the Republic of Colombia and the Seychelles: the sons of Louis XVI usually had all the necessary marks from the pope and a history, since their escape from the Tower, which made their "father's" fate during the revolution pale by comparison. There were, in time, over one hundred dauphins. Not for nothing did Mark Twain's hero in the *Adventures of Huckleberry Finn* consider the matter so amusing that he joked about the "little boy the dolphin."

None of the pretenders' varied and dubious claims would prosper under the reign of Louis XVIII. Nevertheless, in 1824, Louis XVIII, who had suffered from bad health for years, became seriously ill. His eyesight was failing, his right foot and leg were immensely swollen with gangrene; there was gangrene too in his spine. In great pain, he was visibly decaying before his courtiers; at one stage several toes were so rotten they fell away from his foot. When he finally died on September 16, 1824, since he had no children, Louis XVI's youngest brother, Artois, became king as Charles X.

During the reign of Charles X, one man came forward who was to prove far more credible than Hervagault, Bruneau or any of the other claimants. Smooth-talking, knowledgeable and suave, he had first come to the attention of the police in Modena in Italy for claiming that he was "Louis-Charles, duke of Normandy." He rapidly acquired a large circle of discreet devotees who aided his escape when he was threatened with imprisonment, and from his not-too-lonely exile he assumed the name "Baron de Richemont."

When the baron returned to France in 1825 he proved himself a master of disguise, adopting a number of aliases to avoid harassment from the authorities. Richemont could relate a compelling tale about life in Versailles or the Tower, embroidering little-known details about the royal family in great detail, and soon acquired considerable financial support. He did everything possible to further his stay in France and legitimize his cause. In the late 1820s, from his apartment in the Rue de Fleurus in Paris, he bombarded everyone who mattered—including the Duchesse d'Angoulême—with petitions, manifestos and endless letters seeking recognition. Never short of ideas, he made direct appeals to the public so that they would understand how he was maligned and the difficulties of his situation.

The baron's claim for recognition, however, was overtaken by political events. Unlike his wily brother, the ultraroyalist Charles X created widespread discontent in France by trying to introduce measures that echoed the despised *ancien régime* in giving more power to the king and the Catholic Church. On July 26, 1830, with contemptuous disregard for the gains of the revolution, he dissolved the Chamber of Deputies, which had just been elected, restricted the right to vote and took steps to limit press freedom. Across France the reaction was immediate. People poured into the streets, now festooned with the tricolor flags, and civil war broke out in Paris. For three days—*les trois glorieuses*—revolution gripped France once more; 1,800 people died. Artois was forced to abdicate. The crown went to his more liberal cousin, Louis-Philippe d'Orléans, son of "Philippe Égalité," who had voted for the death of Louis XVI. Within two weeks, Artois and the Angoulêmes were forced into exile once more and set sail on the *Great Britain* to England.

Fortunately, in exile they were wealthy. As a precaution, after 1815, Louis XVIII had shrewdly left money in London banks and his younger brother had inherited a few hundred million francs—an attractive magnet for any would-be nephew. It was not long before the Duchesse d'Angoulême was to hear from the Baron de Richemont again. "Everything is over for you," he wrote, now furious that his "sister" had not replied to any of his communications. "If your hatred is extinct, break your guilty silence; this is your only opportunity; it may not happen again . . . because fate again has placed you at the mercy of strangers. You would be better to throw yourself into the arms of your poor brother."

By the early 1830s several versions of the baron's remarkable life story were published. His own account, *Memoirs of the Duke of Normandy son of Louis XVI*, describes breathtaking feats of adventure, portraying him as a romantic hero who survived against the odds, despite far-flung travels to avoid persecution. After his escape from the Tower he distinguished himself, at the mere age of fourteen, in the Egyptian campaign, and later in Italy. His story dovetailed neatly with that of the widow Simon. When he returned to Paris in 1802 he sought her out in the hospital and found her delighted to see "her little Charles." With the authorities on his trail for his participation in royalist conspiracies, he sailed to the Americas where he had yet more flamboyant adventures before returning to Europe. Spurred on by his supporters, the Baron de Richemont soon took an even bolder step. For many royalists, the Orléanist Louis-Philippe had usurped the throne that belonged to the direct descendents of Louis XVI. Consequently, Richemont issued a manifesto challenging the king's position. "As prince and head of the elder branch of the house of Bourbon, I protest against the election of Louis-Philippe," he proclaimed.

By 1833, Louis-Philippe I had had enough. "Louis XVII" was arrested and imprisoned—under the suitably distinguished title of "Ethelbert Louis Hector Alfred, Baron de Richemont." Over the following months the authorities tried to trace his true identity. At one stage they thought he was a certain "Henri Hébert" from Rouen, at another "Claude Perrin" from Lagnieu, or perhaps his brother "Jean," or even "Colonel Gustave," "Henri de Trastamare," or the "Comte de St. Julien" . . . the list was endless. Yet however skillfully the police interrogated "Louis XVII," he always managed to outmaneuver them and consequently over a year elapsed before the case came to trial in October 1834.

Unlike Bruneau, Richemont put on a dazzling display of quick-witted charm in court, which unnerved the authorities. One witness identified the prisoner as Hervagault, a man who had been dead for thirty years according to the police; another decided he was Bruneau; several more—perhaps his associates—insisted he really was the dauphin and with great deference made a series of deep elaborate bows, plumed hats held in a low wide sweep. The prosecution was utterly at a loss when Lasne, the dauphin's former guard in the Temple, arrived in the courtroom. Now a very old man, he recounted simply and with vivid detail how he had witnessed with what agony the *real* prince had died: this prisoner had to be an impostor.

However, all these witnesses were eclipsed as the proceedings were dramatically interrupted. According to the *Gazette des Tribunaux*, a well-dressed man, around fifty-five years of age, rose and demanded the attention of the court "in the name of justice." The president, evidently annoyed at the interruption, asked his name. "I am Morel de Saint-Didier," replied the gentleman, "and I am the bearer of a letter for the gentlemen of the jury written by the *real* Charles-Louis de Bourbon, the son of Louis XVI."

This caused a sensation. The attorney general demanded that the gentleman be arrested. Others wanted to hear the letter. The court retired to deliberate. Finally it was determined that "Monsieur de Saint-Didier shall be heard . . . and that there are no grounds for ordering his arrest." Bowing before the court, Saint-Didier duly submitted the letter and the president broke the seal.

Gentlemen,

If I am rightly informed, the prosecution of Baron de Richemont has been undertaken solely with the view of casting ridicule upon any future pretension to the title of Dauphin of the Temple, *a title which the real son of Louis XVI will not cease to claim to the last moment of his existence.*

The unknown claimant went on to explain that he had all the documents necessary to prove his birth. However, "on every occasion when the royal orphan made an effort to be recognized by his family, a new Louis XVII was put forward, an impostor, like the Baron de Richemont . . . and thus public opinion was misled and the voice of the real son of Louis XVI was stifled." After elaborating this predicament, he continued emphatically:

Gentlemen of the jury and all you Frenchmen in whose hearts reign sentiments of honor and justice, learn that the son of your unfortunate king, Louis XVI, is still living. . . . Yes, Frenchmen, Louis XVII still lives and is relying upon the lively interest which the nation has never ceased to feel for the innocent son of the most unhappy of her kings . . .

Charles-Louis

Duke of Normandy

Paris Oct 28th 1834

The letter caused a great stir. The boldness and confidence of the move put its author in quite a different category to the other claimants. One gentleman, evidently much moved, stood up and declared, "We go from miracle to miracle! If the author is the legitimate heir he *must* have justice." The president brought the court to order and turned to the prisoner, asking if he had any comment to make. Richemont did not waver for a second. "When a citizen lays claim to a name he should at least know it," he replied. "The son of Louis XVI is called *Louis-Charles* and not *Charles-Louis*." There was complete uproar and confusion in court. Which was the impostor? Were they both impostors? How could justice be proved?

Richemont continued to speak eloquently in his own defense. "You have been told that I cannot be the son of Louis XVI. But have you been told who I am? It was not only the right, but also the duty of this court and of all the courts of the Kingdom to tell you who I am . . . but they keep silence. You gentlemen will appreciate the significance of their silence. It is not due to malice, but to *fear*."

However, despite his persuasive defense, Richemont was found guilty of swindling. In November 1834, he was taken to the *Conciergerie* to start his twelve-year sentence. In less than a year, after being transferred to Sainte-Pelagie, he escaped from jail. Hidden by his followers—some drawn from the ranks of the nobility—he remained an elusive figure, occasionally sighted in various towns of France. His anger toward his "sister" for not recognizing him never abated. "Ah, my sister, my sister!—Be gone! You are the cause of all the misfortunes of our family," he railed and began to consider legal proceedings against her, demanding his inheritance.

While the Baron de Richemont was eking out his existence as a shadowy character, hidden from view of the authorities, his challenger, who had so boldly interrupted the court proceedings against him in 1834, went on to become a legend in his own right. This new dauphin came from Prussia, where he had worked as a clockmaker under an assumed name, "Karl Wilhelm Naundorff." He told his story to a local Leipzig paper in the summer of 1831, disclosing his identity as the real Louis XVII for the first time. As the news spread, supporters encouraged him to abandon his life in Prussia and make his way to Paris to seek recognition. When he arrived in May

1833, he was penniless and spoke barely a word of French. Yet unlike any previous pretenders, his credentials were to prove so compelling that he effectively founded a rival royal dynasty and his case was to prove more disturbing to Marie-Thérèse than any of the others.

Naundorff began by trying to make contact with former key members of Louis XVI's household staff. On August 17, 1833, less than three months after arriving in Paris, he obtained an introduction to a former lady's maid to the dauphin, Veuve de Rambaud. As he stepped into the room to greet her, Madame de Rambaud instantly recognized him and was overcome by emotion. They exchanged recollections of happier times at Versailles and with growing excitement she became convinced this was indeed the child she had nursed forty years ago.

She heard of his astonishing escape from the Great Tower. First, a dumb child, named Tardif, had taken his place in November 1794, while he was held secretly elsewhere in the Temple; this was, he said, the silent child reported by Jean-Baptiste Harmand. In early June 1795, there had been a further switch. A child dying of tuberculosis replaced Tardif, only to die a few days later. This child was buried in the garden of the Temple, while the real dauphin was drugged "with a strong dose of opium and placed in the coffin . . . filled with rubbish to give it sufficient weight." On the way to the burial ground, he was rescued by royalists.

This was followed by a whole series of breathtaking adventures in which he was variously kidnapped or imprisoned, then successfully engineered heroic escapes. "My misfortunes have been unparalleled," he declared; some of his supporters had been assassinated and he himself had been attacked. Once, while sailing from Italy, he had been captured by a French ship and his assailants had deliberately cut his face with the intention of disfiguring him. He had been imprisoned once more, only to escape later with the help of the Empress Joséphine.

By 1810, he had made his way to Berlin where the authorities had seized his papers and given him the name of Karl Wilhelm Naundorff. Anxious to keep a low profile, he had established a small business as a clockmaker in the neighboring town of Spandau. In 1818, he had married, he said, "a young woman of the highest class," Jeanne Frederick Einert, and they soon had a family.

Madame de Rambaud was overwhelmed to meet him again after all these years. Soon after her meeting in August 1833, she wrote to the Duchesse d'Angoulême, who was now in exile in Prague, to tell her the good news. "Madame, I am impelled by my conscience to take the liberty of writing respectfully to you to assure you of the existence of your illustrious brother. I have seen him and recognized him with my own eyes," she declared. "His long sufferings, his resignation and submission to the will of Providence, as also his kindness, are beyond belief."

Despite Veuve de Rambaud's evident enthusiasm, the duchess's characteristic approach was one of patient observation: how would the new claimant be seen by others? She waited for more information; caution had proved right in the past and gave her time to calm the emotional turmoil that always accompanied these "dauphin episodes."

It was not long before Naundorff obtained an introduction to the former chamberlain of Louis XVI, Marco de Saint-Hilaire. He, too, was struck with the similarity of this stranger to the dauphin. "The Prince has all the characteristics, mannerisms and inclinations of his illustrious father. He also possesses all his virtues," he enthused. "Whoever has seen him once, cannot doubt his identity." His wife, Madame de Saint-Hilaire, a former maid to Louis XVI's aunt, was equally impressed and noted that Naundorff could answer any question on Versailles without difficulty, even citing the names of twelve of the queen's ladies-in-waiting. Not surprisingly, the "prince" rapidly established a court of loyal followers—including some deserters from Richemont's camp—who generously lifted him from the unsuitable poverty in which he had arrived. Among these supporters were many members of the old court, even Louis XVI's former minister of justice and private secretary, Monsieur de Joly, who at first was extremely skeptical. "Everything which he related to me could only be known by the Dauphin and myself," Monsieur de Joly confided to a friend. "Now nothing in the world could shake my belief that he and the son of Louis XVI are one and the same."

With no response to her letters, Madame de Rambaud became so frustrated by the duchess's refusal to meet her "brother" that she produced a sworn statement. "In case I should die before the recognition of the prince," she wrote solemnly, "I consider it my duty to testify here on oath before God and men that I have seen the illustrious Duc de Normandie." She was persuaded not just by his vivid recall of life with his family but also because he possessed all the appropriate physical characteristics: vaccination marks, moles, the slightly prominent shape of his front teeth, even a scar from a rabbit bite on his lip. She pointed out that she had been with the dauphin from "the day of his birth until August 10, 1792," and knew every last detail of the distinguishing marks on his body. Finally, she set out her most compelling evidence. She had always preserved a treasured relic from the days when she had cared for the young prince: a pretty blue suit, which he had worn only once at Versailles. She placed it in front of Naundorff and set a trap for him by falsely stating that this was a suit he had worn in Paris. To her astonishment, he immediately corrected her, "'No Madame, I only wore it once at Versailles,' and he told me when."

The anxious recipient of such testimony and letters in Prague was soon to feel still more troubled. One of Louis XVI's former private secretaries, Monsieur de Brémond, had become so convinced by Naundorff's claims that he had become his servant. In his letter to the duchess, Brémond probed her conscience, reminding her of the Crown treasure that she had inherited. "This treasure, Madame, *belongs* to the lawful king, and this lawful king, whom you will one day joyfully embrace, is your illustrious brother, the Duc de Normandie. . . . You are no longer entitled to make use of this treasure against him. . . . You are responsible before Almighty God and your lawful king for the use which you make of it. Madame, I have fulfilled my duty."

The duchess was becoming disconcerted; so many credible people whom she trusted were sincere in maintaining that this was, at last, her brother. If they were right, she could be doing him a terrible disservice, one that expressly went against her mother's last wishes. How could so many former servants be so hopelessly deceived? Did people really imagine that she refused to embrace this new "brother" because she did not wish to share her inheritance? The Duchesse d'Angoulême was by now sufficiently unnerved by all these letters from previous members of the royal household that she appointed a friend, a former French minister, to follow him: the distinguished Vicomte de La Rochefoucauld.

The viscount related an account of his first meeting in his letter to her on November 16, 1833. "I found myself in the presence of a man who undoubtedly bears a certain resemblance—taking his age into account—to the more careful portraits of Louis XVII, and who possesses the general features of the Bourbon family." His behavior was "unaffected," and he seemed in no way "confused or self-conscious" as perhaps an impostor might. On the contrary, "his eyes were very penetrating; his features were calm and attentive and showed neither self-consciousness or overeagerness." The "prince" had talked to the viscount at some length about the Duchesse d'Angoulême: "My poor sister has been hatefully deceived; I will enlighten her; I wish even now to save the honor of my family," Naundorff said to the viscount. "I am certain that my sister would recognize me after ten minutes' talk; I propose that she should meet me; I *demand* it of her. Let her go to Dresden—from Prague—under some pretext or other." With tears in his eyes he added, "Monsieur le Vicomte, I am indeed the son of the unfortunate Louis XVI, and the time is not far off when it will be proved."

Naundorff's performance was so utterly compelling that the viscount admitted to the duchess that he was "seized with a sort of dizziness" as he heard him talk so movingly about his family. With his "head and his heart spinning" he realized, "There was nothing in his behavior, in his tone, his manner of speech which suggested impudence or fraud, let alone roguery, and still less blackmail. . . . He is so calm, so convincing, that one is almost convinced oneself."

The duchess agonized over this latest disturbing missive from her own trustworthy confidant. If the pretender was an impostor, he had to be a very clever one to succeed so effortlessly in deceiving so many friends and staff. Quite apart from the myriad of convincing details he had supplied, even his handwriting was similar to members of the Bourbon family and he possessed over a hundred papers and documents that appeared to prove his case. In refusing to see him, she could be spurning the very brother who had already suffered so much in the Tower and who had lived in a wretched exile all these years. On January 12, 1834, the duchess was prepared to receive Morel de Saint-Didier, Naundorff's advisor and lawyer. With penetrating intensity, she cross-questioned Saint-Didier closely about Naundorff, his account of life in the Temple and his escape. Eventually, she agreed to look at the documents but still refused his request for a meeting.

Within two weeks of this meeting, she received a shocking message from her agent, the Vicomte de La Rochefoucauld. Two men had tried to assassinate Naundorff with a dagger. The attack took place on January 28, 1834, in the Place du Carrousel in Paris. "A man came to see me in great haste to inform me that on the previous evening about eight o'clock he [Naundorff] had been stabbed several times. . . . and that one of the wounds seemed to be deep," wrote the viscount. He was suspicious that the attack was fabricated—just another attempt to play with Marie-Thérèse's emotions—and went to check on the patient's wounds for himself. "All his linen was soaked in blood," he wrote. "The wounds are quite close to the heart. . . . The festering of the wound shows that it must be very deep and can have barely escaped being fatal." It was only a silver medallion that apparently saved him. The viscount sent "a clever and discreet surgeon to see him" to note all the "facts with scrupulous exactness."

Madame de Rambaud also wrote to the duchess to put her mind at rest that she had undertaken to nurse her "brother." "I have the joy of seeing him continually," she said. "Day by day, I find in him the same character which he showed in his childhood." The old nurse was totally convinced that she was caring for the genuine prince and she delighted in continued confirmation of this from his behavior. As for the ailing "dauphin" himself, even from his sickbed, his main concern was to meet with Marie-Thérèse and prove he was her brother.

On February 13, 1834, as he was recovering from the attack, Naundorff wrote directly to his "sister." He appealed to her conscience by reminding her of the traumas that he had already endured and painful episodes that haunted them both. "Your Royal Highness no doubt well remembers that night so terrible to us all, when I was awakened roughly and torn from the arms of my virtuous mother." He spoke briefly of the "cruel treatments" he suffered at the hands of Simon, and afterward, when he was locked alone in a little turret, "loaded with all sorts of abuse and ill-treatment by the wretches who surrounded me." After a year of this confinement, he told her, "I was then in a deplorable state, almost dying, my clothes in rags, and covered with vermin." He elaborated details of his escape and promised if she was only prepared to meet, "I am ready to give *my sister alone, by word of mouth, indisputable proofs* which will remove all your remaining doubts" [his italics].

Naundorff stated that he was now convinced that his previous letters to her had been used against him, and others had "taken advantage to ruin me in your opinion." The alleged history of this correspondence was set out and copies of some of the previous letters were attached to his memoirs. He claimed that he had written many times to Louis XVIII before his death and to his "beloved sister." As early as August 3, 1815, he had apparently sent her a letter from Spandau in Prussia: "My very dear sister . . . It is in you that I repose the small share of confidence that I can feel in any human being. I know it is attempted to conceal my existence from you; but a time will come when all traitors will be punished." He had pleaded with her then to help him as an "undeniable witness to my existence."

This appeared to be followed by another letter, dated March 1816, re-opening the rawest of wounds: "My dearly beloved sister, forgive me if, rejecting all court etiquette, the tenderness of a brother who has never forgotten you dictates these lines. For I declare it to you, I am living, I myself, your own brother. . . . Doubt no longer of my existence! Have I not suffered as much as you, and together with you, in the Temple? To convince you of it, must I bring to your recollection, the day when I saw you again with so much delight, after having been cruelly separated from our good mother.... You remember that same day you were dragged before the judges, no one in the world, but I, your brother, could describe to you the place where I saw you afterward. No, none but I could repeat to you the iniquitous interrogatory to which those men, those monsters, dared to subject you, as well as my virtuous aunt."

The following year, as the inquiry into the dauphin's "death" had been coming to a close in France, he had written again from Spandau: "Up to this moment I have received no answer to any of the letters that I have addressed to you or the king. My heart excuses you, but the case is different with respect to Louis XVIII." In this letter he explained "the dishonest intentions and bad faith of his uncle," and why it was in his interest to make her believe that he had died. "Now I ask you, have they ever placed before your eyes a corpse which they told you was mine?"

From his sickbed, recovering from his attempted murder, he now asked, "Madame, were these letters delivered to you? Did your Royal Highness receive no letters from Spandau? What has become of the bearer of the letters? Where is he now?" He implied that Louis XVIII had kept all this secret from her and went on to explain he had been at pains to reach her again in 1818, to let her know of his forthcoming marriage. On September 4, 1819, he had apparently written to inform her of the birth of his daughter, her niece: "The child is as beautiful as an angel." He had explained that he could see his sister's features "in the face of this child." He could not bring himself to call his daughter Marie-Thérèse: "That would bring to my mind too painful recollections." He had chosen the name Amélie, the name Marie-Thérèse had been given on their "unhappy journey" to Varennes.

At the beginning of 1824 he claimed to have written twice to Louis XVIII—stating his intention to come to Paris "and make myself acknowledged." Unaccountably, soon after sending these letters, he said he was imprisoned in Prussia on false grounds of having caused a fire—a charge that was "more ridiculous even than it was unjust." Finally, he spoke of his "tender, respectful, and unalterable attachment, which I have vowed eternally to my sister." He considered that she had been deceived by others regarding him and that she herself "was guiltless of all the ills that I suffered." It was signed, "your unfortunate but worthy brother, Louis-Charles, Duc de Normandie."

Reading and rereading the letters, Marie-Thérèse saw an entire unknown life of a long-lost "brother" unfold before her eyes, complete even with a "niece" who bore some resemblance to herself and numerous "nephews." Was it possible that all these letters from Prussia had been destroyed by interceptors on behalf of the king? Was she in fact the victim of some unseen, controlling power that had shaped her life and influenced her very thoughts for years? Or were these letters extremely clever recent forgeries? It was entirely possible that they had never been sent; that the man now pretending to be her "brother" was cruelly exploiting some of the worst moments of her life to further his own interests: a skilled manipulator quite happy to torment her for his own ends. And what kind of criminal mind would it take to weave such a complex web of deceit, enmeshing even former staff and friends at her expense? She was more tormented by Naundorff than any of her "brothers," never knowing what to believe and, in the end, believing nothing.

In her troubled state of mind, Marie-Thérèse took no action. Since there was no reply from the duchess, later that spring Saint-Didier travelled back to Prague with Madame de Rambaud, who undertook the long journey for her "Prince," despite her considerable age. But the duchess did not want to hear the pleadings of Madame de Rambaud; indeed, she was so confused now, she would not even accept that it was her own dear Madame de Rambaud. It could be almost anyone who was in on the intrigue. She sent a message to Morel stating that "she cannot suppose that a person of her age could have made such a tiring journey; that she had no reason for receiving the person of this name whom you have brought with you." In addition, she had read all the documents he had given her and had "found nothing in them to alter her opinion."

After this, Naundorff's tone changed in his letters to the duchess. "It is sufficiently painful to me to find Frenchmen propagating by *command* [his italics] lies and calumnies against me, but how bitter must be my feelings

[223]

when I see my own sister at the head of my oppressors! My own sister, not content with protecting my enemies, assists them to crush my just cause," he wrote in 1834. "I find myself utterly at a loss, Madam." He was so determined to see her that finally, in the late summer of 1834, he pursued her to Dresden, where he heard she was staying. His purpose was no doubt to engineer a face-to-face meeting, but true to her previous behavior, as soon as she heard of his intentions, she called the carriages and departed immediately.

Naundorff was so eager to confront her that in June 1836 he summoned the Duc and Duchesse d'Angoulême and the former Charles X to appear before the Court of the Seine. It was a civil case in which he was determined to prove his identity. His efforts backfired and he was arrested, pending investigations.

By now, dubious details of his life in Prussia had come to light. In 1824, his shop in Spandau, near Berlin, had burned down. At the time, the Prussian authorities had suspected that he had caused the fire to claim the insurance. A casting mold had also been found. Naundorff had insisted this was used in making clocks; the Prussian police thought he was counterfeiting money. He had been charged with forgery, which he vehemently denied, claiming these were trumped-up charges against him. At his trial in 1825, in spite of the prosecution being unable to establish his real identity, and with his claims to being an aristocrat dismissed, he had been sentenced to three years in prison.

When the French authorities searched his house in Paris in 1836, they seized numerous documents. There were letters to him as Louis XVII from devoted admirers, copies of letters dating from 1815 that he had apparently sent to Louis XVIII and the Duchesse d'Angoulême, and papers apparently proving his identity as the son of Louis XVI and Marie-Antoinette. Had all these, too, been forged? After extensive inquiries, the authorities decided simply to banish him permanently from France. He was deported to England, much to the relief of the Duchesse d'Angoulême, who, at the time, was in exile in Linz on the Danube in Austria. "Thank God, I will not hear of the Prussian again," she said. "But I know it is not entirely over. . . . His threats do not frighten me a great deal. He is a cunning impostor who is being manipulated by political adventurers."

In London, perhaps due to the stress of the previous few months, and the years of lack of recognition, Naundorff's activities became increasingly eccentric. Among other ventures, he founded a spiritual movement based on his mystical experiences. His visions told him the precise location of paradise, which could not be easily proved as it was in the very center of the sun and, although he calculated the distance from earth to paradise, nobody, it seems, was able to make the journey. To supporters who had followed him across the Channel, he remained generous in distributing titles, but as he was no nearer ascending the throne, both he and his titles began to lack credibility. His repeated denouncements of King Louis-Philippe and promises that he would reclaim the throne had led to nothing, and as his courtiers fell away—even, eventually, the loyal Madame de Rambaud, who defected to the Baron de Richemont's camp—his source of income began to dry up. He tried to make money out of his fascination with pyrotechnics and set about creating the perfect explosive device, the "Bourbon bomb," which succeeded in burning his house down, again in suspicious circumstances. Naundorff, too, was badly burned. By now, creditors were closing in on him and he was thrown into a debtor's prison. "The Duke of Normandy: this personage is now among the inmates of the prison in Horsemonger Lane," reported the London *Penny Satirist* in 1843. "His debts are estimated at 5,000 pounds."

However, the Dutch Ministry of War bought his design for the "Bourbon bomb," and Naundorff was invited to develop his research in Holland. In January 1845, when he came out of prison, Naundorff sailed for Rotterdam in search of a new life. He established himself at Delft and his family was preparing to join him when he fell ill. He was in such agonizing pain that poisoning was suspected. Doctors Soutendam and Kloppert, who were appointed to care for him, later recorded that as he lay dying, "the thoughts of the patient lingered mainly on his late unhappy father, Louis XVI, and on the terrible spectacle of the guillotine. He joined his hands to pray and asked, in broken words, for permission to follow his royal father to heaven."

To their amazement, this pattern continued as he degenerated even "until his last gasp." Naundorff, the shadow king, died on August 10, 1845, apparently a convincing prince to the end.

Naundorff was to have one final success. His death certificate was drawn up in Delft and stamped by the Dutch Minister of Justice. It recorded not the death of Karl Wilhelm Naundorff, but that of Louis XVII himself.

The deceased was "Charles-Louis de Bourbon, Duc de Normandie, Louis XVII, who has been known as Charles Wilhelm Naundorff, born at the Château of Versailles, in France, March 27, 1785 . . . the son of his late Majesty, Louis XVI, king of France, and her Imperial and Royal Highness, Marie-Antoinette, archduchess of Austria, queen of France . . . husband of Madame la Duchesse de Normandie, born Johanna Einert, resident in Delft." It is not entirely clear why the Dutch authorities were prepared to issue a death certificate confirming Naundorff to be Louis XVII. There were political tensions between Holland and France, and this would be a small way for the Dutch to ruffle some diplomatic feathers. Alternatively, some historians have hinted that the Dutch may have had evidence supporting Naundorff's claims.

There were now two death certificates for Louis XVII—one in France and one in Holland. His tombstone, too, was engraved "Here lies Louis XVII, Charles-Louis Duc de Normandie, king of France and Navarre." In death, Naundorff had, at last, won the recognition he had so craved.

Shortly after Naundorff's death, with the prospects of two bodies and two death certificates both purporting to be that of the real dauphin, two men came together in 1846 determined to solve the riddle of "the lost dauphin" once and for all. At the cemetery of Sainte-Marguerite in Paris, the priest now in charge, the Abbé Haumet, was only too aware of the inconclusive investigations into the dauphin's burial site thirty years previously. He discussed the case with a friend of his, Dr. Milcent. Although over fifty years had passed since the orphan of the Temple was buried, Dr. Milcent felt sure that he would be able to obtain vitals clues from an examination of the skeletal remains. Even if it meant taking the law into their own hands, they believed that if they could exhume the child's body, the mystery might yet be solved.

Abbé Haumet knew that the gravedigger, Pierre Bertrancourt, claimed he had reburied the dauphin in a private grave to the left of the chapel door. By chance in 1846, the abbé was presented with the ideal opportunity to conduct his own private investigation of this site without being seen, since building repairs were necessary and a temporary hangar was erected near the church. Given the political sensitivity of the case, the abbé envisaged that any formal request to excavate the grave would be refused. Consequently, he and a few loyal friends—two other priests and a colleague of Dr. Milcent—decided to dig up the child's grave secretly one night, without official permission.

About three feet below the ground, much nearer the surface than they had expected, they came across a five-foot-long lead coffin. This immediately puzzled the abbé. Testimony given to the 1816–1817 inquiry suggested that the dauphin had been buried in a pinewood, rather than a lead, coffin. The abbé reasoned that Bertrancourt had transferred the child to a lead coffin to better preserve the body. At five feet, the coffin was also a little larger than they had expected for a boy of ten. Nonetheless, they carefully carried the coffin inside the church and opened the lid.

Inside was the rotting skeleton of a child; the bones had shifted slightly in the slow movement of decay. The abbé and Dr. Milcent immediately noticed that the skullcap had been sawn, above the eye sockets, as Dr. Pellatan had described at the autopsy. They could also see a few curls of reddish-blond hair clinging to the scalp. Although the lead at the base of the casket had partially given way, and bones were missing, the skeleton was sufficiently intact to examine it in detail.

Dr. Milcent found the bones had certain characteristics that suggested the presence of disease, either from tubercular infection or as a result of living in unhygienic conditions. There were also distinctive markings or rotting on both the thigh and shin bones, probably from tumors. All this matched the description from the autopsy. However, Dr. Milcent was puzzled by the length of the leg bones. Louis-Charles was only ten when he supposedly died in the Temple prison in June 1795. Yet the leg bones of this skeleton seemed too long for a ten-year-old. There were, of course, reports at the time indicating that Louis-Charles's limbs had grown disproportionately long—perhaps due to his illness. Even making allowances for this, Dr. Milcent was doubtful that these limbs could have come from a ten-year-old.

The abbé and the doctor were sufficiently concerned that Dr. Milcent summoned another colleague, Dr. Récamier. He too was puzzled, as he wrote to the Abbé Haumet, "Although the ribs . . . were those of a very young subject, the head, the joins on the skull and bones of the trunk appeared more like those of a child of twelve and the arm and leg bones [and the teeth] appeared to belong to a subject of about fifteen or sixteen or more." The presence of the sawn skull suggested this was indeed the child on which the autopsy had been carried out. But surely this long-limbed apparently adolescent child could not be the dauphin? Dr. Milcent estimated that this child could have been as old as sixteen to eighteen. It looked as if the autopsy in 1795 had been carried out on a substitute child after all.

Far from solving the mystery, as he had hoped, the abbé realized that his efforts had compounded it. Madame Simon, the wife of Louis-Charles's "tutor," had consistently maintained that her "little Capet" had escaped. Their evidence now seemed to support her testimony: the body buried by Bertrancourt in the private grave did not seem to be that of Louis XVII. So if Louis-Charles had survived, which of the hundred or more men claiming to be the real dauphin was, in fact, telling the truth? Who had been the man to suffer the agony of not being recognized for who he was, spurned even by his sister? So many of the "lost dauphins" seemed cranks, eccentrics, even madmen. Yet even the sanest and strongest of men might have found the lack of recognition difficult to deal with. The mystery seemed beyond resolution. Abbé Haumet quietly reburied the remains and, fearing a rebuke for undertaking an unauthorized exhumation, decided to keep his results secret.

The Duchesse d'Angoulême was to be spared these latest revelations. She had, at last, found some form of peace. When the Duc d'Angoulême died in 1844, a friend, the Comte Stanislas de Blacas, had helped her to find her a permanent home in Austria. He came across the Château de Frohsdorf—meaning "village of joy"—some thirty-five miles south of Vienna. Gradually, she settled into a quiet routine in her own country home. She was close to her niece and nephew, Henri, the Comte de Chambord, the children of her husband's younger brother, and escorted them sometimes on trips to Venice. To friends such as Madame de La Ferronnays, whom she met occasionally in Italy, she seemed "greatly changed." Her legendary coldness and official ice had softened and she was "kind . . . and anxious to please." The writer Charles-Augustin Sainte-Beuve observed that "even amid the habit of pain," occasionally now "there rose to the surface a sort of joy."

She still kept around her forceful reminders of all she had lost. In the chapel at Frohsdorf she placed treasured mementos of her mother and father that Cléry had finally managed to obtain for her. There was a simple wooden stool that Louis XVI had used in prison, which she now used as a prayer stool, his wedding ring, and a lace cap, yellowed with age, that her mother had once made in the Temple. Sainte-Beuve continues, "She never spoke of the painful and bleeding things of her youth . . . but on January 21 and October 16, the death days of her father and mother, she shut herself up alone." Madame de La Ferronnays, too, was well aware that "the horrible scenes that had marred her childhood" were far from forgotten. "Once, I happened to remark that I hoped someday to have the satisfaction of seeing her nephew, the Comte de Chambord, enter Paris as king, by the Champs-Élysées. 'Oh no, not by the Champs-Élysées, not by there!' she cried in horror." Madame de La Ferronnays, realizing what unbearable memories of her parents' death this place conjured up for Marie-Thérèse, felt so "embarrassed by my lack of tact, I wanted to throw myself in the Grand Canal."

The duchess was never able to put her mind completely at rest about her brother. She did not accept the child's heart from Dr. Pellatan, nor would she meet any of the pretenders. By now she had received letters from twenty-seven men purporting to be her brother. Of these, she told friends,

Naundorff had caused her the greatest uncertainty and distress. With his passing, it seemed that she would no longer be persecuted by his claims; but she was wrong.

Naundorff had left a widow and children, including five boys, for whom "Jeanne Einert, Duchess of Normandy" wanted recognition in France, as she had received in Holland. However, the advantages of pursuing any claim were rapidly diminishing as political events moved on in France. Republican opposition to King Louis-Philippe had increased during his reign and, in 1848, revolution broke out once more. King Louis-Philippe was forced to abdicate, fleeing to England. In the political upheaval that followed, Napoleon's nephew, Louis-Napoleon Bonaparte, seized power, initially as president of the Second Republic. In these turbulent years, the duchess had to face two sets of legal proceedings from would-be brothers. In 1849, Baron de Richemont, who was still living as "Louis XVII" in France, and had the temerity to proclaim his official "recognition" of the Second Republic, launched a legal case against her demanding his inheritance. In September, the following year, Naundorff's widow, "Duchess" Jeanne Einert, asked the French courts formally to invalidate the earlier death certificate of the orphan of the Temple in 1795, legitimize her claim to be the widow of Louis XVII, and restore to her children, the rightful "princes" and "princesses" of the Duc de Normandie, the civil rights and privileges "to which they were entitled."

In May 1851, the duchesse d'Angoulême was summoned to appear before the Court of the Seine to deal with the claims of Naundorff's widow. For most of her life, she had been pursued by "brothers," whose claims she had doubted and preferred to ignore. Now at seventy-two, no longer robust, she had to face yet another threat. It was too much. She refused to attend. "The Duchess of Normandy," Naundorff's widow, produced a number of witnesses who were prepared to identify Naundorff as the missing prince, but the court was not impressed. The public prosecutor dismissed the case on September 5, 1851, saying that on the evidence they had before them, Naundorff's claim to be Louis XVII was not credible. Naundorff's widow was ordered to pay costs. But the Naundorffists were far from defeated. Since the French government would not release Naundorff's original documents, many felt this lent weight to their contention.

All this had taken a toll on the duchess. She was now increasingly confined in her rooms at Frohsdorf. "Madame La Dauphine was, if I may so express it, pathos in person," writes the Comte de Falloux, who met her at Frohsdorf that autumn of 1851. Left standing alone, "amid so many ruins, a ruin herself," she clung to her faith taught her by Aunt Élisabeth. She used to spend nearly the whole day seated at a particular window upstairs. "She had chosen this window because of its outlook on the copses which reminded her of the garden of the Tuileries," continued the count. Even with the passage of fifty years, true solace and peace was only to be found in that distant, perfect world of her childhood when her family was still alive.

On October 16, barely a month since the verdict on the Naundorff case, she was struggling against pneumonia, but she insisted on getting up to observe the death day of her mother. Two days later, as she lay dying, it is said that she asked for her father's watch and wedding ring so she might kiss them. She was still holding the wedding ring when she died. Her epitaph was to read, "Oh, all those that pass by, come and see whether any sorrow is like unto my sorrow!"

Two months after her death, the Second Republic was overthrown and Napoleon III became prince-president of a Second Empire. As the years passed, the remaining pretenders who had made life so difficult for Marie-Thérèse also died, their various claims forgotten, the various graves of these "brothers" bearing sole witness to their story as the world moved on. The Baron de Richemont died in the chateau of one of his supporters in 1853 near Lyon, his case against the duchess never settled. Like Naundorff, his followers arranged a suitable inscription: "Here lies Louis-Charles de France, son of Louis XVI and of Marie-Antoinette. Born at Versailles on March 27, 1785. Died at Gleizé on August 10, 1853."

Even with the death of the duchess, the Naundorff "princes and princesses" would not relinquish their claims. After the fall of Napoleon III, during the Third Republic in 1872, they sought an appeal to the 1851 judgment. They did not ask the court to recognize Naundorff as Louis XVII. Instead, they pleaded that the wealth of evidence to support their claim should be taken into account and an inquiry set up. The testimony of former servants and distinguished members of the former royal court warranted a full investigation. The judges were again unimpressed and threw out the case, passing a posthumous sentence on Naundorff as a calculating impostor. Naundorff's children would not be deterred. Convinced their father was indeed the dauphin, they were determined to return to court and win.

Across the span of years that Marie-Thérèse had been plagued with letters from her living "brothers," her dead "brother's" heart continued its own extraordinary journey through history. Alternately a symbol of a martyred child, a despot's son, a hero or a fraud, this strange relic did not escape the political turmoil in France in the first half of the nineteenth century.

Despite the large number of pretenders who came forward, Dr. Philippe-Jean Pellatan did not lose his conviction that he possessed the heart of the real Louis-Charles. His stolen memento preyed on his conscience and he was determined to return it to the royal family. Since neither the Duchesse d'Angoulême nor Louis XVIII would accept it, when Louis XVIII died in 1824, Pellatan tried once more. He went to see ministers of Charles X to explain what had happened, but Artois, too, seemed to be in no hurry to take his "nephew's" heart.

By May 1828, records show that Pelletan was seriously ill. Now eighty-one years old, he felt more anxious than ever to find a safe place to store the stolen heart. Toward the end of Charles X's reign, unrest was growing in Paris. Pellatan decided to hand over the heart to the archbishop of Paris, Monsieur de Quélin, since he "had never doubted my probity and the truth of everything I had said." At Archbishop de Quélin's request, he wrote out a full statement of the history of the heart, and the archbishop signed an official receipt for the relic on May 23, 1828. Less than four months later, Dr. Pellatan was dead. The heart that he had tried so hard to preserve for posterity was now safely hidden behind books in the library of the archbishop's palace by Notre Dame.

However, when the second revolution—*les trois glorieuses*—broke out in July 1830, the archbishop's palace was invaded. More than two thousand people broke through the Great Gate and looted with ferocity or abandon. It was a night of carnage: everything that it was possible to remove or destroy was attacked. The timelessly beautiful palace with its priceless antiques looked as though a whirlwind had visited, while the morning light showed some of the antique treasures half-burned and piled on fires in the courtyard.

A printer by the name of Lescroart who worked at the archbishop's palace realized the looters were making their way to the library to destroy the books, and he tried to save the precious crystal urn. He made his escape from the palace and was crossing the gardens when he ran into some of the rioters. The crystal urn that he was so desperate to preserve was struck with a saber. The urn shattered into a thousand sharp fragments and the child's heart fell to the ground to be trampled by the unmindful in the darkness.

Lescroart still had the documents that were with the urn and from these he realized that Dr. Pellatan had given the archbishop the sacred relic. He traced the doctor's house in Paris and soon found that although Pellatan was dead, his son, Philippe-Gabriel Pellatan, was keen to help him try to save the heart.

They waited for two days until the streets were quiet and it was safe to return to the archbishop's palace. As luck would have it, there was a storm that night and they were forced to search in the driving rain. Nonetheless, they covered the ground around the palace inch by inch; the garden had turned to mud. "Lescroart showed me the place where he was standing when the vase was broken, and with the help of people who were guarding the entrance door of the archbishop's palace, and the verger, we searched for the remains," Pellatan wrote years later. The heart was nowhere to be seen. "Finally, just as we were about to leave, disappointed, we discovered the *heart completely intact*, in a pile of sand between the boundary gate and the Church. It still smelled of ethyl alcohol" [his italics]. It was damp and surrounded by shards of glass from the crystal urn.

Philippe-Gabriel Pellatan carefully gathered up the heart, and took it home. He knew his father had had no doubts as to its authenticity and that he was obliged to preserve it. He restored the child's heart in a new urn and kept it locked away for years, secret, almost forgotten.

Chapter Ten

THE ROYAL CHARADE

In the history of this sovereign without subjects, an enigmatic history even beyond the tomb, everything totters and collapses as soon as we flatter ourselves that we have laid a course, or erected the frail scaffolding of an argument . . .

—HISTORIAN GEORGES LENÔTRE, 1922

Toward the close of the nineteenth century, the enigma remained unsolved. All possible princes were now characters from history; their strident claims and the testimony from long-dead witnesses gathered dust in police files. The incomplete inquiry during the Restoration, secret exhumations and reburials, and reports of over one hundred pretenders; all these had only served to compound the mystery. However, in 1894, one man took it upon himself to resolve the puzzle, a lawyer, Georges Laguerre. He was well aware of the inconclusive results of Abbé Haumet's secret exhumation of the orphan of the Temple at Sainte-Marguerite cemetery nearly fifty years previously and applied for official permission to investigate the grave again. The previous exhumation, he argued, had been carried out by a priest and a doctor, neither of whom had sufficient forensic expertise to make an informed judgment.

In the fifty years since the last exhumation, forensic analysis was beginning to be applied more systematically to criminal investigation. As early as 1880, the missionary doctor Henry Faulds had published a letter in the

British scientific journal *Nature* suggesting that fingerprints could be used as a basis for identifying criminals. Meanwhile, in France, at the Prefecture of Police in Paris, a clerk, Alphonse Bertillon, had invented an alternative system for identifying individuals, using specific body measurements—of the head, the ear, the trunk, arm length and so on. By keeping accurate records of prisoners, he successfully caught his first repeat offender in 1883 using this method. And at the University of Lyon, Jean Alexandre Lacassagne, a professor of pathology, was also pioneering a scientific approach to police work. In a high-profile case in 1889, he solved a brutal murder by studying the victim's body. Advances such as these highlighted the possibility that forensic analysis might bring some bearing on the case of the lost dauphin.

By the 1890s, although there was still great interest in the fate of Louis-Charles, the political sensitivities of his case had subsided and the authorities gave permission for an official investigation around the chapel door in Sainte-Marguerite cemetery. This was the same site as the 1846 exhumation, but Georges Laguerre was better prepared than his predecessor. He drew together a large team of distinguished specialists, including Dr. Bilhaut, children's surgeon at the International Hospital, Professor Amoedo of the Paris School of Odontology, and Dr. Felix de Backer, director of the *Revue Antiseptique*.

As Georges Laguerre's team dug down by the chapel wall on June 5, 1894, they found an oak box inscribed "L. . . . XVII" in which Abbé Haumet had replaced the child's remains. It was very fragile, having almost rotted away, but the bones Haumet had described in 1846 were revealed yet again for the curious: journalists, priests, even members of Naundorff's family who had gathered to witness this historic event. The oddly shaped skeleton took form once more. The sawn skullcap with its wisps of reddish-blond hair, the long limbs, the underdeveloped ribs, fragments of spine: the bizarre shape slowly emerged. A photograph was taken of the skullcap as a record.

From the jaw alone, it was possible to estimate the age of a child. The odontologist, Professor Amoedo, could see that the boy had had no milk teeth when he died, suggesting he was over twelve years old; in fact, the eruption of the wisdom teeth indicated that he could have been as old as eighteen. There was also the question of the overall size of the skeleton. Dr. de Backer had found that the average stature of a sixteen-year-old Parisian boy was 158 centimeters. Their calculations of the height of this child showed he had been no less than 153 and possibly as much as 165 centimeters. From this they reasoned that he had been at least fourteen when he had died. Finally, they considered the development of the skull. During childhood, the size of the cranium, which encloses the brain, is large compared with the bones of the face. These proportions gradually change until, by adult life, the cranium and facial bones are of equal proportions. Dr. de Backer and Dr. Bilhaut again estimated that this was the skull of a child of fourteen or older. Yet the skull was "sawn in two by a very expert hand," just as Dr. Pellatan had described at the autopsy. A baffling result.

The forensic team could not be sure that the bones they had recovered from the box were all from the same skeleton. The cemetery had been a dumping ground for a large number of bodies over this period. As early as 1804, the mayor of Paris had complained that too many bodies had been buried at Sainte-Marguerite, which was in danger of running out of space. The problem had been compounded by Paris hospitals dumping—without much ceremony—dissected cadavers used in anatomical research. Many of these bodies were not even wrapped but were piled in pits and barely covered with earth. "The edges of the pits are dripping with blood," the mayor had complained. "It is the most disgusting picture that can be seen." This overuse of the cemetery meant that it was difficult to guarantee the integrity of any particular skeleton.

Yet as the doctors scrutinized the child's skeleton, they concluded it was unlikely to be a mixture of bones from several people. Apart from one humerus, or upper arm bone, the remainder of the decaying bones were an identical brown color and showed the same amount of ossification, or bone formation. In addition, measurements of the arm and leg bones revealed that they were perfectly in proportion, as if they had originated from one person. All this pointed to a disturbing conclusion. The body they had exhumed matched the description of Pellatan's 1795 autopsy and the 1846 exhumation and yet could not be that of a ten-year-old boy. Since this could not be the real dauphin, was it an ill-fated substitute? Could the real Louis-Charles have escaped after all?

At this time in the late nineteenth century, historical documents continued to surface that lent weight to the idea that Louis-Charles had miraculously survived. The publication in 1893 of some of the correspondence of an English aristocrat, Charlotte Lady Atkyns, provided fine fuel for conspiracy theorists. During the French Revolution, Lady Atkyns, who was an ardent royalist, had watched the unfolding misfortune of the royal family with horror and had become committed to helping them. In the autumn of 1793 it is thought she had even travelled to Paris and managed to enter the queen's cell in the *Conciergerie* disguised as a guard, where she swore to the queen she would do everything in her power to rescue her son. She had enlisted the help of Comte Louis de Frotté, a royalist who was behind the insurrection in Normandy, and a lawyer, the Baron de Cormier.

At first, she thought she had succeeded. By October 1794, Cormier had written to her with extraordinary news: "I must write you a few words in haste. . . . I believe I am able to assure you, declare to you most positively, that the *Master* and his *property* are saved. . . . I can give no details; it is only full in the face that I can open my heart to you" [his italics]. This news also appeared to be confirmed in a letter from Comte Louis de Frotté: "Everything is arranged; in short, I give you my word that the king and France are saved . . . and we ought to be happy." Later it emerged that she had been duped by Cormier, who had been only too happy to take her money in return for his false assurances. Lady Atkyns came to believe that the dauphin had escaped, "but a higher power than mine took possession of him." Her correspondence suggested the prince had indeed been rescued from the Tower sometime before the autumn of 1794.

A few years later, further intriguing documents were produced that also appeared to show that the dauphin had escaped. A manuscript of a secret meeting of leading members of the Directory, held on April 28, 1796, was printed in the *Revue Historique* in Paris in 1918. The text appeared to be the minutes of a discussion between General Barras and the four other Directors in which they implied that Louis XVII had been abducted from the Temple in 1794.

The conversation set out in this curious document revealed that the prisoner of the Temple had been entrusted to the care of a banker named Petitval. However, on April 20, 1796, his chateau had been attacked and Petitval and members of his household had been most brutally murdered as they tried to flee. The most likely motive for the attack was that he had discovered that the child he was guarding was not the real dauphin and he had to be silenced. Whatever the reason, General Barras and his colleagues spoke as though confidently assured that the dauphin was not among the murdered victims, since he had escaped earlier. This manuscript published by *Revue Historique* has not been authenticated, nor have its origins been established. Whether a forgery or not, this fantastic tale also served to perpetuate the belief that the dauphin had been saved.

The failure of the 1846 and 1894 exhumations to find the body of the dauphin, the testimony of old Madame Simon, the persistent rumors of an escape at the time of his alleged death, the letters from Cormier and Frotté, the document in the *Revue Historique*: all this lent weight to the idea that a switch had been made and that Louis-Charles had been rescued. In 1922, the popular French historian Georges Lenôtre tried to draw these threads together in a definitive study of the lost dauphin: *Louis XVII, The Riddle of the Temple*. Sifting through the vast body of records and archives on the case, he reached the controversial conclusion the dauphin had indeed escaped at a date prior to August 1794. He argued that when Jean-Jacques Laurent was appointed by General Barras as guardian after the death of Robespierre, he soon realized the boy in his care was an impostor. He informed Barras, who panicked, fearing this would precipitate a political crisis. Barras made Laurent swear to secrecy and ordered the substitute who was held in the Great Tower to be kept completely out of sight.

In reaching his conclusions, Georges Lenôtre took account of the large body of circumstantial evidence lending support to the idea that a substitute was held in the Tower: the obstinately mute child seen by Jean-Baptiste

Harmand early in 1795, the suspicious death of the kindly Dr. Desault who had been treating the orphan of the Temple, the hurriedly produced death certificate which many believed was a forgery. Above all, Lenôtre was influenced by the compelling evidence that Laurent had persistently refused permission for Marie-Thérèse to see her brother. The only credible reason for this, he claimed, is that she would have instantly recognized that the boy prisoner was a substitute. After all, Laurent appeared to be genuinely sympathetic to both Louis-Charles and his sister and had been instructed to improve the conditions under which the boy was held. Yet despite her repeated pleading and the pitiful isolation of the boy, he would not allow them the comfort of even a brief meeting, although this would hardly have undermined prison security. He concluded that the only explanation for this quite unnecessary cruelty toward them was to conceal the substitution.

However, in 1924, shortly after Georges Lenôtre's publication, René Leconte, in his book *Louis XVII et les Faux Dauphins,* noticed a crucial detail that had been overlooked by other researchers. As he pored over the photograph of the skull that had been taken during the 1894 exhumation, he realized it did not match Pellatan's original description. Dr. Pellatan had described his sawn section of the skull as being "level with the eyebrows." When René Leconte scrutinized the picture of the skull, he realized that this skull had been sawn at a much higher point, well above the eyebrows, across the top of the forehead, almost at the hairline. The body that had been exhumed in 1894 and 1846, he reasoned, could not have been the one on which Dr. Pellatan had undertaken his autopsy. Since so many bodies used in anatomical research had been buried at Sainte-Marguerite, Leconte reasoned that it was at least plausible that another unfortunate child whose skull had been sawn had come to rest on the same site. He concluded that the nineteenth-century exhumations could no longer be taken to support the claim that a substitute child had been buried. The exhumations had simply failed to find the right body that Pellatan had dissected, which was almost certainly lying undiscovered, deeper underground.

By the beginning of World War II, the seemingly unsolvable puzzle continued to attract experts. Hundreds of books had been written as historians, forensic specialists, royalists and cranks all pored over the evidence, producing one "definitive" book after another. With so many claims and counterclaims, agents and double agents, substitutes for the substitutes, not to mention the pretenders themselves, there seemed no limit to the possible fates for the prince. The matter seemed impossible to resolve conclusively on the historical evidence alone. And while the courts of France had dismissed the claims of Hervagault, Bruneau, Richemont, Naundorff and others, many still believed it was at least plausible that one of the pretenders was telling the truth. But which one?

As forensic techniques improved, there was still the possibility of solving the puzzle scientifically. In the first half of the twentieth century, Professor Edmond Locard, an eminent French criminologist who had studied under the two great masters, Alphonse Bertillon and Jean Alexandre Lacassagne, was pioneering the use of trace evidence—such as hair, fibers, flakes of skin, even grit and dirt—in forensic cases. He showed that when a person comes into contact with another person or place there is invariably a transfer of evidence. "Every contact leaves a trace," he famously declared.

From a sample of hair alone, gathered near the crime, Locard could analyze external features such as the length, color, degree of curliness, texture, diameter of shaft, even the shape and condition of the root. In addition, under the microscope in his laboratory, he could also compare three main internal features of the hair shaft. The outer layer, or cuticle, comprises external scales, which overlap like tiles on a roof. The chief part of the fibrous stem is made up of spindle-shaped cells that contain the color pigment. Apart from the color itself, the distribution of the pigment can show differences between individuals. Finally, running down the center of the shaft there can be a spongy, air-filled core, known as the medullary canal. Comparisons of hair samples could be used to exclude a subject, or if there was a match to a crime scene, as contributing evidence.

By the early 1940s, it occurred to the French historian André Castelot that this technique could be applied to the case of the lost dauphin. He approached the famous criminologist, now established as the director of the Scientific Police Laboratory at Lyon. Locard agreed that if Castelot could trace authentic hairs from Louis-Charles and others claiming to be the dauphin, then he was prepared to compare them under the microscope.

Following a detailed investigation, Castelot did find samples of Louis-Charles's hair that Marie-Antoinette had taken from her son while they were imprisoned in the Temple. Incredibly, these locks of hair had been found in Robespierre's rooms. After his death at the guillotine in 1794, a deputy called Courtois had been ordered to search his rooms and draw up an inventory of his belongings. Among the objects that he had found were items that had formerly belonged to Marie-Antoinette, which had been confiscated at the *Conciergerie*. Robespierre had abhorred the queen and all she stood for and now, like grisly charms and tokens of his power, symbols of the dead queen were found under his mattress: a lock of the queen's hair, some curls that she had treasured of Louis-Charles's hair, and her last letter to her sister-in-law, written a few hours before her death. Castelot was able to trace the history of these hairs as they were handed down over the years until by the 1940s they had ended up in the care of a priest, the Abbé Ruiz.

In addition to these hairs taken from the dauphin by his mother, Castelot was also able to trace the hairs that were cut from the orphan of the Temple in 1795 during his autopsy by Dr. Pellatan. These were the hairs that commissioner Damont had been permitted to keep, and which he had tried to give to Marie-Thérèse after the Restoration; she had rejected them because she thought they were a slightly different color to her brother's hair. These hairs had been passed down in the Damont family and had eventually been entrusted to a close family friend.

Castelot took the hairs to the laboratory in Lyon where Dr. Locard's team examined them under the microscope. He soon found that the sample of Louis-Charles's hair that had been found under Robespierre's bed displayed a very rare feature. The medullary canal did not run centrally down the shaft, but was slightly displaced to one side, or "ex-centered." When he compared this to the hair sample taken during the autopsy on the orphan of the Temple, the results were astonishing. In this hair, the medullary canal ran centrally down the shaft. The hair samples simply did not match. This appeared to provide strong corroborative evidence that the young boy who died in the Temple prison in 1795 was not the dauphin, but a substitute.

Inevitably, skeptics queried the authenticity of the hair samples. However, André Castelot was able to trace another sample of Louis-Charles's hair, taken before his imprisonment in the Temple. It was in the collection of the Marquis de Tinguy, whose forebears had been friends of the royal family and had been given a lock of the dauphin's hair in the early 1790s. When examined in Dr. Locard's laboratory, this hair, too, like the sample found under Robespierre's mattress, showed the distinctive anomaly: an ex-centered medullary canal.

By chance, the historian Castelot was able to take his investigations a stage further. He was contacted by a representative of the Naundorff family called Baron de Geniebvre. The baron had hair samples from Naundorff, which had been cut as a memento by his oldest son shortly before his death in Delft in 1845. Some of these locks of hair had been given to a staunch Naundorff supporter, Mlle. de La Tour du Pin, and these were later passed down to the Baron de Geniebvre.

Castelot asked Dr. Locard to compare these hair samples with those from the dauphin that he had already analyzed. As he looked down the microscope, to his amazement, Dr. Locard could see at once that these hairs from Naundorff showed the same rare displacement of the medullary canal that he had observed in the two samples from Louis-Charles. The hair samples were identical. It seemed that Castelot and Locard had solved the puzzle at last. The real dauphin appeared to be none other than Naundorff himself.

These tests, carried out by one of the leading forensic experts in the field, produced a clear-cut result and caused a stir when it was published in 1943 in the journal *La Gerbe*. The man dismissed as a crank by his contemporaries, by his "sister," and by the French courts in 1851 and 1872 now apparently had scientific evidence to back up his claim to be the rightful dauphin. André Castelot was forced to concede that the latest research, the finest objective analysis available at the time pointed to the inescapable conclusion that a huge injustice may have been done.

. . .

After World War II, the case of the lost dauphin was no longer simply a piece of idle historical controversy. The war had changed the political landscape in France. General de Gaulle, leader of the Free French Forces, had pledged himself to the reestablishment of democracy in France and firmly declared that the French people alone should determine the future constitution of the country. There were some in France who felt the French monarchy should be restored to bring stability, continuity and strong government in the aftermath of a traumatic war. Newspaper articles began to appear debating the issue; there were even rumors that General de Gaulle might be sympathetic to the restoration of the monarchy. As France began to make its first tentative step toward making peace with its royal past, the nineteenth-century law banishing the heads of the former French ruling houses and their descendents from residing in France was repealed in 1950. There was, however, a crucial unresolved issue. If the monarchy were ever to be restored in France, who would have the legitimate claim to be king? The royalist battle lines were being drawn.

One of the first to return from his exile in Lisbon was the glamorous Comte de Paris, a direct descendent of the Orléanist Louis-Philippe, the last king of France who had been forced to abdicate in 1848. The count returned to France in 1950 in the bright spotlight of public interest and quickly claimed for himself the title of the head of the Bourbon family and pretender-in-chief of the French throne. He had inherited a considerable fortune and settled into a large country house near Versailles, determined to reestablish the prestige of the Bourbon dynasty. His book, *Entre Français*, published in 1947, argued strongly in favor of the restoration of the monarchy in the postwar reconstruction of France. The count assiduously courted De Gaulle, and their cordial relations created a great deal of press speculation. At one point, De Gaulle caused a stir by writing personally to the count on the eve of the wedding of his son, Prince Henri de France. "Is De Gaulle a royalist?" asked the *Daily Telegraph* in London the next day, summing up the excitement in the Paris papers.

However, there were other Bourbon princes who openly challenged the dashing Orléanist Comte de Paris as pretender-in-chief. Centuries-old wounds between different branches of the family had not yet healed. While some French royalists rallied to the Orléanist line, others could not accept the "theft" of the throne from Charles X by Louis-Philippe in 1830. In their eyes, this treachery had been compounded by the actions of his father, Philippe Égalité, who had shamefully voted for the death penalty in the trial of Louis XVI. Since the Duc and Duchesse d'Angoulême had died without issue, as had their nephew, Henri, comte de Chambord, the title of head of the Bourbon family had passed to the Spanish Bourbons. Their descendents did not accept the Orléanist count as the senior Bourbon and revived the bitter family feud that had lasted for generations.

During the 1950s, the Comte de Paris and his rival princes, these dazzling figures imbued with centuries of prestige and charm, fought out their claims and counterclaims as pretenders to the throne with the world's press in enraptured admiration. On the Côte d'Azur, in the fashionable resorts of St. Tropez and elsewhere, would-be kings of France mingled with film stars, glitterati and European high society. They were courted by press and society magazines eager to satisfy the insatiable public interest in the lifestyles of members of European royalty and in the long-running disputes between the various pretenders. The ordered perfection of many a royal event, a wedding, gala or public ceremony was all too often spoiled by petty disputes as to which prince should take precedence over the others. To add to the intrigue, the sparring Orléanists and Bourbonites were opposed by the Bonapartists, who maintained that the great-great-grandnephew of Napoleon was in fact the rightful heir: Prince Louis Napoleon Bonaparte. Bonaparte had supported the resistance movement during the war and had been living unofficially in France since the liberation. And while the Orléans, Spanish Bourbons, and Bonapartes fought over their claims to the throne in the unlikely event of any restoration, the finishing touch came when all these pretenders received an unwelcome challenge from yet another unexpected source: the Naundorffs.

Nearly two hundred years had elapsed since the death of the orphan of the Temple. Yet Naundorff's descendents still legitimately bore the name of the Bourbons and were determined to obtain recognition in France that they were the true descendents of Louis XVII. Once again, they resorted to legal action. On May 5, 1954, the Paris appeals court was asked to hear a case against the decision of the French court in 1874 not to recognize Karl Wilhelm Naundorff as the rightful heir of Louis XVI and Marie-Antoinette. Naundorff's descendents wanted to overturn the earlier verdicts and prove their claim.

The press was delighted with this new dimension to the question of succession. In contrast to the well-heeled and aristocratic Comte de Paris and other equally plausible Bourbon princes, some of Naundorff's descendents, their pedigree notwithstanding, had hit hard times. One had died in a French poorhouse in 1944, and it soon emerged that the senior surviving member of the Naundorff family and would-be heir to the throne was currently employed as a Parisian circus manager: René Charles de Bourbon. "Circus manager who wants to be king" blasted the headlines of the *Manchester Guardian* in May 1954. In "Royalist outrage in Paris," the *Times* reported on the circus manager who had the temerity to stand up in a French court and claim any prospective royal prize for himself.

On May 20, 1954, the *Times* in London summarized the arguments of the distinguished barrister Maître Chresteil, leading counsel for the Naundorff family in the Paris courts. Chresteil drew attention to the death certificate, issued in Delft in 1845, recognizing Naundorff as Louis XVII, and asked the court to invalidate the earlier death certificate drawn up in 1795 at the Temple. He cast suspicion on the mysterious disappearance of "202 of Naundorff's documents confiscated by the Paris Police in 1836." These documents could still be produced, Chresteil argued, with a "little goodwill" from the archives of the Ministry of Justice, and would surely prove the validity of his claims. Inevitably, the numerous members of the old court who recognized Naundorff as Louis XVII were presented as evidence: Madame de Rambaud, Monsieur Saint-Hilaire, even the duchess's own envoy, the Vicomte de La Rochefoucauld. Naundorff's repeated efforts to secure a meeting with the Duchesse d'Angoulême were also cited in his favor. His "sister's" persistent refusal to receive him was explicable, according to Chresteil, "only by her reluctance to call into question the legitimacy of the reigning family."

Finally, the latest forensic evidence on Naundorff's hair was also presented to the court. Events had moved on rapidly since André Castelot and Edmond Locard's studies in the early 1940s, which had appeared to show that Naundorff's hairs displayed the same rare anomaly as that of the real dauphin. At the time, skeptics had questioned the accuracy of the tests and the genuineness of the hair samples. Castelot himself had been eager to check his results, and consequently had approached the Dutch authorities for permission to exhume Naundorff's remains. On September 27, 1950, over a hundred years after his death, Naundorff's body was exhumed from its burial site at Delft in Holland.

The remains were analyzed by a Dutch anatomist, Dr. Hulst, who hoped to obtain evidence that, one way or the other, would prove Naundorff's claim. First, he tried to ascertain the exact cause of death, since it was widely rumored that Naundorff had been poisoned. Naundorff's humerus, or upper arm bone, was removed and tested for the presence of arsenic. Although trace amounts were found, these were too low to have been the cause of death. Hulst reasoned that the arsenic had been absorbed into the bone from the lead coffin after his death. Dismissing any conspiracy theories, he said Naundorff was more likely to have died from typhus than from anything else. From his analysis of the teeth and jaw, Hulst could show that Naundorff was around sixty when he died; this tallied neatly with the correct age for the dauphin had he survived until 1845. He took hair samples to send on to Dr. Locard in Lyon, and Naundorff's body was returned once more to its grave by his tombstone as Louis XVII.

When Dr. Locard analyzed the reddish-brown hair taken from Naundorff's exhumed body, he made a startling discovery. These hairs were quite different from the ones he had examined earlier from Baron de Geniebvre, for they did not show the rare anomaly in the medullary canal found in Louis-Charles's hair. With this new result, Naundorff's hair did not match that of the real dauphin. So how could the early tests have given the wrong result? Castelot knew that Baron de Geniebvre had received these hairs from an ardent Naundorff supporter, Mlle. de La Tour du Pin. He speculated that she had accidentally mixed the Naundorff sample with hair from the real dauphin that she possessed—a mistake done quite genuinely since she believed that Naundorff was Louis XVII.

In court, Naundorff's lawyers argued that these forensic tests did not prove that Naundorff was an impostor. After all, hair could easily have become damaged over time. There were discrepancies, too, in the analysis of the dauphin's hair: the samples taken in the early 1790s did not match the hairs taken during the autopsy in 1795. Recent studies had shown that the medullary canal can be fragmented and differ from one hair to another on the same person, or even be absent entirely! The forensic examinations of Naundorff's grave and the exhumations at Sainte-Marguerite cemetery had all produced interesting information, reasoned Maître Chresteil, but none of it provided definitive proof as to the fate of the dauphin.

However, as the trial gathered pace, Maître Garçon and Maître Malzieux, counsel for the Bourbon family, tore into Naundorff's case. Apart from the lack of forensic evidence to support his claims, the historical evidence, too, was flawed. According to the *Times* on May 21, 1954, Maurice Garçon began by tracing the captivity of Louis-Charles in the Tower and analyzing the inconsistencies in the arguments used to show that the boy who died there in 1795 was a substitute. For example, the guardian, Laurent, had insisted on having an assistant, but surely would not have wished for a witness if he had been planning the prisoner's escape? As for the child's solitary confinement, this was not to conceal the fact that he was an impostor, argued Maître Garçon, but merely because the revolutionaries had wished to democratize the wolf cub by making him "forget his family and antecedents." Regarding his rapid degeneration, "no doctor would support the claim that it was impossible for a relatively healthy child to die of tuberculosis of the bones, after thirty-three months of imprisonment in a cold, damp tower."

Then he scrutinized Naundorff's own characteristics and history. Despite his remarkable physical resemblance to the Bourbons, the pretender had a vaccination scar only on his left arm whereas Louis-Charles was known to have had scars on both of his arms. Quite apart from this, was it credible, he demanded, that in 1833, after a gap of over nearly forty years, Louis XVII should suddenly reappear in Paris, barely able to speak French? On the contrary, he was a cunning impostor who had duped ardent royalists into giving him their life savings, and had spent three years in prison for counterfeiting money. He had failed, in spite of repeated efforts, to convince his "sister," who considered his letters "a pack of lies." As for his death certificate as Louis XVII, this too could be explained. When he had arrived in Holland from England, the police had confiscated his passport because of a mistake at the Dutch consulate in London. When Naundorff died, the police did not want to reveal that they had seized his passport, since this was illegal, and so they had turned a blind eye when he was buried under a false name. His case had already been thrown out twice before by the French courts and was, in short, nothing but a scandal and a fraud that had lasted 150 years!

On July 7, 1954, after weeks of argument by some of the country's top lawyers, a packed courtroom waited for the verdict. The court ruled that although the historical record was far from complete, the story usually told in the history books is correct: Louis-Charles did not leave the Tower but died there at the age of ten on June 8, 1795. There was insufficient evidence to support the claim that Karl Wilhelm Naundorff, the watchmaker who died in Delft, was indeed the dauphin. Quite the reverse, he was nothing but a bold adventurer, capable of cunning and deceit on a grand scale. The appeal by the Naundorff family against the 1874 decision was dismissed.

This third court verdict was a crushing blow to the Naundorff family's hopes. Yet they still refused to accept defeat and remained convinced that the French authorities had deliberately withheld information to prevent the truth about Naundorff's claim from being established. From Paris they continued to act as though there was no doubt that the blood that flowed through their veins was of the royal line, traced back through the mists of time to French kings of undisputed glory. They persisted in proclaiming their royal identity and publishing documents to support their cause.

As for the remaining Bourbon, Orléans, and Bonaparte princes, as time progressed it became clear that postwar royalism in France was little more than a fantasy. The Comte de Paris himself, an effete figure at the best of times, became increasingly distanced from the president while desperately trying to maintain his image of the leader of a great royal house, irrespective of the cost. His palaces, his luxurious way of life and the needs of his large family slowly consumed his immense fortune. Gradually, the count realized that his dream of leading France was slipping away from him, and his monthly newsletter, embellished by the *fleur-de-lys*, was finally shut down. By 1967, the count's political aspirations had become the butt of jokes even for De Gaulle. When he was asked whether the count would make a good president, De Gaulle is alleged to have replied, "Yes . . . of the Red Cross."

Meanwhile, almost unbelievably, the soil at the cemetery of Sainte-Marguerite was to be turned over yet again as the 1970s brought further investigations at the site. Although the French court had ruled in 1954 that Louis XVII had died in the Temple prison, historical and forensic evidence to support this was still not conclusive. Questions about the 1846 and 1894 exhumations at Sainte-Marguerite remained unanswered. Was the skeleton of the fourteen-year-old boy uncovered in the 1846 and 1894 exhumations a substitute or just the wrong corpse? Why had Louis-Charles's body still not been found? To try to resolve these issues, in 1970, Michel Fleury, Director of Historic Antiquities of the Île-de-France, obtained permission for yet another excavation at Sainte-Marguerite cemetery.

He undertook a full investigation of the area where the gravedigger, Pierre Bertrancourt, claimed to have reburied the child. Once more, the earth to the left of the chapel door was removed, exposing the foundations. His team painstakingly sifted through the soil, delving much deeper underground than in previous exhumations. They were looking for a ten-year-old male skeleton showing signs of tubercular lesions and with a sawn skull. Yet they failed to find any remains that matched this description. The work continued in 1979 and one skeleton was retrieved: Lot 1, forty-one pieces, which proved by the maturation of the bone to belong to an adult, over eighteen years. Fleury could only conclude that the gravedigger had made a mistake; boasting or deliberately deceiving his wife and friends—perhaps in the hope of making money.

His team turned their attention to the common grave, the official burial site of the dauphin. This was difficult to investigate, since a nursery for small children had been built above the grave. Although a few human remains were retrieved near the edge of this site, none of the bones came from a ten-year-old boy buried almost two hundred years previously. After detailed research, Michel Fleury was forced to concede that the body of Louis-Charles could not be found. The earth, which had swallowed the final evidence of his troubled life, remained impenetrable, yielding none of its secrets. The forensic science had drawn a complete blank. The mystery was unlikely to be resolved unless there was some new evidence or an unexpected advance in forensic science.

As for the child's heart in the crystal urn, this too continued its eventful history. After the July revolution of 1830, it remained with Philippe-Gabriel Pellatan for the next fifty years until his death in 1879. Pellatan's executor tried once more to return the heart to the royal family and approached the Comte de Chambord, Marie-Thérèse's nephew, who was still living in exile at the Château de Frohsdorf. After checking on its authenticity, the count did finally agree to accept the heart, but before he could receive it, he too died in 1883.

In Paris, the boy's heart passed into the hands of a distant relative of Pellatan's wife: a Monsieur Édouard Dumont. He approached the Spanish Bourbons, since, on the death of Marie-Thérèse's nephew, many royalists now recognized the duke of Madrid, Don Carlos de Bourbon, as head of the senior branch of the Bourbon family. The duke scrutinized the detailed records of the heart's history from the Pellatan family and from the archbishop of Paris and finally wrote to Édouard Dumont on June 15, 1895, to confirm his acceptance: "I cannot thank you enough for conserving for my family the heart of my great-uncle, Louis XVII."

Later that month, a ceremony was held in Édouard Dumont's house at

Neuilly-sur-Seine to hand over the precious relic to representatives of the Spanish Bourbons. It was quite a gathering: notaries were present to make official records of the transfer, as well as journalists and representatives of the Bourbon and Pellatan families. The ceremony was to take place in front of a portrait of Dr. Pellatan Sr., in recognition of his great struggles to return the heart to the royal family. Édouard Dumont wished him to be present in some way "at the triumph of his actions," reported the local paper, the *Littoral de la Somme*. After so many years of distrust and neglect, the heart was at last acknowledged, even welcomed by its new owner. "Oh, gentle child's heart! Sacred heart of a martyr, rest at last close to your own family! Rest in peace, sir, my king!" said Monsieur de Junquière, representative of the Spanish Bourbons, in an emotional speech. He turned to Édouard Dumont, on behalf of the Pellatan family, and said, "You have shown . . . that throughout all revolutions and years of exile, close to the heart of a real Bourbon, the heart of real France still beats."

The duke of Madrid deposited the heart in the chapel of the Château de Frohsdorf in Austria. Here, next to Marie-Thérèse's treasured mementos, the stool that her father had made and her mother's lace cap, the heart in the crystal urn was all but forgotten. And there it was to remain, untouched and unseen, for the best part of fifty years, until Europe was transformed once more and Austria became part of the Third Reich.

During World War II, the Château de Frohsdorf was first occupied by the Germans and then on liberation was looted by the Soviet army, who turned it into a military hospital. After the war, Marie-Thérèse's former home was unrecognizable, having the sad air of something about to be demolished. The chapel was desecrated; it had been used for storage, the stained-glass windows were broken, the marble altar was shattered, and rubbish was piled high. A worn emblem of the crown and *fleur-de-lys* still clung to the doorway, but the child's heart, which had survived two revolutions, was nowhere in sight.

Chapter Eleven

RESOLUTION

*I do not know whose heart this is, but it is certainly symbolic
of children anywhere in the world who have suffered.*

PRIEST AT THE BASILICA OF SAINT-DENIS,
DECEMBER 15, 1999

Some thirty kilometers east of Brussels, in Belgium, lies the ancient
Flemish town of Leuven. It was once part of the empire of Marie-
Antoinette's mother, Maria-Theresa, and the ghosts of the old Habsburg
empire still seem to linger in the narrow streets and squares that bear their
names; there is even a college named in honor of the Empress Maria-Theresa.
Now the charm of the old town, with its shady maze of cobbled streets and
tall, narrow, red-tiled houses, each with its profusion of geraniums tumbling
precipitously from window ledges and balconies, contrasts with the noisy,
almost carnival atmosphere of the market square.

Away from the excitement of the old city, on the outskirts of town, lies
the sprawling, modern campus of the University Hospital, the largest hospital in Belgium. At the top of the hill in a large concrete block is the
Center for Human Genetics. Crisscrossed by a series of long corridors, the
windows open out onto an endless series of laboratories providing a view of
technicians in masks and gowns absorbed in their specialist tasks. At the
far end of the building, approached through all this gleaming paraphernalia
of late-twentieth-century science, is a bright, airy room overlooking the
campus. Outside is a secretary screening the calls; inside, a neat array of

studies, piles of papers, classical music playing softly. It is the office of Professor Jean-Jacques Cassiman.

Now in his fifties, Cassiman is of medium build, with a thick crop of dark brown hair, tanned face, and watchful dark eyes. As a specialist in genetics, for much of his career he has been in charge of all the molecular diagnostics for the University Hospital. He also leads a research team trying to understand the role of genetic change in life-threatening diseases such as certain cancers and leukemia.

In 1992, Cassiman received a call out of the blue from a Dutch historian who introduced himself as Hans Petrie. Petrie had been intrigued by the Naundorff case for years and was studying it for a thesis at the University of Groningen in Holland. He explained the history of Louis-Charles and wanted Cassiman to use genetic testing to find a solution to the dauphin mystery. From his interpretation of the historical data, he was doubtful that Naundorff could be the prince, and thought that genetic testing would finally settle the issue, one way or another.

By studying the archives, Hans Petrie had traced the very lock of Naundorff's hair that had been removed from his coffin during his exhumation in 1950. These hairs, he explained to Cassiman, were now stored in a sealed envelope in the archives of the dutch city of Delft. "Could these hairs be compared genetically to those from the dauphin or other members of his family to solve the mystery?" Petrie asked.

Professor Cassiman was only too aware of the advances in genetics over the last fifty years that might make this possible. In 1953, while Naundorff's descendents were stealing the headlines as they prepared their third attempt to prove their royal pedigree in court, a scientific discovery, barely reported in the press, was to transform twentieth-century science. In the same year, James Watson and Francis Crick at Cambridge University had discovered "the secret of life": DNA.

It had long been suspected that a substance, invisible to the naked eye yet found in the nucleus of every living cell, called DNA, or deoxyribonucleic acid, was the magical ingredient that could make us all unique, carrying chemical messages of inheritance from generation to generation. Watson and Crick deciphered the structure of DNA as an elegant double helix made of two spiralling strands of alternating molecules of sugar and phosphate. They showed that the strands are joined, like the steps on a ladder, by molecules known as bases which form a code along the lengths of DNA: A for adenine, T for thymine, G for guanine and C for cytosine. Watson and Crick's landmark paper in the science journal *Nature* soon led to a revolution in our understanding of genetics.

With the molecular basis of DNA defined, questions inconceivable just a few years before could now be explored. By the late 1970s, advances in genetics were being applied to detect individual variation in DNA, the unique genetic blueprint for each individual. Incredibly, 99.8 percent of a person's DNA is the same in everyone; this is what makes us human, with the same basic structure of organs and bones, rather than some other creature. However, the remaining fraction of a percent can vary greatly from one person to another. In 1984, Professor Alec Jeffreys at Leicester University developed a method of identifying individual differences in DNA. He discovered that within the highly variable regions of DNA there are repeated sequences of bases, such as ATGATGATGATG and so on. The number of repeats can vary enormously from one individual to the next. He realized that if he could find a way of counting the number of repeats then he would have a unique "genetic signature" for an individual.

He designed a specific DNA "probe" that could attach to these sections of repeated or stuttered DNA. The probes were radioactively labelled so that wherever they bond to the DNA there would be radioactive emissions. This was then exposed to X-ray film to provide an image of this DNA as a series of dark bands, not unlike a supermarket bar code, different for each individual. "It was a eureka moment," says Jeffreys. "We had a unique 'DNA fingerprint' of an individual."

As news of the breakthrough spread, Jeffreys was approached by the local Leicestershire police who were trying to solve the double murder of two young women. Jeffreys's team was able to extract a "DNA fingerprint" from a tiny semen sample collected at the crime scene. Blood samples were taken from almost four thousand local men, until finally they found an exact match to the DNA collected at the crime scene. This led to a successful conviction in 1987 and, within a year, DNA testing was being used in many criminal cases around the world.

Alec Jeffreys went on to develop increasingly sophisticated techniques of DNA fingerprinting and was soon to apply this to solve historical mysteries, notably the case of Dr. Josef Mengele, the Auschwitz "Angel of Death." Mengele had evaded capture after World War II and escaped to South America until his death in 1979. He was buried as Wolfgang Gerhard, but exhumed six years later. In 1990, Jeffreys extracted trace amounts of DNA from his bone and compared it to DNA from Mengele's family. The presence of all the paternal bands in his son provided very strong evidence that this was indeed the Nazi war criminal.

The DNA in the Mengele case was successfully extracted from bone that had been buried for six years. In 1992, in an ambitious and high-profile case, this genetic technology was to be applied to solve the mystery of the death of the Russian czar and his family more than seventy years previously. As with the dauphin, this story too was one of royalty imprisoned and in danger, and they too came to a bloody and mysterious end and spawned famous pretenders. The Russians had uncovered nine bodies in a shallow grave near Yekaterinburg in Siberia which matched the description of the Russian royal family murdered by the Bolsheviks in 1918. The bodies showed evidence of a brutal death: bayonet marks and bullet wounds to the skulls, bones crushed and damaged by sulphuric acid. A British forensic team was collaborating with the Russians to carry out forensic tests. They hoped to extract DNA from the bones found in the Siberian grave and compare it to DNA from living descendents of the Russian royal family, including Prince Philip, the duke of Edinburgh, to confirm the identity of the bodies.

By the early 1990s, Professor Cassiman was leading one of the few teams at the forefront of this genetic technology in Europe. "Jeffreys's work opened the door," he says. "He established the principle—there are areas of DNA with extreme variation in composition and this can be used to identify individuals." At the request of the Belgian criminal justice system, Cassiman had set up a specialist forensic laboratory at Leuven to advise on criminal cases, and his team was also involved in archaeological research into human remains found at a site near Brussels. He was intrigued as Hans Petrie explained the story of the lost dauphin and the pretenders and agreed to take on the case. "It was a scientific challenge," he says. "We wanted to be able to show whether the Prussian clockmaker was Louis XVII or not."

Cassiman explained to Petrie that they would stand a greater chance of success if they tried to extract a particular type of DNA known as mitochondrial DNA. This is contained outside the nucleus of each cell, in slender structures known as the mitochondria, the powerhouses of each cell which convert nutrients into energy. Unlike the vast majority of DNA inside the nucleus of the cell which is inherited from both parents, mitochondrial DNA, or mtDNA, is inherited *only* from the mother—the so-called umbilical line passed unchanged from mother, grandmother, great-grandmother and so on. Since mtDNA comes only from the maternal line, genes can be traced over the generations much more easily than genes that may have come from either the mother or father.

All the mementos lovingly saved by various members of the dauphin's family in times of crisis now took on a new significance. Invisible to the naked eye, the genetic essence of the maternal line might perhaps be revealed within locks of hair or other relics that had been so carefully treasured. Cassiman was hoping to find samples of hair or bone from Marie-Antoinette or her female relatives, even blood samples from living female Habsburg descendents, to compare to DNA from Naundorff's hair. If Naundorff was Marie-Antoinette's son, the mtDNA extracted from his hair should be an exact match to mtDNA from Marie-Antoinette's line.

In the autumn of 1992, the sealed envelope bearing Naundorff's hair was duly conveyed to Cassiman's laboratory in Leuven by the mayor of Delft and other dignitaries from Holland. Before they went ahead with their investigation, they wanted permission from the Naundorff family. There were two lines of descent, headed by different Naundorff-Bourbons. The oldest surviving member of the senior branch of the family, Charles-Louis-Edmund de Bourbon, who was in his seventies, lives out his days in Marly-le-Roi, near Versailles, firmly in the belief that he is of royal blood. His followers still recognize him as King Charles XII, and, in 1990, founded the Institut Louis XVII in Rue des Moines in Paris to promote the Naundorffist cause. There is also a Dutch-Canadian branch, headed by Charles-Louis de Bourbon, who lives in Ontario, Canada. Both sides of the family were aware that Cassiman could potentially rule out their claim and yet were in full agreement. For Naundorff's descendents it was a chance, finally, to prove their royal connections. They called Cassiman to confirm that they were happy for the tests to proceed.

In gloved hands in a special laboratory at the Center for Human Genetics dedicated to DNA extraction, the seal on the envelope from Holland was broken. Inside were a handful of red-blond hairs pressed tightly together. All the equipment was sterilized to avoid any contamination; all the chemicals used to remove impurities were specially filtered. To obtain Naundorff's DNA, the hair shafts had to be dissolved completely. They could extract DNA even from just one hair. "This can give you nanograms of DNA," said Cassiman. "It's a little—but just enough." Gradually the clue to Naundorff's identity was reduced to a few mere drops of colorless solution in a test tube.

Since the DNA samples were so small, Cassiman used a new technique to amplify the DNA, known as PCR or polymerase chain reaction. Millions of copies of a specific section of DNA can be chemically synthesized in a short time in a small PCR machine. This technique has transformed research with very degraded DNA samples, since tiny sections of DNA can be singled out and copied millions of times to provide a large enough sample for identification.

Although there are sixteen thousand base pairs in the whole of the mitochondrial DNA, Cassiman's aim was just to isolate a particular region of the mtDNA known as the D loop, comprising 1,100 base pairs. They needed to determine the exact sequence of bases A,C,T,G, and so on, along the length of two specific regions of Naundorff's mtDNA, known as HVR1, or hypervariable region 1, and HVR2, or hypervariable region 2. This would show the maximum variation from one individual to another.

Once these two sections of mtDNA had been copied millions of times in the presence of labelled nucleotides, they were taken to yet another specialist laboratory to the sequencer, which could read the sequence of bases along the length of the two sections of mtDNA. "You put your samples into the machine and run it on a gel. The laser will detect the type of fluorescence that passes through and give a readout of different colors that correspond to the difference bases," says Cassiman. If they were successful, the sequence of Naundorff's mtDNA would finally emerge as a unique sequence of As, Cs, Ts and Gs.

While this research was under way, Cassiman and Petrie had to track down biological samples from Marie-Antoinette or her maternal relatives for comparison. They announced details of the genetic testing in the Dutch and Belgian newspapers in the hope that private collectors might come forward with suitable artifacts or mementos. Some of the responses took them by surprise. One collector arrived with a handkerchief stained with blood—supposedly from Marie-Antoinette herself. The cloth was said to have been soaked in her blood at the time of her execution. "I didn't think that was likely to be true," said Cassiman, "so I did not pursue it."

However, they soon discovered that there was a way to obtain DNA from Marie-Antoinette and her family. The Empress Maria-Theresa, Marie-Antoinette's mother, had kept a rosary, which was thought to contain a lock of hair of each of her children. This rosary, which the empress had used in her prayers for keeping count of her devotions, was now held in the Elisabethinen convent in Klagenfurt, Austria. It was here that her oldest daughter, the invalid, Maria-Anna, had spent the later years of her life. When she died in 1789, the monastic order had received a number of her belongings, including her mother's bead string. Cassiman and Petrie obtained permission to test samples of this hair and, in March 1995, Cassiman set off for Klagenfurt.

The rosary was very ornate, shiny black beads interlaced with decorated gold medallions. It had not been opened for two hundred years. "We had to do this in a scientific way with as little chance as possible of contaminating the hairs with modern DNA," explains Cassiman. "The whole thing was very well planned; there were a number of witnesses. The archivist at Klagenfurt authenticated the rosary. A jeweller was brought in to open it because the people at Klagenfurt did not want to destroy the clasp." There were sixteen medallions, one for each of Maria-Theresa's children. Each medallion had an inscription of the name of the child. Marie-Antoinette's hair was deemed too precious, but the convent did give permission for hairs of two of her sisters to be taken.

Before Cassiman's eyes, the first medallion was opened. It was a tense moment; nobody really knew what was inside each medallion hiding its two-hundred-year-old secret. Cassiman could see a tiny metal grid that kept the hairs in place. When this filter was lifted the medallion was full of light brown hairs. They had been cut to the right length and carefully pasted in place, one by one. These hairs were from another of Marie-Antoinette's older sisters: Johanna-Gabriela, who died in 1762 at the age of twelve. When Cassiman saw the fragile state of the hairs in the rosary he was doubtful about achieving success but was intrigued by the challenge.

The next medallion was the same: painstakingly filled with brown hairs of yet another sister, Maria-Josepha, the ill-fated beauty who had died suddenly of smallpox in 1767 just before her wedding at the age of sixteen. The empress had ordered Maria-Josepha to pray in the royal crypt beside a relative who had just died of smallpox, but the coffin lid had not been properly fastened and this intimate proximity was enough to ensure that the unseen deadly virus would accompany her dutiful prayers and exact a terrible price for her obedience. Cassiman selected two or three hairs from Johanna-Gabriela and Maria-Josepha, carefully placed them in sterile containers and conveyed them himself back to his laboratory in Leuven.

Meanwhile in Holland, Hans Petrie was making headway tracking down locks of Marie-Antoinette's own hair. A collector near Nijmegen had seen their newspaper advertisements and phoned Petrie to tell him that there was a collection of curios from Marie-Antoinette in the museum of the University of Nijmegen. Petrie went immediately to find out what was there. To his great delight he found many evocative trinkets, including samples of her hair, carefully set in a frame decorated with the lilies of the Bourbons. The hairs were held firmly in place by silk thread, fastened by a seal bearing the handwriting of Henri, the Comte de Chambord, declaring that if the seal and thread were intact, the hair was authentic. The documents with the frame showed that these hairs were originally owned by the dauphin's sister, Marie-Thérèse. The memento had been passed down in the family until eventually sold to a Dutch collector at an auction in France and, in time, had been bequeathed to the university.

At around the same time, a second source of Marie-Antoinette's hair came to light in another private collection in Cannes in southern France, owned by the Marquise Jane de Bernardières. These locks of hair were dried in a medallion and their origin could only be established from oral testimony passed down through the generations of the families who owned the piece. Nonetheless, when these light brown hairs arrived in a sealed envelope from southern France, Cassiman could see they looked very similar to the hairs from Holland.

By 1995, however, despite their success in gathering hairs from Marie-Antoinette and her maternal relatives scattered all over Europe, the scientific team had run into a problem. They had taken no less than sixty-two different extracts of Naundorff's hair. Yet each time they were frustrated to find they obtained a different mtDNA sequence. The DNA in Naundorff's hairs was too contaminated and too degraded to give a reproducible result. In Holland, Petrie was aware of the disappointment. Knowing that they now had hairs from Marie-Antoinette and her sisters, he was determined to find another source of biological material from Naundorff.

Petrie knew from the official description of Naundorff's exhumation in 1950 that in addition to a lock of his hair, a bone was also taken from his coffin, the humerus, or upper arm bone. At the time, this had been used to determine whether Naundorff's death was due to poisoning, but Petrie could not trace what happened to this bone afterward. He tried many different museums and collections, but after a three-year search the trail went cold. In desperation, he went back to the main Dutch forensic laboratory in The

Hague. Petrie had already spoken to this laboratory once and had been assured that Naundorff's bone was not there. He decided to try one last time—and this time he was lucky.

Naundorff's arm bone, sawn in two, was indeed waiting to be discovered and rescued from such an unsuitable royal resting place, in a neatly labelled sealed jar in the Dutch forensic laboratory at Rijswijk. It was not on display, but kept in the archives of the pathology department, a mere curio among countless other curios that had accumulated over the years. Cassiman's colleague, Ronny Decorte, hurried to Holland to collect the crucial specimen, and samples of Naundorff's bone and the Habsburg hairs were also sent to a second genetics laboratory in Nantes, France, where tests were to be carried out independently for comparison.

In the dedicated extraction laboratory, the surface layers of Naundorff's arm bone were removed with a sterile saw to ensure there was no contamination from handling the bone. Els Jehaes, who was working on her Ph.D., undertook much of the testing on Naundorff. Carefully, she removed four internal segments of bone, barely a centimeter each. These were placed in liquid nitrogen and ground to a powder in a freezer mill in preparation for DNA extraction. The fine grey dust of his bones now held the key to whether this was, indeed, the arm bone of the ill-fated and perhaps much-maligned prince.

"We repeated the extraction several times—thirteen in all," says Cassiman. "Not all the sequences were complete; there were some that were contaminated, but we got an identical sequence *nine* times." If a result is reproducible several different times, from different bone samples, he explains, this helps to confirm the authenticity of the sequence. What is more, the samples of bone analyzed in the laboratory in Nantes produced the exact same sequence: the unique trace of Naundorff's mitochondrial DNA.

This sequence had to be compared to that obtained from the hairs of Marie-Antoinette and her maternal relatives. When they looked at these hairs under the electron microscope it was clear that some were damaged; the outer envelope of the hair was frayed or broken. There were, however, some hairs that were still intact. Starting with the young aunts of Louis

XVII—hairs from Johanna-Gabriela and Marie-Josepha—the scientific team successfully extracted four DNA samples. Of these, to their delight, three sequences were identical: the unique trace of the maternal mtDNA sequence of the Habsburg family. It was the first time his team had successfully extracted an mtDNA sequence just from a sample of hair.

However, when these mtDNA sequences from Marie-Antoinette's sisters were compared to those from Naundorff's bone—there was a surprise. In hypervariable region 1 in the mtDNA there was only *one* nucleotide difference at position 16260. "One nucleotide difference is insufficient to exclude Naundorff as a son of Marie-Antoinette," Cassiman said. "We had a problem. One difference is not enough to conclude anything. We didn't have enough proof."

To obtain more evidence, they analyzed the mtDNA at another region, between hypervariable regions 1 and 2. This part is less variable between individuals and is usually not analyzed. However, they did find one other difference, at position 16519. With two nucleotide differences between Naundorff's bone and Marie-Antoinette's sisters, this strongly favored the conclusion that Naundorff was not Louis XVII.

"The chances that Naundorff was indeed a son of Marie-Antoinette were now very slim," says Cassiman, "although I wouldn't say he was completely excluded on the basis of this result." They went in search of more proof. Cassiman's first step was to check that the mtDNA sequences obtained for Marie-Antoinette's two sisters were authentic. Attempts to obtain DNA for comparison from hair samples of other descendents of the Empress Maria-Theresa proved unsuccessful; however, he did have the hairs that were thought to have come from Marie-Antoinette herself. "These were important because there was fairly good evidence that this was indeed hair from Marie-Antoinette," says Cassiman. "If the sequence from these hairs had been different from her sisters, that would have been worrying." They tested both the Marie-Antoinette hairs from Cannes and from Nijmegen and successfully obtained an unambiguous sequence identical to her sisters' hair. He now had a third confirmation of the Habsburg sequence.

There was one final check. They knew that Marie-Antoinette had living maternal relatives who could provide fresh DNA for a comparison: Queen Anna of Romania and her brother, André de Bourbon-Parme. Cassiman wrote to Queen Anna explaining the tests and requesting a sample of her blood; the team in Nantes obtained samples of hair from her brother. Both these mtDNA sequences proved to be identical. Comparison of their mtDNA sequence with that of Naundorff revealed that there were *four* nucleotide differences between these living relatives and Naundorff's mtDNA. This made it even more unlikely that Naundorff could be a relative.

"The result, however, was troublesome," admits Cassiman. Although the living Habsburg relatives had the same two differences in their mtDNA as the hairs of Marie-Antoinette and her two sisters, in addition there were two further differences in their mtDNA. This was puzzling, since the results should have been identical. Studies on mtDNA had established that mutations usually occur only once in thirty-three generations. This suggested there had been two mutations in the nine generations that separated Marie-Antoinette and her two sisters from Queen Anna and her brother. Although this was possible, it was very rare. "This result bothered me and we hoped to find an explanation," said Cassiman. "We believed in the conclusion that we had to rule Naundorff out, but we were left with this problem of two additional nucleotide differences. That frustrated me—not that we did not solve the Naundorff problem—but that we did not get clean results. As scientists we want one hundred percent."

Cassiman and his team wrote up their results for publication in the *European Journal of Human Genetics* in 1998. Since Naundorff's bone showed two nucleotide differences from the sequences of the two aunts and the mother of Louis XVII and four differences from the sequences of living maternal relatives, he concluded, as had the French courts in 1851, 1872 and 1954, that "it becomes very unlikely that Karl Wilhelm Naundorff is the son of Marie-Antoinette." After a lifetime of acting the part of the prince, of looking like the prince, there, in the center of his being, the genetic essence of his bones denied it all. Naundorff was a great impostor, betrayed, apparently, by his arm bone.

Naundorff's descendents, however, do not accept this scientific evidence.

They want Naundorff's grave in Holland exhumed once more to obtain more bones for testing. "The only way now that the relatives can still claim that Naundorff was the son of Marie-Antoinette," says Cassiman, "is if they can prove that the bone taken from his coffin in 1950 is *not* his bone!" Ever more convoluted explanations were needed for Naundorff to be the missing prince. Cassiman told them, "If you want to exhume, fine, go ahead. But the story is finished. There are no grounds to take it any further." There was just one outstanding question. If Naundorff was not the missing prince, then who was?

With Naundorff's claim out of the picture, Cassiman suddenly found he was a target for other hopeful counts and princes, descendents of the numerous pretenders. All the old romantic escapades and escape stories to shame Hollywood were resurrected. "There was a Belgian count who visited me who had contacts in Argentina," recalls Cassiman. He believed the dauphin had fled from France and died in Argentina where his skeleton was buried in a mass grave. "They had been dowsing with a pendent over the grave to try to establish which of these skeletons might be the lost dauphin. They had even carried out tests on a skeleton with strange results which they wanted me to look at." On another occasion, he received a call from a woman who claimed to be a descendent of Marie-Thérèse. According to her account, Marie-Thérèse escaped and a substitute girl was locked in the Tower who later went on to live in Austria and marry the Duc d'Angoulême. The *real* princess fled to Poland where she had children and her descendents now lived in Munich. Cassiman shook his head at these fanciful stories.

In the case of the Russian royal family, the British forensic team had been able to positively identify the skeletons found in Siberia. They found that one woman and three of her children in the grave were maternally related to Prince Philip, the duke of Edinburgh, a grand-nephew of Czarina Alexandra. This genetic evidence, taken with the historical record, provided convincing proof that this miscellaneous collection of bones was, in fact, the once all-powerful czarina and three of her beautiful daughters. However, genetic tests on bones thought to be from Czar Nicholas himself yielded a rare anomaly and proved inconclusive. The case was only resolved when the Russian authorities finally agreed to exhume the czar's brother, Georgij Romanov. Tests showed he had exactly the same rare anomaly, providing almost 100 percent confirmation that it was indeed the czar in the grave. In 1998, the Russian royal family had a state funeral in St. Petersburg. The genetics in the czar's case had led to a satisfactory conclusion—but how could Cassiman resolve the case of the dauphin?

There was one other way forward. "Hans Petrie kept talking about a missing heart," recalls Cassiman. Petrie knew that during the autopsy on the boy who died in the Temple in June 1795, his heart had been stolen. DNA analysis on this heart might show whether the orphan of the Temple was maternally related to Marie-Antoinette and, if confirmed, put an end to the theory of a substitute. Cassiman was tantalized by the fact that he now had the mitochondrial DNA signature of the Habsburg maternal line— it would be so easy to compare. But where was the heart?

By chance, shortly after announcing his results on Naundorff in 1998, Cassiman received a phone call from an eminent French historian in Paris called Philippe Delorme. Delorme introduced himself, and it was soon clear that he had a deep interest in the case and had studied the life of Louis XVII closely. He knew exactly where the heart could be found and was sure he could get a piece. And he was right.

With painstaking research, Philippe Delorme had traced the whole incredible story of the child's heart: Pellatan's "pious theft" during the French Revolution, his Herculean efforts to return the heart to the royal family, Tillos's theft from Pellatan, the dramatic loss of the heart in the July Revolution of 1830, and its eventual transfer to the Château de Frohsdorf, where it was again caught up in war with the advances of first Hitler's troops and then the Soviet army. However, during World War II, Delorme told Cassiman, the heart had been rescued by the duke of Madrid's descendents and ended up in the care of his granddaughter, Princess Marie-des-Neiges Massimo. Eventually, in April 1975, the princess had returned the boy's heart to France. In a solemn ceremony, the heart had been given to the Duc de Bauffremont, who runs the Memorial at Saint-Denis, the private organization that oversees the royal graves. More than 150 years since Pellatan had first tried to place the relic in the royal crypt, the heart of the orphan of the Temple had finally arrived at the Basilica at Saint-Denis. It had been placed in an underground chapel in the crypt, *La Chapelle des Princes*, and, said Delorme, it is still there to this day.

After speaking to Cassiman, Delorme immediately went to see the Duc de Bauffremont. He explained that his historical research had shown that it was indeed the same child's heart from the Temple prison in 1795 as the one now in the Basilica. Despite its astonishing past, this stolen heart, the only vestiges of the child who died in the Tower, could yet reveal the true story of the dauphin. The Duc de Bauffremont was intrigued and agreed to the tests.

In June 1999, the three men gathered round the tiny heart in its urn hidden away in a side chapel at Saint-Denis. For Philippe Delorme, it was an emotional moment as the wrought-iron gate to *La Chapelle des Princes* was unlocked and they walked carefully in the half-light between the dusty coffins, seeming almost to walk through time itself as they travelled back two hundred years, reaching the shelf on the far wall where the crystal urn with its secret waited. "It was scarcely like a heart, it was so small and dry, and yet, at the same time, it was such a powerful symbol," thought Delorme. True scientist, Cassiman remained unmoved at the sight—to him it was nothing more than a biological specimen. The urn was sealed, so he could not examine the heart directly; he suspected that it was in bad shape, given its eventful history. Delorme asked what their chances were of obtaining any DNA. Cassiman could guarantee nothing, but agreed they would at least try.

There were earnest discussions about the protocol, permissions and the nature of the genetic tests; because of the public interest in the case, they decided notaries should record every detail of the procedure. Cassiman agreed to look for another genetics team that could also carry out independent tests. "They asked me specifically—don't take a Frenchman." Cassiman smiled. "There were too many vested interests in the story in France!" He nominated a German laboratory at Münster University, led by Professor

Bernard Brinkmann. Brinkmann's team was one of the few in Europe that had considerable expertise in the use of mitochondrial DNA in forensic cases.

With arrangements complete, on December 15, 1999, after a short ceremony at Saint-Denis, the boy's heart in the crystal urn was placed in a hearse and travelled through the streets of Paris once more on its final journey. At the nearby Thierry Coté Medical Laboratory, Cassiman soon found his initial doubts were not justified. It was possible to see every detail of the heart, the muscular structure, the coronary arteries, all the vessels and compartments; it was extremely well preserved. However, time had turned it to stone and it could only be cut with a saw. Doctor Els Jehaes severed the bottom tip of the heart and also took a sample of the aorta, the great artery coming from the heart. These segments were then carefully divided: one specimen for Cassiman and his team in Belgium, the other for Professor Brinkmann in Germany, and then the jars were sealed.

Cassiman himself carried the five hundred milligrams of the boy's heart back to Leuven, past the old town and Maria-Theresiastraat to the Center for Human Genetics on the edge of town. He took the sealed tube up to the sixth floor, along gleaming corridors lined with canisters of gas, fridges and freezers. It was here that the carefully labelled locks of hair from Marie-Antoinette were stored, along with the locks from the dauphin's aunts. Now the segments of the child's heart, too, joined them in a freezer awaiting examination.

Once the notary arrived to witness the breaking of the seal of the jar in Leuven, the heart was taken to the extraction laboratory. To get at the child's DNA, first they had to destroy the heart tissue, removing cell walls, proteins, and any other material. The fragments of heart were cut into very small pieces with a sterile saw and then crushed, either with a pestle and mortar, or frozen in liquid nitrogen and broken up with a hammer. "It was like grinding meat," says Cassiman. Gradually, the child's heart was reduced to a fine dust in a sterile tube. Standard chemical procedures were used to clean it and break down the cell walls with special enzymes. To Cassiman's surprise, the heart contained relatively high amounts of DNA. As before, this was put in the PCR machine to copy the genetic signature of the child millions of times. These samples were then placed in the sequencing machine, to read the order of the 1,100 bases in the two key sections of mitochondrial DNA.

In the sterile modern laboratory, under the bright fluorescent lights, faint echoes from another age emerged as the secrets of the heart finally yielded to modern science. Cassiman was able to obtain three identical sequences of mitochondrial DNA from the child's heart—the essential clue to his identity.

"As soon as we had the little boy—we could see his sequence was identical to the living relatives," says Cassiman. To double-check, they compared it manually—base by base. It was an *exact* match. "We had worked for years on the Naundorff case and come out with a result which I was not one hundred percent pleased with scientifically," says Cassiman. "Our results had made the point that Naundorff was not Louis XVII—but not to our satisfaction. We had the problem of the two additional changes in the mtDNA in the living relatives of Marie-Antoinette, compared to the sequences from Marie-Antoinette's and her sisters' hair. Now we had the heart, everything fell into place because it matched the living Habsburg relatives perfectly! This confirmed for me that we had not got a complete result from the older relatives."

There was just one final test. Could he get the Habsburg sequence found in the boy's heart and Marie-Antoinette's living relatives from the older biological specimens—the hairs of Marie-Antoinette or her sisters? They had spent some time developing their methodology and developed a probe that would allow them to amplify shorter sequences in the PCR machine. The original tests had been done on longer DNA fragments that were over 250 base pairs. They now recognized that it was easier to accidentally include a contaminant in the longer fragments, and miss some of the key positions that make up the true sequence. With the new probes, they could break the DNA into tiny fragments, a mere 100–200 base pairs, to obtain a more accurate result.

The hairs of Marie-Antoinette herself did not contain sufficient DNA to get a full result. But in the freezer outside the laboratory they had just one hair shaft left—from her sister Johanna-Gabriela. "I felt if we could confirm the same sequence that we found in the living relatives in that one hair then I would be satisfied," declared Cassiman.

He repeated the cycle: extraction, analysis, PCR and sequencing. Once he had the results he sent them to the computer in his office where he had stored the results from the boy's heart. Here in his orderly office, sunlight streaming through the windows, classical music playing softly as he worked, Cassiman could study the result, base by base. The distinctive genetic signature from the single hair of Marie-Antoinette's sister—the Habsburg maternal line—was lined up against the heart of the son she had lost. Using the ghostly imprint of the genetic material of mother and son, united for the first time in two hundred years as an electronic signal in the laboratory computer, together they were able to reveal what really happened. The sequence from Johanna-Gabriela, the aunt the dauphin had never met, was an exact match to the heart of the boy. The DNA signatures for the critical region of mitochondrial DNA were *identical*.

On April 3, Professor Brinkmann came to Leuven to compare data. "They had the same results—and that was interesting," Cassiman said, with classic understatement. "Not only did we have sequence alignment and identity from the heart with living and deceased relatives, but we also had independent confirmation from another lab." From a scientific point of view, the puzzle was solved. Meanwhile, Delorme had been waiting anxiously in Paris. He was delighted when a fax finally arrived from Cassiman confirming all of his historical research.

On April 19, 2000, Professors Cassiman and Brinkmann, Philippe Delorme and the Duc de Bauffremont assembled in Paris to hold a press conference to announce their findings. Members of both lines of the Bourbon family were present; Prince Louis de Bourbon, duke of Anjou, one of the closest living relatives of Louis-Charles, arrived from Spain for the occasion. There were also representatives of Naundorff's family. A large crowd of TV crews, international press, and photographers had gathered to hear the results.

Cassiman and Brinkmann carefully outlined the steps in the scientific testing. "The comparison of the DNA appeared to show beyond all reasonable doubt that the heart came from a child that was maternally related to the Habsburg family," Cassiman told the reporters. "The sequence for the Habsburg family is unique, since it has not been observed in a collection of more than one thousand seven hundred European mtDNA sequences. All this, taken with the historical record, provides strong evidence to support the proposition that this is the heart of the lost dauphin."

With his customary scientific caution, he also explained the limitations of the testing. "The science does not *prove* beyond doubt that the heart belonged to Louis XVII, or even to a son of Louis XVI and Marie Antoinette," he said. "The scientific tests can only show that the heart in the crypt has to belong to the son of a maternal relative of the Habsburg family." When asked whether it was possible that the heart could have come from some other unknown son of Marie-Antoinette herself, he replied, "Marie-Antoinette may have had a relationship with the Swedish count—Axel Fersen—but there is absolutely no historical evidence of a secret son who died at the same age, whose heart could have been taken in this way. Scientifically, I can't disprove this, but it does not fit with the historical data." Marie-Antoinette's life was so public, another child would have been impossible to conceal.

There was also the question of whether the heart could have belonged to the older son of Marie-Antoinette, the first dauphin, Louis-Joseph, who died of illness in Versailles before the revolution in 1789 at the age of eight. "This too was unlikely," Delorme reasoned, "because the heart removed from Louis-Joseph was embalmed. When a heart is embalmed it is cut open down the middle and filled with herbs and embalming liquid." Yet the heart on which Cassiman conducted his tests had clearly not been embalmed; the aorta was cut roughly and the tissues were fragmented and dried as is consistent with the heart's tumultuous history. Consequently, he explained, although Louis-Joseph's heart was lost after the Revolution and has never been found, it is most unlikely to be from Marie-Antoinette's older son.

Some reporters asked about the independence of the tests, given that they were paid for by the royal family trust. Cassiman laughed at this suggestion; he was paid around 1,500 pounds, which barely covered laboratory costs, and he had undertaken the research primarily for the scientific challenge. He pointed out there are only a few forensic laboratories in Europe that can test mtDNA; the two laboratories were specifically chosen because they were not French and had no interest in the outcome. Others still speculated that the extraordinary history of the heart must cast doubt on the findings. Professors Cassiman and Brinkmann dismissed this criticism, explaining that two independent teams had come to exactly the same result.

"And is this ninety-nine percent sure?' pressed the reporters.

"Yes, I'm satisfied," replied Cassiman. "If you take our results with the historical evidence—and if that is correct—then our results are one hundred percent. Everything seems to indicate that it was the young dauphin who died alone in the Temple prison in tragic circumstances."

"This is the end of two hundred years of uncertainty," declared Delorme. "It puts to an end a mystery that has absorbed so many of us. The DNA analysis shows the child's heart is from a member of the Habsburg family. The historical research shows that this heart came from the orphan of the Temple. Since, apart from Marie-Thérèse who survived, the only other relative of Marie-Antoinette in the Temple in 1795 was Louis-Charles, now we have an answer. It was Louis XVII, the little king of France without a crown, who died in the Temple prison. It's definitive."

All other claimants, however plausible, were shown to be impostors. Each one in his secret heart had acted out a fantasy, laughing at the credulous world. They had all tried to exploit the circumstances of Louis-Charles's death for their own financial, political and social gain; all apparently equally happy to submit his sister, Marie-Thérèse, to further anguish as they pursued their dubious ambitions. Each must have died, surely aware that they were passing a lie on to their descendents. It is perhaps hardly surprising that after two hundred years, Naundorff's descendents do not accept these genetic findings and are hoping to fund further tests. From the Institut Louis XVII in Paris, they continue to assert their royal pedigree on their website, www.louis-xvii.com.

As for the other stories that had been cited for so long as evidence of Louis-Charles's escape, these, too, fell into place. Widow Simon, the shoemaker's wife, fearing retribution at the Hôpital des Incurables for the brutish treatment her husband had measured out to the dauphin, had evidently invented her own escape story and repeated it so often that she came to believe it. The silent child seen in his cell in the Tower by Jean-Baptiste Harmand and many others was no substitute but in fact the young prince himself, then so traumatized by his tormentors that silence seemed the only way he could deal with an inexplicable and hostile world. In the words of Dr. Pierre Desault, shortly before his own death—almost certainly of natural causes—Louis-Charles had been reduced to "a child who is now mad, dying, a victim of the most abject misery and of the greatest abandonment, a being who has been brutalized by the cruellest of treatments and who it is impossible for me to bring back to life. What a crime!" As for the various documents appearing to provide proof of the dauphin's escape, like Naundorff's forged letters apparently setting out a twenty-year correspondence with his "sister," all this amounted to no more than the cruel and Machiavellian twists of the human mind exploiting tragedy for self-interest. No worse perhaps than the fact that a nation in a moment of madness was quite prepared to sacrifice one small boy for the greater good and that one small boy, alone and defenseless, turned out to be quite a hero of whom his mother would have been most proud.

"For me it's a very important day," said Delorme, "a very moving day for a historian. It's an affair that has lasted two centuries. There have been around eight hundred books written on the subject and we never managed to find the response. I think now we are bestowing justice on this child. Until now, his death was stolen. It was not admitted that he died in such a horrible way."

"More than two centuries of mystery have ended here today," declared Prince Louis de Bourbon. The discovery should be dedicated to the "memory of an innocent child who was a victim of history," he said, and called on the French authorities to bury Louis XVII's heart next to the tombs of his father and mother in the royal crypt. He was not alone in the desire to give the heart, the only surviving remnant of Louis-Charles's body, a proper memorial. "We would like to see him buried between his mother and his father, which would be very fitting," said the Duc de Bauffremont.

The next day the child's heart made headlines around the world. Whatever the motive that prompted Dr. Philippe-Jean Pellatan to steal the child's heart—whether royal fervor, curiosity or a desire to make money—it is ironic that an act of thievery should lead two hundred years later to such a satisfactory resolution. As Pellatan had consistently maintained, the child who lived and died alone and in such misery in the Temple, unrecognizable as a royal prince and heir, his sickly body covered in sores and ulcers, was indeed the ten-year-old dauphin. At last, the tragic circumstances of Louis-Charles's death were now proved to the world.

As for his heart, this has been returned to Saint-Denis. It is still hidden from public gaze, having finally come to rest in the shadow world of the crypt. The urn has been resealed and the heart itself, with the tip carefully sawn away, bears the hallmarks of twentieth-century science. More than two hundred years have passed since the owner of the heart suffered in silence, paying a high price for the extravagant mistakes of his forebears. But now justice was done: he has been given a voice, the secrets of his life and death are exposed, and his life, in some small way, is resurrected at last.

NOTES ON SOURCES

Chapter One: "The Finest Kingdom in Europe"

An intimate account of Marie-Antoinette's early years in France has been written by her First Lady of the Bedchamber: Campan, Madame. *Memoirs of the Private Life of Marie Antoinette, Queen of France and Navarre.* 2 vols, 1824. For Marie-Antoinette's personal correspondence to her mother see: Bernier, O. *Imperial Mother, Royal Daughter: The correspondence of Marie-Antoinette and Maria Teresa* (London, Sidgwick and Jackson, 1986); and also Arneth, A., and Geffroy, M. A., eds. *Correspondance Secrète entre Marie-Thérèse et le Comte de Mercy-Argenteau avec les letters de Marie-Thérèse et de Marie-Antoinette.* 3 vols., Paris 1874. See also: Weber, J. *Mémoires concernant Marie Antoinette Archiduchesse d'Autriche, Reine de France,* 1822.

Of the many biographical works exploring Marie-Antoinette's early days in the French court and events leading to the revolution, I would particularly recommend: Fraser, A. *Marie Antoinette* (Weidenfeld and Nicolson, 2001); Dunlop, I. *Marie-Antoinette* (London: Sinclair-Stevenson, 1993); Lever, E. *Marie-Antoinette: The Last Queen of France,* trans. Temerson, C. (New York: Farrar, Straus & Giroux, 2000); Seward, D. *Marie Antoinette* (London, Constable, 1981). A description of the French palaces is given in: Dunlop I. *Royal Palaces of France* (London: Hamish Hamilton, 1985).

For a full discussion of France's financial problems during Louis XVI's reign and how this issue became politicized see: Schama, S. *Citizens: A Chronicle of the French Revolution* (London: Penguin, 1989). See also Bosher, J. F. *French Government Finance 1770–1795* (Cambridge, Cambridge University Press, 1970).

Chapter Two: "Grâce pour Maman"

Marie-Thérèse wrote a short but vivid narration of the royal family's experiences during the revolution, which covers the period from their forced departure from Versailles until the reported death of her brother in 1795. This was written in two parts. The second part was written first, toward the end of Marie-Thérèse's period of imprisonment in the Tower: *Mémoire écrit par Marie-Thérèse-Charlotte de France sur la captivité des princes et princesses, ses parents, depuis le 10 août 1792 jusqu'à la mort de son frère arrivé le 9 juin 1795.* The original version of this manuscript was first given to her guardian, Madame de Chanterenne, who made a copy when Marie-Thérèse left the Temple at the end of 1795. A revised edition, apparently incorporating some changes requested by Louis XVIII, appeared in 1817, published by L. E. Audot. Subsequent editions aiming to be based more closely on her original manuscript also appeared in 1862, published by Poulet-Malassis and in 1892 by Costa de Beauregard. The first part of Marie-Thérèse's narrative, starting with her departure from Versailles, was written after her marriage to the Duc d'Angoulême: *Journal de Marie Thérèse de France, Duchesse d'Angoulême, 5 Octobre 1789–2 Septembre 1792,* introduced by Baron Imbert de Saint-Amand, 1893.

For an analysis of events leading up to and during the French Revolution, in addition to the biographies and Simon Schama cited above, see: Cobban, A. *A History of Modern France* (London: Penguin, 1961); Cronin, V. *Louis and Antoinette* (London: Collins, 1974); Roberts, J. M. *The French Revolution* (London: Oxford University Press, 1978); Cobb, R. *The French and their Revolutions,* ed. Gilmour D. (1998); John Murray, London: A unique colorful nineteenth-century account is given by Carlyle, T. *The French Revolution A History* (1889), reprinted ed. Fielding & Sorensen, (London: Oxford University Press, 1989).

Chapter Three: The Tuileries

Apart from the journal of Marie-Thérèse, another firsthand account of events at the Tuileries and the flight to Varennes is provided by Madame de Tourzel, who remained with the royal family as governess until she was forced to leave the Tower in September 1792: Tourzel, *Mémoires de Madame la Duchesse de Tourzel, Gouvernante des Enfants de France de 1789 à 1795* (Paris, 1883).

For perspectives on this period see also Loomis S. *The Fatal Friendship: Marie Antoinette, Count Fersen and the Flight to Varennes* (1972). Soderhjelm, A. *Fersen et Marie-Antoinette* (1930); Farr, E. *The Untold Love Story, Marie Antoinette and Count Fersen* (London: Allison & Busby, 1997); Oscar, B., *The Flight to Varennes and other Historical Essays* (1892); Chateaubriand, Vicomte René de, *Mémoires d'Outre-Tombe* (Paris, 1949); and Fersen, Count, *Le Comte de Fersen et la cour de France,* ed. R. M. De Klinckowstrom (Paris, 1877–78).

The royal family's "silent decoronation" on their return from Varennes is discussed by Yalom, M. *Blood Sisters. The French Revolution in Women's Memory* (London: HarperCollins,

1995). For the rise of the revolutionary in Paris see Rose, R. B. *The Making of the Sans-culottes: Democratic Ideas and Institutions in Paris 1789–92* (Manchester: Manchester University Press, 1983).

An absorbing analysis of the destruction of Marie-Antoinette's image in the popular press and *libelles* is in: Thomas, C. *The Wicked Queen: The Origins of the Myth of Marie Antoinette*, trans. J. Rose (New York, Urzone 1999). This includes *The Love Life of Charlie and Toinette* [1779], *The Royal Dildo* [1789], *The Royal Orgy* [1789] and many other pamphlets. See also Fleischmann, H. *Les Pamphlets Libertins Contre Marie-Antoinette* (Paris, 1908).

Chapter Four: "God Himself Has Forsaken Me"

The king's valet, Cléry, was a key witness to the life of the royal family in the Tower and events leading to the execution of Louis XVI. See his memoirs: Cléry, J. *Journal de ce qui s'est passé à la Tour du Temple pendant la captivité de Louis XVI, roi de France, par M. Cléry, valet de chambre du roi et autres mémoires sur le Temple.* (Paris: C. Bertin, 1861). See also an account from François Hüe: *The Last Years of the Reign and Life of Louis XVI*, trans. R. C. Dallas (1806); and from the Abbé Edgeworth: Edgeworth de Firmont, Abbé. *Mémoires* (Paris, 1816) and Turgy, L. F., *Fragment historique sur la captivité de la famille royalle* (Paris 1818).

Of the many works which deal with the king's trial in addition to the biographies cited above see also: Jordan, D. *The King's Trial* (Los Angeles, 1979). Hardman, J. *Louis XVI* (New Haven and London: Yale University Press, 1993); Allen, R. *Threshold of Terror: The Last Hours of the Monarchy in the French Revolution* (Sutton. Stroud, Glos., 1999).

Chapter Five: The Young "Sans-Culotte"

Many historians have tried to investigate Louis XVII's period of captivity with Simon as tutor such as: Lenôtre, G. *The Dauphin, Louis XVII. The Riddle of the Temple*, trans. F. Lees. (London: Heinemann, 1922) and Buckley, E.R. *Monsieur Charles. The Tragedy of the True Dauphin, Louis XVII of France* (London: Witherby, 1927). For more modern interpretations, Cronin [above] in his biography *Louis and Antoinette* also includes a short account of this period. The most recent analysis drawing together the evidence on Louis XVII's captivity in the Tower is by French historian Philippe Delorme: *L'affaire Louis XVII* (Paris: Tallandier, 1995).

For more information on Marie-Antoinette's trial and final months: Lenôtre, G. *La Captivité et la mort de Marie-Antoinette* (Paris, 1902). Furneaux, R. *Last Days of Marie Antoinette and Louis XVI* (London: Allen & Unwin, 1968); & Yalom [above].

Note: there has been some debate about the authenticity of the queen's last letter to her sister-in-law. In the letter she says she dies in the "Catholic, Apostolic and Roman religion" and yet had received no spiritual consolation "not knowing if there still exist any priests of this religion." However, there is evidence that she did receive the ministration of the Abbé

Magnin, in which case she could not have said that she did not know if any true Catholic priests existed. Others argue that the letter is indeed authentic and she specifically failed to mention that she had seen a nonjuring priest since this would put him at risk.

Chapter Six: The Orphan of the Temple

The most comprehensive source on the imprisonment of Louis XVII once separated from his family is Beauchesne, *Alcide de Louis XVII: His Life, His Suffering, His Death.* 2 vols., trans. W. Hazlitt (London: Harper and Bros., 1853). After the Restoration, Beauchesne interviewed many surviving witnesses and guards who had worked at the Temple. Although their interviews are couched in the royalist sentiments of the time, they provide a detailed perspective on this period of Louis XVII's captivity, as reported by the only witnesses, his guardians. Beauchesne's extensive study has provided much of the material and anecdotes debated by numerous historians over the years when trying to resolve the fate of Louis XVII. See also Lenotre and Delorme above.

For a compelling analysis of events leading the downfall and death of Robespierre, see Schama and also Hardman, J. *Robespierre.* (Edinburgh: Pearson, 1999). For Princess Élisabeth's support for her brother and a description of her death: *Life and Letters of Ma{cf4}dame Elizabeth de France*, cited in Wormeley, K. P., *Ruin of a Princess* (New York: Lamb Publishing, 1912), also Debriffe, M. *Madame Élisabeth: la princesse martyre* (Paris, Le Semaphore, 1997).

Dr. Philippe-Jean Pellatan's admission that he stole the heart of the child who died in the Temple and his detailed statement on the history of the heart while in his possession is in *Documents Concernant Le Coeur de Louis XVII. Revue Retrospective* 1.3.1894 (Paris). *Mémoire Historique sur les derniers jours de la vie de Louis XVII et sur la Conservations de ses précieux restes.* Biographical details and Pellatan's correspondence relating to the heart are included in the Appendix.

A full investigation into the strange odyssey of the heart taken from the orphan of the Temple has been carried out by historian Philippe Delorme, who was also instrumental in trying to obtain genetic testing. He summarizes his conclusions in *Louis XVII: La Verité. Sa mort au Temple confirmée par la science* (Paris: Pygmalion, G. Watelet, 2000). See also Delorme's website: www.chez.com/louis17.

Chapter Seven: Farce and Fraud

Different perspectives on Marie-Thérèse's life in exile are provided by: Saint-Amand, Baron Imbert de. *The Duchesse d'Angoulême and the Two Restorations*, trans. J. Davis, (London: Hutchinson & C., 1892); Turquan, J. *Madame Royale, The Last Dauphine*, trans. T. Davidson, (London: Fisher Unwin, 1910); Weiner, M. *The French Exiles 1789–1815* (London: Murray, 1960); Mansel, P. *Louis XVIII* (Blond & Briggs, 1981). For Sainte-Beuve's observations see:

Prescott-Wormeley, K., trans. *The Ruin of a Princess* (New York: Lamb Publishing Co., 1912).

Colorful details of the pretenders can be found in many sources. Hervagault's life is described in: Morton, J.B. *The Dauphin, A biography of Louis XVII.* (London: Longmans & Co, 1937); Minnigerade, M. *The Son of Marie Antoinette and the Mystery of the Temple Tower.* (London, Jarrolds, 1935); Welch, C. *The Little Dauphin, Louis XVII.* (London: Methuen, 1908); and also Lenôtre and Buckley [above].

Chapter Eight: Return of the Lilies

For a detailed analysis of the inconclusive evidence of the dauphin's death and the problems facing the official inquiry into his case, in addition to Beauchesne and Lenôtre see Francq, H. G. *Louis XVII, The Unsolved Mystery* (Leiden: E. J. Brill, 1970).

An account of the colorful life of Mathurin Bruneau is given by Morton, Lenôtre and the police records on his case: *Procès de Mathurin Bruneau se disant Louis XVII, par devant le Tribunal de police correctionale de Rouen* (Marseille: A. Ricard, 1818).

The controversy over Tillos's theft of the heart and Pellatan's countless fruitless attempts to return it to the royal family are described in: *Dépôt conservation du Coeur de Louis XVII, incident du vol qui m'en a été fait et de la restitution* . . . etc. in *Documents Concernant Le Coeur de Louis XVII. Revue Retrospective* 1.3.1894 (Paris), pp. 8–19.

Chapter Nine: The Shadow King

The dauphin's identification as Eleazer Williams: Evans, E. E. *The Story of Louis XVII of France* (London: Swan & Sonnenschein, 1893); Stevens, A. de Grasse. *The Lost Dauphin or Onwarenhiiaki, The Indian Iroquois Chief* (Orpington: G. Allen, 1887); Richemont's claims are set out in: *Mémoires du Duc de Normandie, fils de Louis XVI, écrits et publiés par lui-même* (Paris: July 1831) and also Richemont, *Mémoires du contemporain que la Révolution fit orphelin en 1793 et qu'elle raya du nombre des vivants en 1795* (Paris: Maistrasse-Wiart, 1846); Creissels, L., *Louis XVII et les Faux Dauphins* (Paris: Albin Michel, 1936).

Biographies of Karl Wilhelm Naundorff include: Madol, R. H. *The Shadow King. The Life of Louis XVII of France and the Fortunes of the Naundorff-Bourbon Family* (London: Allen and Unwin, 1930; Allen, P. *The Last Legitimate King of France, Louis XVII* (London: Dent & Sons, 1912); Eckard, J. *The King Who Never Reigned: Being Memoirs upon Louis XVII* (London: Eveleigh Nash, 1908). Manteyer, G. P. *Les Faux Louis XVII. Le roman de Naundorff et la vie de C. Werg* (Paris: Librarie Universelle Gamber, 1926); Decaux, A. *Louis XVII retrouvé. Naundorff roi de France* (Paris: L'Elan, 1947; Bazan E. P. *The Mystery of the Lost Dauphin*, trans. A .H. Seeger. (New York: Funk and Wagnalls, 1906); Treherne, P. *Louis XVII and Other Papers* (London: Fisher Unwin, 1912; Weldon, G. *Louis XVII of France, Founder of Modern Spiritualism* (London: Virtue & Co., 1896.

Naundorff's extraordinary letters to his "sister" Marie-Thérèse and numerous other details of correspondence relating to his identity are cited in: Perceval, C. G. *An Abridged Account of the Misfortunes of the Dauphin* (London: Fraser, 1838). This also includes a translation of Naundorff's own account of his life history.

For details of Péllatan's transfer of the heart to Archbishop de Quélin see *Narration simple et vraie des démarches que je n'ai cessé de faire . . . pour déposer le précieux objet . . .* etc. in *Revue Retrospective* cited above, pp. 29–34, and correspondence between Pellatan and Quélin pp. 51–57. A statement from Pellatan's son, Philippe-Gabriel, sets out details of the raid on the archbishop's palace and the subsequent recovery of the heart, see pp. 57–59.

Chapter Ten: The Royal Charade

A report on the exhumations at Sainte-Marguerite can be found Francq and also in the journal *La Ville de Paris*, August 27 and 28, 1884, Nos. 1364 and 1365. The more recent investigations at the site have been described by the late Michel Fleury: *Rapport par M Fleury sur les résultats du sondage effectué au cimetière Sainte-Marguerite . . .* Procès-verbal de la Commission du Vieux, Paris, séance du 10.12.79; and also *Le Cimetière Sainte Marguerite: Osteo-Archeologie des Dernières Fouilles {Septembre 1979}* Procès-Verbal séance du 3.11.80.

An introduction to early developments in forensic science: Beaven, Colin. *Fingerprints: Murder and the Race to Uncover the Science of Identity* (Fourth Estate, 2002). Castelot's research into the validity of Naundorff's claims is set out in: Castelot, A. *Louis XVII, L'Enigme Résolue.* (Brussels: Chabassol, 1947), and Castelot, A. *Louis XVII* (Paris: Perrin, 1968). See also, Le Conte, R. *Louis XVII et les Faux Dauphins* (Paris: P.U.F., 1924). Further information on Charlotte, Lady Atkyns can be found in: Barbey, F. *A Friend of Marie-Antoinette (Lady Atkyns)* (London: Chapman Hall, 1906).

The changing attitudes to the various French pretenders in postwar France is reported in many newspapers of the time: The *Times*, "French Royalist Manifesto" (11/23/37); The *Times*, "Proposed Repeal of Exiles." (6/23/49); *Manchester Guardian*, "French Pretender back in France" (5/18/50); *Daily Telegraph*, "Royalist France" (3/1/55); *Daily, Telegraph*, "Is de Gaulle a Royalist?" (7/3/57); *Daily Telegraph*, "Royalism in France" (3/10/55); The *Times*, "Deep-seated loyalties of the Vendée," (11/10/58); *Sunday Telegraph*, "Prominent Pretender," (11/11/62); *The Guardian*, "De Gaulle 'sees count as his heir' " (1/21/69).

For the developments in the Naundorff family's legal case during the 1950s see contemporary press reports: The *Times*, "Temple Prison Report Recalled" (5/13/54); The *Times*, "Naundorff's life history" (5/20/54); The *Times*, "Inconsistencies in the Naundorff Claim" (5/21/54); *Daily Telegraph*, "Bourbon Claimant," (5/24/54); *Manchester Guardian*, "Circus Manager who wants to be King" (5/6/54); The *Times*, "A Dauphin who knew no French"

(5/26/54); *Manchester Guardian*, "Bourbon claimant Fails" (7/2/54); N. Y. *Herald Tribune*, "Court Rules Dauphin Died in Prison in 1795" (7/2/54).

A full account of events as the heart of the orphan of the Temple was given to the Spanish Bourbons, including relevant correspondence, is in: *Louis XVII Fin de L'Odyssée d'un Coeur Royal* Supplement to *Littoral de La Somme* (11/16/1895).

Chapter Eleven: Resolution

I am indebted to Professor Jean-Jacques Cassiman, Dr. Hans Petrie and Sir Alec Jeffreys for fascinating interviews explaining the scientific background and the genetics history. Their research is published in the following scientific papers:

For testing on the heart of the orphan of the Temple: F. Jehaes, H. Pfeiffer, K. Toprak, R. Decorte, B. Brinkmann, and J. J. Cassiman: "Mitochondrial DNA analysis of the putative heart of Louis XVII, son of Louis XVI and Marie Antoinette," *European Journal of Human Genetics:* 9 (2001): 185–190.

For the earlier testing on Naundorff: E. Jehaes, R. Decorte, A. Peneau, H. J. Petrie, P. Boiry, A. Gilissen, J. B. Moisan, H. Van den Berghe, O. Pascal, and J. J. Cassiman: "Mitochondrial DNA analysis on remains of a putative son of Louis XVI and Marie Antoinette" *European Journal of Human Genetics* 6 (1998): 383–395. For a very different perspective on this science from Naundorff's descendents see their website at: www.louis-xvii.com

Jeffreys's breakthrough on genetic fingerprinting is described in: E. Hagelberg, I. C. Gray, and A. J Jeffreys. "Identification of the skeletal remains of a murder victim by DNA analysis," *Nature* 352 (1991): 427–429. For details of the groundbreaking Mengele case see: A. J. Jeffreys, M.J. Allen, E. Hagelberg, and A. Sonnberg: "Identification of the skeletal remains of Josef Mengele by DNA analysis," *Forensic Science International* 56 (1992): 65–76.

The scientific testing on the czar and his family is set out in: P. Gill, P. L. Ivanov, C. Kimpton, R. Piercy, N. Benson, G. Tully, I. Evett, E. Hagelberg, and K. Sullivan "Identification of the Remains of the Romanov family by DNA analysis," *Nature Genetics* 6 (1994: 130–135.

For contemporary press reports of the genetic testing see: The *New York Times*, "A Genetic Denouement to the Tale of Prince's Death" (4/20/00); *Washington Post*, "Tell-tale Heart Finds Its Place in History" (4/20/00); *The Guardian*, "DNA tests get to the heart of a 200 year old mystery" (4/20/00); *Irish Times*, "Boy's heart survives centuries to solve royal mystery" (4/26/00); *Associated Press*, "Case closed: Last Bourbon heir died in 1795" and "Long Dead Boy Identified as Louis XVII" (4/20/00).

BIBLIOGRAPHY

Allen, R. *Threshold of Terror: The Last Hours of the Monarchy in the French Revolution.* Sutton. Stroud, Glos, 1999.

Arneth, A., and Geffroy, M.A., eds. *Correspondance Secrète entre Marie-Thérèse et le Comte de Mercy-Argenteau avec les lettres de Marie-Thérèse et de Marie-Antoinette.* 3 vols. Paris, 1874.

Barbey, F. *A Friend of Marie-Antoinette (Lady Atkyns).* London: Chapman Hall, 1906.

Bazan E. P. *The Mystery of the Lost Dauphin*, trans. A.H. Seeger. New York: Funk and Wagnalls, 1906.

Beauchesne, Alcide de. *Louis XVII. His Life, His Suffering, His Death*, trans. W. Hazlitt. 2 vols. London: Harper and Bros., 1853.

Beaven, C. *Fingerprints: Murder and the Race to Uncover the Science of Identity.* Fourth Estate, 2002.

Bernier, O. *Imperial Mother, Royal Daughter: The correspondence of Marie-Antoinette and Maria Theresa.* London: Sidgwick & Jackson, 1986.

Bosher, J. F. *French Government Finance 1770–1795.* Cambridge: Cambridge University Press, 1970.

Buckley, E.R. *Monsieur Charles. The Tragedy of the True Dauphin, Louis XVII of France.* London: Witherby, 1927.

Campan, Madame. *Memoirs of the Private Life of Marie-Antoinette, Queen of France and Navarre.* 2 vols. 1824.

Carlyle, T. *The French Revolution: A History.* 1889. Rev. ed. Fielding & Sorensen, Oxford University Press, 1989.

Castelot, A. *Louis XVII, L'Enigme Resolue.* Brussels: Chabassol, 1947.

Castelot, A. *Louis XVII.* Paris: Perrin, 1968.

Chateaubriand, Vicomte René de. *Mémoires d'Outre-Tombe.* Paris, 1949.

Cléry, J. *Journal de ce qui s'est passé à la Tour du Temple pendant la captivité de Louis XVI, roi de France, par M. Cléry, valet de chambre du roi et autres mémoires sur le Temple.* C. Bertin, Paris, 1861.

Cobb, R. *The French and Their Revolution,* ed. D. Gilmour. London: John Murray, 1998.

Cobban, A. *A History of Modern France.* London: Harmandsworth Penguin, 1961.

Creissels, L., *Louis XVII et les Faux Dauphins.* Paris, Albin Michel, 1936.

Cronin, V. *Louis and Antoinette.* London: Collins, 1974.

Debriffe, M. *Madame Elisabeth: La Princesse Martyre.* Paris: Le Semaphore, 1977.

Decaux, A. *Louis XVII retrouvé. Naundorff roi de France.* Paris: L'Elan, 1947.

Delorme, P. *L'affaire Louis XVII.* Paris: Tallandier, 1995.

Delorme, P. *Louis XVII, La Verité: Sa mort au Temple confirmée par la science.* Paris: Paris Pygmalion, G. Watelet, 2000. See also Delorme's website: www.chez.com/louis17.

Dunlop, I. *Marie-Antoinette: A Portrait.* London: Sinclair-Stevenson, 1993.

Dunlop, I. *Royal Palaces of France.* London: Hamish Hamilton, 1985.

Eckard, J. *The King Who Never Reigned: Being Memoirs upon Louis XVII*. London: Eveleigh Nash, 1908.

Edgeworth de Firmont, Abbé. *Mémoires*. Paris, 1816.

Evans, E. E. *The Story of Louis XVII of France*. London; Swan & Sonnenschein, 1893.

Farr, E. *The Untold Love Story, Marie Antoinette and Count Fersen*. London: Allison & Busby, 1997.

Fersen, Count. *Le Comte de Fersen et la cour de France*, ed. Paris: R. M. De Klinckowstrom, 1877–78.

Fleischmann, H. *Les Pamphlets Libertins Contre Marie-Antoinette*. Paris, 1908.

Fleury, M. *Rapport par M Fleury sur les résultats du sondage effectué au cimetierè Sainte-Marguerite*. Procès-verbal de la Commission du Vieux Paris, séance du 10.12.79.

Fleury, M. *Cimetière Sainte Marguerite. Osteo-Archéologie des Dernières Fouilles {Septembre 1979}*. Procès-Verbal séance du 3.11.80.

Francq, H.G. *Louis XVII, The Unsolved Mystery*. Leiden: E.J. Brill, 1970.

Fraser, A. *Marie Antoinette*. London: Weidenfeld and Nicolson, 2001.

Furneaux, R. *Last Days of Marie Antoinette and Louis XV*. London: Allen and Unwin, 1968.

Gill, P., P. L. Ivanov, C. Kimpton, Piercy R., Benson N., Tully G., Evett I., Hagelberg E., and Sullivan K. "Identification of the Remains of the Romanov family by DNA analysis," *Nature Genetics* 6 (1994): 130–135.

Hagelberg, E., I. C., Gray, and A. J. Jeffreys. "Identification of the skeletal remains of a murder victim by DNA analysis," *Nature* 352 (1991): 427–429.

Hardman, J. *Louis XVI*. New Haven & London: Yale Univ. Press, 1993.

Hardman, J. *Robespierre*. Edinburgh: Pearson, 1999.

Hüe, F. *The Last Years of the Reign and Life of Louis XVI*, trans. R. C. Dallas. 1806.

Jeffreys, A. J., M.J. Allen, E. Hagelberg, and A. Sonnberg. "Identification of the skeletal remains of Josef Mengele by DNA analysis," *Forensic Science International* 56 (1992): 65–76.

Jehaes, E., H. Pfeiffer, K. Toprak, R. Decorte, B. Brinkmann, and J.J. Cassiman, "Mitochondrial DNA analysis of the putative heart of Louis XVII, son of Louis XVI and Marie Antoinette," *European Journal of Human Genetics* 9 (2001), 185–190.

Jehaes, E., R. Decorte, A. Peneau, H. J. Petrie, P. Boiry, A. Gilissen, J. P. Moisan, H. Van den Berghe, O. Pascal, and J. J. Cassiman, "Mitochondrial DNA analysis on remains of a putative son of Louis XVI and Marie Antoinette," *European Journal of Human Genetics* 6 (1998): 383–395.

Lafont d'Aussonne, G. *Mémoires sur les Malheurs de la Reine de France.* 1824.

Le Conte, R. *Louis XVII et les Faux Dauphins.* Paris, Presses Universitaires de France, 1924.

Lenôtre, G. *The Dauphin, Louis XVII. The Riddle of the Temple*, trans. F. Lees. London: Heinemann, 1922.

Lenôtre, G. *La Captivité et la Mort de Marie-Antoinette.* Paris, 1902.

Lever, E. *Marie-Antoinette: The Last Queen of France*, trans. C. Temerson. New York: Farrar, Straus & Giroux, 2000.

Loomis, S. *The Fatal Friendship: Marie Antoinette, Count Fersen and the Flight to Varennes.* New York, 1972.

Madol, R. H. *The Shadow King. The Life of Louis XVII of France and the Fortunes of the Naundorff-Bourbon Family.* London: Allen and Unwin, 1930.

Mansel, P. *Louis XVIII.* Stroud: Sutton Publishing, 1999.

Manteyer, G. P. *Les Faux Louis XVII. Le roman de Naundorff et la vie de C. Werg.* Paris: Librarie Universelle Gamber, 1926.

Marie-Thérèse. *Mémoire écrit par Marie-Thérèse-Charlotte de France sur la captivitée des princes et princesses, ses parents, depuis le 10 août 1792 jusqu'à la mort de son frère arrivée le 9 juin 1795; & Journal de Marie-Thérèse de France, Duchesse d'Angoulême, 5 Octobre 1789–2 Septembre 1792*, introduced by Baron Imbert de, Saint-Amand, 1893.

Mason, L., and T. Rizzo. *The French Revolution, A Document Collection.* New York, Houghton Mifflin Co.1999.

Minnigerade, M. *The Son of Marie Antoinette and the Mystery of the Temple Tower.* London: Jarrolds, 1935.

Morton, J. B. *The Dauphin, A biography of Louis XVII.* London: Longmans & Co., 1937.

Oscar, B. *The Flight to Varennes and Other Historical Essays.* 1892.

Paine, T. *Political Writings*, ed., B. Kuklick. New York and London: Cambridge Univ. Press, 2000.

Pellatan, Dr. Philippe-Jean. His admission that he stole the heart of the child who died in the Temple and his detailed statement on the history of the heart while in his possession is in *Documents Concernant Le Coeur de Louis XVII. Revue Retrospective* (Paris, 3/1/1894). *Mémoire Historique sur les derniers jours de la vie de Louis XVII et sur la Conservations de ses précieux restes.* The controversy over Tillos's theft and Pellatan's fruitless attempts to return the heart to the royal family is in the same document, pp. 8–19: *Dépot conservation du Coeur de Louis XVII, incident du vol qui m'en a été fait et de la restitution* . . . For details of Pellatan's transfer of the heart to Archbishop de Quélin see pp. 29–34: *Narration simple et vraie des démarches que je n'ai cessé de faire . . . pour déposer le précieux objet.* A statement from Pellatan's son, Philippe-Gabriel, sets out details of the raid on the archbishop's palace and the subsequent recovery of the heart, see pp. 57–59. For a full account of events as the heart of the orphan of the Temple was given to the Spanish Bourbons, including relevant correspondence: *Louis XVII Fin de L'Odyssée d'un Coeur Royal*, supplement to *Littoral de La Somme* (11/16/1895). Biographical details and Pellatan's correspondence relating to the heart are included in the *Appendix of Revue Retrospective.*

Perceval, C. G. *An Abridged Account of the Misfortunes of the Dauphin.* London: Fraser, 1838.

Procès de Mathurin Bruneau se disant Louis XVII, par devant le Tribunal de police correctionale de Rouen. Marseille: A. Ricard, 1818.

Richemont, Baron de. *Mémoires du Duc de Normandie, fils de Louis XVI, écrits et publiés par lui-même.* Paris, July 1831.

Richemont, Baron de. *Mémoires du contemporain que la Révolution fit orphelin en 1793 et qu'elle raya du nombre des vivants en 1795.* Paris: Maistrasse-Wiart, 1846.

Roberts, J. M. *The French Revolution*. New York and London: Oxford Univ. Press, 1978.

Rose, R. B. *The Making of the Sans-culottes: Democratic Ideas and Institutions in Paris 1789–92*. Manchester: Manchester University Press, 1983.

Rousseau, J. J. *The Social Contract, or Principles of Political Right*, trans. M. Cranston, London: Penguin, 1968.

Saint-Amand, Baron Imbert de. *The Duchesse d'Angoulême and the Two Restorations*, trans. J. Davis. London: Hutchinson & Co., 1892.

Schama, S. *Citizens: A Chronicle of the French Revolution*. London: Penguin, 1989.

Seward, D. *Marie Antoinette*. London: Constable, 1981.

Soderhjelm, A. *Fersen et Marie-Antoinette*. 1930.

Stevens, A. de Grasse. *The Lost Dauphin or Onwarenhiiaki, the Indian Iroquois Chief*. Orpington: G. Allen, 1887.

Thomas, C. *The Wicked Queen: The Origins of the Myth of Marie Antoinette*, trans. J. Rose. 1999. New York: Urzone Inc., 1999.

Tourzel. *Mémoires de Madame La Duchesse de Tourzel, Gouvernante des Enfants de France de 1789 à 1795*. Paris, 1883.

Treherne, P. *Louis XVII and Other Papers*. London: Fisher Unwin, 1912.

Turgy, L. F. *Fragment historique sur la captivité de la famille royalle*. Paris, 1818.

Turquan, J. *Madame Royale The Last Dauphine*, trans. T. Davidson, London: Fisher Unwin, 1910.

Voltaire. *Philosophical Dictionary*, trans. T. Besterman, New York: Penguin, 1972.

Weber, J. *Mémoires concernant Marie-Antoinette Archiduchesse d'Autriche, Reine de France*. 3 vols., 1822.

Weiner, M. *The French Exiles 1789–1815*. London: Murray, 1960.

Welch, C. *The Little Dauphin, Louis XVII*. London: Methuen, 1908.

Weldon, G. *Louis XVII of France, Founder of Modern Spiritualism*. London: Virtue & Co., 1896.

Wormeley, K. P. *Ruin of a Princess*. New York: Lamb Publishing, 1912.

Yalom, M. *Blood Sisters, The French Revolution in Women's Memory*. London: HarperCollins, 1995.

INDEX